THE ELEVENS OF ENGLAND

The Elevens of England

by

G. Derek West

Darf Publishers Limited
London
1988

FIRST PUBLISHED 1988

ISBN 1 85077 206 1

Printed in Great Britain by A. Wheaton & Co. Ltd., Exeter

The Elevens of England

List of Illustrations

Foreword

WHEN I began exploring the history and development of cricket many years ago, I gradually became aware of an increasing number of references to an organization called the All England Eleven. Founded in 1846 and flourishing for over a quarter of a century thereafter, the AEE was an Itinerant Eleven, engaged for most of the season in travelling to all parts of the United Kingdom to play matches against local sides. Soon, I read, a rival team was established, and later a whole array of itinerant elevens sprang into being. The references to the AEE emphasized the overwhelming importance of this organization's contribution to the development of cricket. Eager to know more about the various "Elevens of England" and the vital role some of them played in the history of the game, I began searching for a book on the subject, only to find that not one had ever been published. I soon discovered some of the reasons why. The subject is highly complex, and although the reminiscences of several of the cricketers of the time are available in print, much of the material is not easy of access. Unfortunately, my attempts to trace such items as original score-books and account-books proved fruitless. Some of the former were apparently destroyed shortly after they were completed, but it is possible that examples of both and other interesting documents may have been preserved by the heirs or descendants of the cricketers and team managers.

One difficulty occasionally arises out of the nomenclature applied in contemporary newspapers, annuals, and books of scores, which assign different titles to one or both sides in the same match. Particularly misleading was the somewhat indiscriminate use of such terms as "England", "All England", "An All England Eleven", and "An Eleven of All England" to designate a team and lend lustre to the occasion of a match. Journalists and cricketers evidently were not always concerned with the niceties of accurate distinction. A perfect example occurs in the diary kept by a member of one of the first teams touring abroad. The diarist calls the side the AEE, although some of the tourists did not belong to that organization in England. Perhaps it was force of habit, since the writer was a genuine All England man himself.

There are, then, some problems in dealing with the subject, but nevertheless a treatment of the "Elevens of England" provides a mirror of the historical period to which they belonged—not merely a series of reports, scores, and statistics, interesting though they be, but also a study of the personalities and of the organization of the society in which they lived and moved, the clothes they wore and the equipment they used, and the prevailing attitude adopted towards the professional cricketer. The events of the period when the Itinerant Elevens flourished provide a perfect illustration of the biblical adage that "there is no new thing under the sun", and there is a familiar ring about some of the details in this segment of the social history of the Victorian age. Nowadays, some of our politicians, commentators, and journalists dilate upon the divide between North and South, but as far as the world of cricket was concerned, this concept was already in existence to a marked degree in the 1860s, a period which also saw the birth of that long-standing tradition of internecine strife between the committee of a famous northern county and some of its leading players.

As far as I am aware, many of the illustrations have rarely or never been reproduced since they were originally published. The portraits of individual cricketers went through two, and in some instances three stages. First, there was a photograph, but since the technical process for converting original photographs into plates was not in use at that time, a copy of the player's likeness was engraved on wooden blocks, from which prints were made and published in one of the leading illustrated journals of the 1860s. Later, a number of these saw the light of day again—as a type of lithograph, according to a dealer who was offering them for sale. I have seen a representation of all three stages for one of the subjects. In addition to preserving the physical appearance of some of the principal players, these portraits also provide a valuable record of the cricketing dress they wore.

I have incurred many obligations during the preparation of this study. In particular, I should like to express my gratitude to Michael Blumberg, the editor of *Cricket World*, for his assistance in the publication of this book; the late James D. Coldham, for his constant encouragement and advice and for drawing my attention to numerous facts and details; Stephen Green, the Curator and Librarian at Lord's, whose expertise and resources were always made available to me; Paul Lewis, the Librarian of Ridley College, St Catharines, Ontario, who readily gave me access to the Karl Auty Library; Roger F. Mann, whose collection of photographs and extensive knowledge were placed at my disposal; Nicholas Potter, of the Burlington Gallery, who provided one of the illustrations; Peter Wynne-Thomas, who was a mine of information, whenever I addressed an enquiry to him. Finally, I must not fail to acknowledge the courteous assistance rendered to me over the years by the staff of the British Library Newspaper Library at Colindale.

Caversham, Berkshire, 1988   G. DEREK WEST

CHAPTER ONE

William Clarke and the All England Eleven

THE first of the Elevens of England was the brain-child of a former bricklayer, but ultimately all were his progeny: one begat another, and all were descended from the first. Some flourished, enjoying years of life, others blossomed only to wither on the vine, and a few were almost still-born. The first, conceived in the ripeness of time, was the greatest, even though its existence was prolonged for years after its usefulness had vanished, until it became a mere anachronism. Yet its influence on the development of English cricket was of inestimable value in converting what was largely a local pastime into a national sport with an ever expanding programme of first-class matches.

Popular interest in cricket was burgeoning by the 1840s, thanks to a combination of several factors. Not least was the contribution made by *Bell's Life in London*, the leading sporting newspaper of the day, with its increasing coverage of matches. This, in turn, was assisted by the introduction of the penny postage in 1840, creating a cheap, rapid means of forwarding match reports to the press and, at the same time, facilitating the arrangement of fixtures between clubs. The army, too, played its part, when the military authorities decreed in 1841 that all barracks should be provided with a cricket ground, thus producing a notable increase in the number of playing arenas, since garrisons were quartered in many sizeable towns. Finally, of major importance was the vast improvement in transport achieved by the construction of the railways, which were replacing the more hazardous, expensive stage-coach lines in many areas. The hour had come for cricket to be spread throughout the length and breadth of the land, and the erstwhile labourer possessed the acumen to devise a plan for capitalizing on the situation.

The son of a bricklayer, William Clarke was born at Nottingham, on December 24, 1798, and began his working life by following in his father's footsteps. For Clarke, however, there was more to life than the laying of bricks. There was sport, especially cricket, but opportunities for earning a living as a professional cricketer pure and simple were virtually non-existent

1

in those days. Finding his trade distasteful, Clarke abandoned trowel and hod in favour of the more congenial occupation of mine host of *The Bell Inn* in his native town. When he was nearly forty, he married the widowed landlady of *The Trent Bridge Inn*, and shortly afterwards he enclosed and developed some of the nearby land, thus creating what was to become the famous Trent Bridge Ground. Playing cricket from an early age, he earned a high reputation in the North—which then and much later included the Midlands, as far as cricket was concerned—but was almost unknown in the South and did not appear at Lord's until July 11 and 12, 1836, when he assisted the North in their victory over the South by six wickets.

Clarke stood 5ft. 9in. tall and, at the age of forty, weighed nearly 14st. His age and weight were no great handicap in those days, when cricket was a more sedate game, but his activities extended beyond "the tented field". He was very knowledgeable in the art of betting on the horses—for Clarke had ever a keen financial brain—and he was much addicted to the game of fives, which he played with consummate skill. Increasing stoutness inevitably told against him, but he continued indulging his second favourite sport for hours on end. So great were his exertions that, when sheer exhaustion interrupted the frenzied chase and compelled him to rest by leaning against the side of the fives-court, he imprinted a kind of sweaty silhouette of himself on the wall! His passion for fives, however, was not without its cost: before he was thirty, he suffered a grievous injury, when an accident deprived him of the sight of his right eye.

This mutilation did not prevent Clarke from participating in either fives or cricket, though his younger colleague George Parr made the wry remark that "in his latter days he played not by *sight* but by *sound.*" It may have impeded his batting, but it never impaired his skill with the ball. As a bowler he was extraordinary. At a time when round-arm bowling had come into fashion, Clarke revived and perfected the under-arm delivery of the past. Approaching the wicket at a gentle trot, he bent back his elbow at the last moment to bowl from almost under his right arm-pit, making the ball rise steeply from the ground. At times, however, he delivered from the level of the hip, propelling the ball in the style of a man tossing a quoit. He varied his length and action as much as his pace, which was generally slow with the occasional faster ball, and, on pitching, "the leathern sphere" moved sharply from leg to off. The twist was so prodigious that he preferred bowling from the Pavilion end against the slope at Lord's.

Adept at discovering his opponents' weaknesses, Clarke customarily observed them practising before the wickets were pitched and made mental notes for future reference. Once play had begun, he sent down a series of nagging deliveries calculated to cause his adversaries to lose their patience—and almost inevitably their wickets. His principal gratification was the entrapment of all opposing batsmen, and when victims were destroyed by his guile, his delight at their discomfiture was reflected in the half-grim, half-smiling expression he habitually wore. To the supremacy of his bowling must be added his matchless skill at setting the field. He was "a crafty and fox-headed cricketer altogether," but, like many a bowler, he was often extremely reluctant to relinquish the ball, claiming he was "always expecting to get a wicket his next over."

All in all, Clarke was quite a character and the subject of many anecdotes. Very abstemious during the hours of play, he usually restricted his luncheon to a cigar and a bottle of soda-water. By contrast, he sometimes consumed a whole goose entirely by himself at the evening meal. There were, however, more serious flaws than occasional gluttony in his make-up. He could be a very difficult companion, often morose and, in the contemporary idiom, "queer-tempered." Impatient, autocratic by nature, totally incapable of suffering fools gladly, he frequently behaved with crushing rudeness ("What's the first thing I should do to become a good cricketer, Mr Clarke?"—"Get your nails cut!"). Worse still, a vindictive, even cruel streak lurked beneath the surface, manifesting itself in one deplorable incident. A railway porter discovered him enjoying an illicit cigar in a non-smoking compartment—for Clarke, as we have seen, was fond of a good cigar. Failing to persuade the offender to change his seat or extinguish the "weed", the official placed one hand on the window-sill and waved the other to summon the station-master. Quick as a flash, Clarke stubbed out his cigar on the back of the unfortunate porter's hand, declaring with affected innocence that he was merely obeying orders, and that if the porter's hand happened to be in the way, it was the porter's own fault . . . A wonderful performer on the field was Clarke, but his far from likeable personality was destined to bring him much grief.

Clarke's difficulties, however, belonged to the future, beyond the year of 1846, which marked a watershed in his career. Engaged as a ground bowler at Lord's, he moved to London and, at the age of forty-seven (!), made his first appearance for the Players against the Gentlemen. Much more momentous was his scheme which, maturing in the same year, made that immeasurable contribution to the development of cricket. Impossible to say how long his thoughts had been turning in that direction, but Clarke obviously had his finger on the pulse and, fully aware of the public's increasing interest, devised a plan to take cricket to all quarters of the land. His motives were anything but altruistic. As shrewd a businessman as a bowler, he recognized the potential of a financial speculation advantageous to himself and, incidentally, to some of his fellow cricketers. Local clubs, he reasoned, would welcome the chance of meeting and contending against some of the players who had acquired a national reputation through the medium of the press, and would be willing to pay for the privilege of basking in their reflected glory—in which Old Clarke showed his keen perception of the foibles of human nature. So, he founded his All England Eleven, and this choice of name, with all its implications of exclusive excellence, was a stroke of genius. Dingley Dell or All-Muggleton would be flattered in the belief of facing the *élite* of the land, and Clarke would usually do his best to see they were not disappointed. Even-sided contests were naturally out of the question, and a well established custom was followed by arranging for the local sides to be represented by more than eleven players.

Too prudent to draw up a full fixture list before testing his scheme in practice, Old Clarke began with a small pilot run towards the end of the season. The inaugural match took place on the Hyde Park Ground, Sheffield, on August 31 and September 1 and 2, 1846, when the AEE met 20 of Sheffield. Representing the visitors (in the batting order of the first innings) were the following:

W. Clarke (captain), James Dean, sen., W. Dorrinton, Fuller Pilch, Mr Alfred Mynn, J. Guy, W. Martingell, T. Sewell, sen., G. Butler, Mr V. S. C. Smith, and W. R. Hillyer.

There is no need to justify the inclusion of Alfred Mynn, still regarded as the leading all-rounder for the Gentlemen, while the other amateur, Mr Smith, assisted Oxford four times in the varsity match (1844–47). The true strength of Clarke's side, however, lay in the nine professionals, all of whom had appeared for the Players against the Gentlemen in one or both fixtures that season. Young George Parr, later to be Old Clarke's successor as secretary of the AEE, was a notable absentee, suffering from a feverish cold, caught while playing cricket.

The Eleven took first innings and, seemingly desirous of personally launching the team on its maiden voyage, Clarke opened the batting with Dean. Unfortunately, he failed to score, and his side were dismissed for 80. The home team, all twenty of them, could only achieve a total of 72. All England fared slightly better on second hands with 106, but it was not enough, and they lost by five wickets. Perhaps Old Clarke underestimated the strength of the Sheffield team, which contained such good men as G. Chatterton, H. Sampson, and G. H. Wright, who later appeared for the AEE. All three, in their time, assisted the Players against the Gentlemen—the supreme accolade in those days—though possibly not so often as they deserved. As northern men, their remoteness from Lord's was disadvantageous in the matter of selection for such representative matches. Also playing for the home side was little James Dearman, well known in Sheffield for his prowess, but remembered now only for the two crushing defeats inflicted upon him by Alfred Mynn in single-wicket contets in 1838 and for his pluck in adversity (Dearman had "delighted the spectators throughout by his unflinching bottom").

Lest it be thought that the totals in this historic match were abysmally low, let it be remembered that the odds were heavily weighted against batsmen in 1846 and many years later. Care and preparation of the turf were rudimentary, and no modern cricketer would tolerate the uneven, grassy pitches and fields, which were the rule rather than the exception. Lord's was particularly bad in this respect ("all ridge and furrow"), and one of the leading professionals remarked some years later "that the ground was not a billiard-table, except as regards the 'pockets'." Overs consisted of four balls, and sight-screens had not been invented. There were few boundaries as they are known to-day: most hits had to be run out, and there were instances of seven or eight runs scored from one stroke during this period of the game's history. This was exhausting both physically and mentally for batsmen, whose concentration was sapped by fatigue and breathlessness. A firm defence was consequently much admired, and individual scores in double figures were considered worthy of mention in match reports, even though the rate of run-getting was often very slow. Playing for the AEE against twenty opponents in 1848, George Parr—long regarded as the premier batsman in England—took six hours to score 25 in an innings interrupted several times by rain. In 1857, against a team of sixteen, James Grundy went in first and carried his bat for 51, compiled in five-and-a-quarter hours. Even this feat pales in comparison with a performance by John Lillywhite, the man responsible for the quip about the 'pockets' at Lord's. No slouch with the bat as a rule, Lilly occupied the crease for nearly two hours while scoring 6 runs against a side of sixteen in 1858! These and other examples of slow scoring illustrate another handicap suffered by batsmen playing for an eleven against "odds": it was far harder to score runs against as many as twenty-two opponents in the field than against another eleven.

Licking their wounds, the AEE departed from Sheffield for an encounter with 18 of Manchester, on September 3, 4, and 5. Clarke, it may be assumed, did not wish to see his team incur the humiliation of another defeat, and perhaps he delivered a pep talk to his men. At any rate, the AEE made 228 (Fuller Pilch 62) to achieve a handsome victory by an innings and 31 runs. Encouraged by this success, the Eleven made their way to Leeds where, on September 7, 8, and 9, they took on 18 of Yorkshire in what proved to be a sterner struggle. In their first innings, Clarke's team were all out for 102, with only two batsmen reaching double figures. On second hands, the total was 125, the top score from the bat being 19 not out, but Extras amounted to 45 (22 wides, 23 no balls)! The Eighteen were dismissed for 72 and 86, the AEE winning by 69 runs. All England were unchanged for all three matches, but Clarke put himself on only once in the opponents' six innings, so perhaps he was content to concentrate on the management of the matches. Hillyer (56 wickets) and Dean (36) bore the brunt of the bowling.

Unpleasantness and ill-feeling marred the final match of 1846. The AEE openly questioned the fairness of the bowling of J. R. Ibbetson, who captured in all 12 wickets. Unfortunate it was that such an accusation should be levelled against Yorkshire's most successful bowler, but so much rancour was engendered that both umpires were changed during the match. Of the 23 no balls in the Eleven's second innings, no less than 16 were delivered by Ibbetson. Doubtless, this unnerved him, for he also bowled 7 wides! This incident was characteristic of the arguments and quarrels rife during much of the Eleven's existence, though it would be unjust to claim that the AEE were directly involved in *all* of them.

Evidently well satisfied with his experiment, Clarke decided to develop the operation by extending the fixture list. He would be willing henceforth, on terms acceptable to himself, to take his team anywhere by rail and sometimes by stage-coach to play against "odds". Many of the opponents were often comparatively mediocre performers and, according to their strength, Clarke would agree to contend against sides consisting of sixteen, eighteen, twenty, and even twenty-two players. To redress the balance still more, local teams sometimes engaged the services of one or more professional bowlers. Usually referred to as "Given Men", they were often of such calibre as to merit selection for the AEE itself, and occasionally they would assist the opposition in one match and Clarke in the next. Another tactic employed by managers to strengthen local sides was the adoption of some such title as "Twenty-two of ——— and District", a fairly elastic term to justify the inclusion of good players, whose actual connection with the town or club was rather tenuous. This was a ploy sometimes viewed with mixed feelings by the AEE. Not all the fixtures over the years were of this type: from time to time, Clarke got up important matches against only fourteen or sixteen opponents, and there were some genuine first-class contests with teams fielding only eleven men.

By twentieth-century standards, Clarke's players were rather elderly— sure evidence of the more sedate tempo of the game—and of the original Eleven appearing in that historic first encounter at Sheffield, only two (Martingell and Mr Smith) were still under thirty. Nevertheless, the title used to designate the team was largely justified, even though it smacked of arrogance and aroused some hostility. Many of Clarke's men *were* the best in England, and if the massive Alfred Mynn and the mighty Fuller Pilch were entering their twilight, their fame alone was sufficient to attract the public. In Joseph Guy the team possessed one of the finest batsmen of the time, renowned for the strength of his defence and his stylish scoring strokes. For him Clarke had the deepest admiration ("Joe Guy, sir; all ease and elegance, fit to play before Her Majesty in a drawing-room"), though Joe sometimes gave the impression of deliberately sacrificing scoring opportunities in order to exhibit those powers of defence of which he was so proud. As regards the bowling, there was Clarke himself and Billy Hillyer of Kent, nicknamed "Topper", often regarded as one of the best of the early round-arm bowlers. Usually designated for the sake of convenience as a medium-pacer, he varied his speed considerably: in 1840, he played for the Fast Bowlers against the Slow, but in 1842 for the Slow Bowlers against the Fast. "Topper" produced a lot of movement with the action of his arm, often making the ball pitch on the off-stump and veer away sharply towards the slips. There were several all-rounders, the most noteworthy being James Dean, sen., of Sussex. "Joyous Jemmy" was good enough with both bat and ball to merit selection in any representative team for a number of years. Though no stylist like Joe Guy, he was generally a safe batsman, who made some good scores. A fast, accurate bowler in the 1840s, his constitution later told against him, for Dean ran easily to fat. Try as he might, he was eventually defeated in his struggle to shed superfluous flesh and took on the semblance of "a broad, half-filled sack". Jemmy's increasing bulk slowed down the pace of his bowling, and his waddling approach to the wicket was once compared to "the rolling of a hedgehog which exploded when it reached the crease".

CHAPTER TWO

The All England Eleven, 1847–1851

IN 1847, Clarke extended his fixture list and roll of players, and advanced the commencing date of his programme to August 12. Ten matches, all against "odds", were played in the North and Midlands, resulting in three victories, three defeats, and four unfinished. Mr Smith and Butler dropped out of the side, but nine new players were introduced. Some made only one appearance, the most noteworthy being the Sussex professional, John Wisden, nicknamed in his youth "The Little Wonder", and later "The Cardinal". In spite of his diminutive stature and lack of weight (5ft. 4½in., and 7st., increasing eventually to nearly 11st.), Wisden developed into a bowler "very fast indeed and ripping", and a good batsmen with the straightest of blades. His favourite scoring stroke, becoming obsolescent with the wide-spread wearing of leg-guards, was the hazardous "draw", in which a delivery on or near the leg stump was deflected under the striker's front leg or between the rear leg and the wicket. During the next few seasons, Wisden played much more often for the AEE and was a valuable member of the side. Had Clarke been gifted with the power of hindsight, however, he would probably have never engaged the services of "The Little Wonder".

Another recruit was the pioneer of round-arm bowling, Old Lillywhite (F.W.), who played four times for the AEE after appearing as a Given Man against them. For the first seven matches, Clarke included the amateur, Mr O. C. Pell, who played four times for Cambridge in the varsity match (1844–47) and twice for the Gentlemen against the Players (1847–48). The demands of the legal profession obliged Mr Pell to abandon cricket after 1848.

Participating, like his friend Alfred Mynn, in all ten fixtures, was one of two important additions to the team, the amateur Nicholas Felix (real name Wanostrocht). Of Flemish extraction, he had many varied talents—schoolmaster, painter, musician, sportsman, author of *Felix on the Bat*, the most successful of the early instructional manuals on cricket, and other works, inventor of batting gloves and a bowling machine called the

Lithograph after N. Felix's watercolour of the All England Eleven, 1847.
J. Guy, G. Parr, W. Martingell, A. Mynn, W. Denison, J. Dean, W. Clarke, N. Felix, O. C. Pell, W. R. Hillyer, F. W. Lillywhite, W. Dorrinton, F. Pilch, T. Sewell, sen.

Catapulta. A superb, left-handed batsman with a brilliant cut, Felix had a long first-class career, lasting from 1831 to 1852. Surrey and Kent shared his services, and he assisted the Gentleman against the Players twenty times. Cricket was not his only game, for this active, little man was highly proficient at billiards and fives, the last, perhaps, creating a bond between him and Clarke. Aged forty-two when he joined the AEE, his fame equalled Alfred Mynn's, and his value to Clarke was not confined merely to batting. Aware of his gifts as a public speaker and his tact, Clarke invited Felix to be the President of the AEE. The post was no sinecure, and Felix took his duties seriously, calming Clarke's quarrelsome nature, smoothing over difficulties, writing letters to *Bell's Life* in defence of his captain's actions and the honour of the Eleven, and endeavouring to prevent any serious dissension among the members. What arrangements Clarke made with such gentlemen as Messrs Smith and Pell is not known, but it is certain that Felix and Mynn—both impecunious men—received payment for playing for the AEE. As a historian, too, Felix played his part, recording the Eleven's doings in his sketch-books of 1851 and 1852, but one of his greatest legacies to posterity is the well known picture of the team painted in 1847. At times, the artist showed a tendency to idealize his subjects, and occasionally he got the perspective wrong. In the team picture of 1847, Jemmy Dean is shown standing in the centre and slightly to the rear of the group. According to the Surrey all-rounder, William Caffyn, it "is a good likeness, but makes him appear absurdly small as compared with some of the other players".

The other addition to the team, *the* most important of all, was George Parr, "The Lion of the North". Born at Radcliffe-on-Trent, Nottinghamshire, on May 22, 1826, Parr made his *début* for the Players against the Gentlemen at the same time as William Clarke in 1846 and appeared in twenty-two of these matches up to 1865. He assisted the AEE in nine of their ten fixtures in 1847, and in his first match George scored 100, an ominous sign for local sides in the future, since centuries were comparatively rare in contests against "odds". His aggregate of 404 runs in 15 completed innings yielded an average of 26.93—enormous in those days. The tall, lugubrious Fuller Pilch, the darling of a previous generation, scored 178 runs in 16 completed innings for an average of 11.12. Small wonder, then, that Parr was considered as Fuller's natural successor for the title of premier professional batsman of England, a position he occupied unchallenged until about 1860, when other players began staking their claims. Over medium height and muscular, George adopted a somewhat crouching stance at the crease. His defence was very strong, his cuts (right foot advanced), late cuts and drives were all executed with power, but the splendour of his batting was his leg-hitting, for which he was famous. "His method", said William Caffyn, "was to reach out with the left leg straight down the wicket, bending the knee, and to sweep the ball round in a sort of half-circle behind the wicket." Sometimes, according to the pitch of the ball, the stroke was made in the direction of square leg. There were, it seems, occasional murmurs that Parr used to hit straight balls to leg, a habit considered gross bad form in those days, but Caffyn firmly scotched this slander. George, a farmer's son, was able to devote his life to cricket, and he was destined to exert as great an influence as Old Clarke on the progress of the national game. Like the veteran, too, he became rather "queer-tempered" as he grew older, and many problems—some of his own making—would lie across his path. Fearless on the field of play, George had a morbid dread of thunderstorms and was always convinced that any ship on which he was a passenger—to Ireland, North America, or Australia—was certain to founder and be engulfed by the waves. As the years passed, he developed the custom, much to his younger team-mates' amusement, of always carrying an old leather hat-box with a dent on one of its sides. Its contents were an unrevealed mystery, and nobody, not even an hotel waiter, was ever allowed to touch it. About three years before his death in 1891, Parr was persuaded to accompany a team on an annual tour and turned up at the station with the identical hat-box, completely unchanged. He expressed some surprise, when an old friend from the All England days recognized it instantly. Could it have contained nothing more sinister than his best hat? George, who eventually succeeded Old Clarke as manager of the AEE, took on some of the veteran's characteristics. He, also, did not suffer fools gladly and was sometimes caustic and irascible, feeling no doubt the burdens of office. Clarke found his relaxation on the fives-court; George's delight was a day's shooting, either on his own or with a friend, yet he was able to enjoy some conviviality with chosen companions. He was very fond of gin-and-water.

First-class contests were few and far between in the early days of the AEE—occasional county matches, though there was no championship, Gentlemen *v* Players, North *v* South, "England" *v* a team of worthy opponents. All these yielded wages for the professionals, so Clarke, when establishing his arrangements, took pains to try and avoid any conflict of dates. Nevertheless, the fixture list rose to sixteen in 1848, with eight victories and five defeats. Most games were played in August and September, but the programme was much more ambitious, with three significant developments. First, Clarke began operations nearer the beginning of the season by getting up two matches in the second half of June. Secondly, though the majority of contests took place in the North and Midlands, no less than four were played in the South, at Gravesend, the Oval, Chelmsford, and Itchen, near Southampton. Thirdly, the calibre of the opponents was good enough in two of the matches for them to be classified subsequently as "important". One was staged at the Oval, in August, when the AEE met 14 of Surrey and were defeated by 8 wickets.

The other, the final fixture of the programme, was played on Day's ground at Itchen, at the end of September, the opponents being 14 of Hampshire. A hard-fought, low-scoring contest ended in a draw, with Hampshire 19 short of victory and only 1 wicket to fall. This match was got up for the benefit of the ground superintendent, Daniel Day, a Surrey man, who had migrated to Hampshire and who later played for the AEE. Daniel, a good fast bowler and an average batsman, evidently believed there was a cricket ground in the hereafter: according to legend, he gave instructions for his bat to be placed in his coffin.

Throughout 1848, Clarke relied mainly on many of those who had played for him previously, but he introduced two newcomers, who appeared in many of the matches. One, another talented amateur, was Mr R. T. King, who represented Cambridge against Oxford (1846–49) and assisted the Gentlemen against the Players five times (1847–51). Mr King took holy orders in 1851 and was unfortunately lost to cricket. A fine, forcing batsman and a fastish bowler, he was famous as a specialist fielder at point.

A more notable recruit was Thomas Box, who had assisted his native Sussex as far back as 1828, and who appeared twenty times for the Players against the Gentlemen (1834–53). No longer young when he joined the AEE, Tom was a useful batsman and was regarded for many years as the best professional wicket-keeper in England. He had taken some hard knocks, for stumpers had little or nothing in the way of protective equipment during his youth. A handsome man, whose good looks were marred by an injury to his nose sustained in a match at Lord's, Tom was very proud of his fine head of hair, which he wore rather long. This harmless vanity once caused him to become the victim of an extremely cruel practical joke, when a naïve barber, assured that Tom was a lunatic with over-heated brains, was cozened into giving his unsuspecting customer the shortest of prison crops! A regular for several seasons with the AEE, Box was employed in his latter days at Prince's Cricket Ground, where his stumps were lowered for the last time in sad but appropriate circumstances. Middlesex were playing Nottinghamshire in July 1876, and on the final day Tom collapsed with heart failure in the act of changing the figures on the score-board. The attack proved fatal, and the match was abandoned as a mark of respect for the veteran.

Three other prominent professionals made a fleeting *début* for the AEE in 1848. One was George Chatterton, the Sheffield all-rounder, who was not far behind Tom Box as a wicket-keeper, and who had played for the Eleven's opponents in the inaugural match of 1846. He was a member of the ground staff at Lord's for several years and was often employed as an umpire.

Another new face was Edmund Hinkly, a fast, left-handed bowler from Kent, who marked his greatest performance that year. Playing for his county against the flower of England at Lord's, he captured 6 wickets in the first innings and all 10 in the second. One of his victims in both hands was George Parr, who came to regard Hinkly as his bogeyman, for George often succumbed to Edmund's expresses. Hinkly's career at the top was of short duration, and he drifted away into a series of engagements as a club professional and coach.

Alfred John Day Diver was the most noteworthy of the three new arrivals making a brief appearance in the Eleven in 1848. Originally a cook's apprentice in his native Cambridge, he played more frequently for the AEE in later years and often assisted his county. A good man to have on any side, he was capable of preserving his wickets for long periods while accumulating a respectable score. His style, neat and precise, was too formal and mechanical for some onlookers, prompting the Rev James Pycroft to characterize him as "one of those very correct and proper people whom we always much approve but never want to see again". At the outset of his career, little "Ducky" Diver was quite a useful bowler, fastish round-armed, adding slow, underhand lobs in the 1850s. Still later, he more or less abandoned bowling to convert himself into a specialist long-stop. His knowledge of cricket was vast, and from 1856 until his death twenty years later, he was employed at Rugby School, achieving lasting fame for his coaching abilities and dry, poker-faced wit.

By now, the salad days of the AEE were over, and Clarke could clearly contemplate the development of events with satisfied equanimity. So successful was the pattern established in 1848 that he had no hesitation in expanding his programme to an even greater extent. The list for 1849 comprised twenty-one matches, of which the Eleven won fourteen and lost only two. Clarke still adhered to the policy of avoiding as far as possible any conflict with grand matches, but saw no reason for imposing other limits on his team. Apart from a few intermissions, principally in June and July, the AEE were occupied throughout the whole season, fulfilling their first five engagements in May. As previously, the North and Midlands formed the principal arena of their activities, but the team ranged as far north as Edinburgh and as far south as Brighton. Four important contests were played, three of them against teams of only eleven players, including two counties (Kent and Sussex), resulting in three victories for the AEE and one draw. In one of these, George Parr made his highest score for the AEE in important and first-class matches (86 not out—worth at least double that by modern standards).

The backbone of the Eleven in 1849 consisted of Messrs Felix and Mynn, Clarke himself, Box, Guy, Hillyer, Martingell, and George Parr, while Pilch, Wisden, and George Chatterton made frequent appearances. Some of the old faces were missing or little in evidence. Sewell had left the team, never to return, and William Dorrinton, another of the "originals", had died the previous November from colds and fevers contracted, it was alleged, while travelling about with the AEE and playing on wet grounds. Old Lillywhite (five matches in 1848) made a solitary and final appearance for the Eleven, and Jemmy Dean played but once. Both were ground bowlers at Lord's, owing their first allegiance to MCC, but there can be little doubt that their relations with Clarke had deteriorated. With Dean this is far from easy to understand, for Jemmy of the ready smile was good nature personified, and it must be asumed that he suffered some hard times with his abrasive taskmaster. Old Lillywhite was a different matter. Older than Clarke, he was vain, self-opinionated, fond of having his own way, and a clash of wills was inevitable.

Three other professionals receiving their first engagements with the AEE in 1849 were Henry Sampson, Thomas Adams, and John Bickley. The first, like George Chatterton, had assisted the Eleven's opponents at Sheffield in 1846. A short, powerful man, skilled at single-wicket contests, Sampson was a strong, determined batsman with plenty of Yorkshire grit. He played for Clarke only a few times and was never a regular member of the AEE.

Tom Adams, of Kent, was a good, forcing batsman and a useful bowler, who—unusual in those round-arm days—delivered over the wicket. Like Tom Box, he was blessed with a fine head of hair, which he wore long and tended with much care, training it to hang down each side of his face in a curl known as a "love lock" or "kiss me quick". Adams played for Clarke in over half of the fixtures of the following season, but only infrequently thereafter. He lived into his eighties, having carefully preserved one of his old top hats, in which he used to store his long clay pipes.

John Bickley, of Nottinghamshire, was a fast bowler whose walking approach to the wicket concealed his speed and his ability to make the ball fizz off the pitch at an alarming pace, veering from leg to off. Cricket was not his only sport, for he was also an excellent sprinter and jumper. Some of his contemporaries held a high opinion of his talents, but Bickley was one of those trundlers who never receive the recognition they seem to deserve. He was engaged as a bowler for several seasons in the 1850s at Enville Hall, the residence of the Earl of Stamford and Warrington, a noted patron of the noble game.

By 1849, the commercial advantages accruing from Clarke's operations had attracted the adherence of Fred Lillywhite, who was resolved to glean a share of the harvest. One of Old Lilly's sons, Fred made his mark as a journalist, author, compiler of *Lillywhite's Guide to Cricketers*, and publicist of the monumental *Scores and Biographies*, earning the undying gratitude of future historians. His enthusiasm for cricket knew no bounds, but his talent was negligible, so he became an inveterate hanger-on, condemned to obtaining a vicarious satisfaction from associating with the great and sharing their triumphs and vicissitudes. Fred was one of the earliest printers of score cards, produced on a portable press, and he toured the country with Clarke's men and later other teams, recording their deeds. His activities were not always appreciated by the players or the home authorities, and at times the famous portable press was denied admission to the ground—perhaps at the insistence of a local printer eager to profit from the visit of the famous Eleven. This was a source of great frustration to Fred, creating difficulties for him in fulfilling contracts made to supply enthusiastic subscribers with a complete record of the Eleven's doings throughout any one season.

There was no stopping Clarke now. Still more engagements were accepted in 1850—twenty-four, including four important matches—and in the following year he attained the astonishing aggregate of thirty-four fixtures, with five important contests. This was a record never equalled in subsequent seasons.

Clarke was ever on the look-out for new talent to replace his ageing stars, and there were five promising recruits in 1850. Most prominent was William Caffyn, a rising Surrey "crack", who played in four matches, becoming a regular member of the team from 1851 to 1854. Destined to become one of the leading all-rounders of the country, Caffyn was a sparkling batsman whose brilliant cuts won him high acclaim—though he tended sometimes to play by guess—and a first-class medium-pace bowler. He was one of the leading lights of his county side for over ten years.

Almost as eminent as Caffyn, but rarely assisting the AEE, was John Lillywhite, another of Old Lilly's sons. Short, stocky, broad-shouldered, renowned for his full-blooded drives and cuts, John was also an occasional and effective trundler, known as "The Mud Bowler" for his success on wet wickets. Short-sighted from birth, he once recalled that in his school-days he had to wear spectacles to read and write, adding whimsically that he had also "got many a pair on the cricket field". He was nevertheless an excellent batsman, scoring a century against a twenty-two on his final appearance for the Eleven in 1864.

Three others engaged on occasions by Clarke were Thomas Hunt, George Henry Wright, and Thomas Sherman. Hunt hailed from Derbyshire, but played most of his cricket in Sheffield and Manchester. A portly, handsome man, a fine batsman, dubbed "The Star of the North" by his admirers, Hunt was a champion performer in single-wicket matches. Wright was a stolid Yorkshire batsman with a long reach, extolled also for his fielding at point. Sherman, a fast bowler from Surrey, lived to a great age (almost eighty-six) and left some interesting reminiscences. Greatness eluded him, probably because of his temperament. Tom was an awkward customer, attributing his early omission from his county team to the machinations of "powerful enemies", though he was occasionally called upon in emergencies. He rarely played for Clarke.

The Eleven received more regular service from most of the six newcomers of 1851. A prime example of Clarke's ability to spot a talented player was George Anderson. A canny Yorkshireman from the Bedale district, George did not immediately accept the offer of regular employment with the AEE. After appearing eleven times in 1851, he became a permanent member, missing few matches between 1852 and 1866, and even played as late as 1870. A tall, handsome man, a cut above the average professional of his time, George was a fine, forcing batsman, highly respected by his contemporaries, always impeccably turned-out and "as clean as a new-scraped carrot". Off the field, he favoured suits of heather mixture and was often mistaken for an army officer in mufti. He became a great friend of George Parr, who for reasons best known to himself, affectionately nicknamed him "The Old Scotchman". Anderson was a moderate indulger in liquor and tobacco, but he had a very sweet tooth for cheesecake and pastry of all kinds.

Another famous *débutant* of 1851 was Julius Caesar of Godalming, a pillar of the Surrey eleven for many years. A strong man of medium height, a droll companion, and a skilful pugilist, "Julie" was a carpenter and joiner by trade. His batting was a happy blend of stubborn defence and free hitting, and he was a merciless punisher of the "slows", being an early practitioner of the pull stroke. Though not much of a bowler—except in his own estimation—he was worth his place in any side for his fielding, especially at point, long-stop, or long-slip. For all his humour, he was easily depressed by a run of low scores and was obsessed by a conviction that any strange house in which he slept was liable to catch fire. A favourite drinking partner of George Parr's, "Julie" was an early and prolonged sufferer from the martydom of gout, which effectively ended his career in the mid-1860s. He rarely missed a match with the AEE between 1853 and 1855 and continued to appear frequently up to the end of 1863.

Old Clarke's son, Alfred, was a regular member of the AEE and Nottinghamshire from 1853 to 1864. No bowler like his father, Alfred was a competent, stylish batsman and a quietly safe fielder, performing his part "without any useless display". As an expert at reading time-tables, he was often entrusted with the task of planning all the Eleven's journeys by rail.

Another Nottinghamshire man joining the AEE in 1851 was Robert Crispin Tinley, who came from a well known cricketing family, but achieved more fame than his brothers, Frank and Vincent. As a batsman, "Cris" was not much more than a cross-batted slogger, but his quickness of eye often made up for his lack of science, and he was a dangerous opponent, feared for destroying a bowler's length. In his prime, he was recognized as one of the finest fielders at point, and his bowling was frequently in demand. Originally fast and round-armed, he later became Old Clarke's successor as a purveyor of crafty under-hands. George Parr, with his propensity for

MOURE & WILLIAMSON

George Anderson, Yorkshire and the All England Eleven. Toured Australia, 1863–64. One of the Yorkshire 'rebels' of the mid–1860s.

Thomas Lockyer, Surrey, United All England, and United South of England Elevens. Toured North America, 1859, and Australia, 1863–64.

bestowing nicknames on his team-mates, called Tinley "The Spider", and many a victim became enmeshed in the treacherous web of his spinning deliveries. He was a holy terror against twenty-twos and once reduced a Balaclava veteran to a defenceless state of stuttering impotence.

James Grundy, also of Nottinghamshire, appeared occasionally for the AEE in 1851 and the following year. A neat, erect, strongly built man, Jemmy was almost as good an all-rounder as William Caffyn. As a batsman, he possessed a sound defence and made many long scores, though at times he displayed a too obvious dislike of pace. His bowling was fast-medium with an easy, effortless action, pitching slightly short of a length with pin-point accuracy. Always attacking the stumps, he scorned any suggestion that he should give the batsman a chance to hit out and be caught. "Nay, I shan't!" was Jemmy's invariable reply, "I shall gi'e him a *good* 'un; if he wants to hit me, let him come and do it!" He usually bowled with his cap tucked into his belt and always acted as his own statistician, keeping a mental note of his analysis throughout the innings. Jemmy was a great favourite at Lord's, where he was employed as a ground bowler for twenty-one seasons (1851–1871). He was very fond of mutton chops, particularly the fatty bits, which he cut off and devoured with gusto.

The last important newcomer of 1851 was Thomas Lockyer, of Surrey, a hard-hitting batsman, an occasional bowler, and the prince of wicket-keepers, almost always first choice for the Players against the Gentlemen from 1854 to 1866. Tall, brawny, with exceptionally long arms, Tom was one of the first stumpers to take leg-side deliveries instead of relying on his long-stop. Though usually a good-natured man, he was considered to be a little "queer-tempered" on occasions, because he liked to get away on his own to smoke a quiet, reflective pipe. In those days before the invention of sweaters, Tom was instantly recognizable by the white, flannel jacket he always wore to keep out the cold. He had an extensive knowledge of the game and was a sublime exponent of the arts of gamesmanship. With cat-like vigilance he would watch and wait, holding on to the ball and stumping an unwary batsman caught in the act of lifting a foot to ease his stance or scratch his leg. He was even known to draw an opponent's attention to a bit of dirt on the pitch, whipping off the bails after the victim had left his crease to deal with it. "I wait for a chance," was Tom's dictum, "especially when we play against twenty-two, for then we can't afford to be particular." Lockyer evidently did not relish playing for the AEE, appearing only once during Old Clarke's time, and rarely thereafter.

For Clarke, at the end of 1851, everything was *couleur de rose*: a record number of matches in the season, a dominating position in the world of cricket, and plenty of promising youngsters to replace the veterans and bring new blood into the Eleven. Clarke could afford to relax and bask in the warm sunshine of his own making. Or so he thought. Had he looked towards the horizon, he would have seen a small cloud arising out of the sea. As yet no bigger than a man's hand, it gradually grew larger, and the lowering sky turned dark with the coming storm.

CHAPTER THREE

Finance and Fateful Fifty-two

A shrewd, hard-headed businessman like Old Clarke would surely have kept careful accounts of his venture with the AEE, but his ledgers, like many other written and printed records of cricket at this period, have unfortunately not been preserved or located. Concrete information relating to financial transactions and arrangements for the management of an itinerant eleven is rather sparse and vague, consisting of brief items scattered throughout a wide variety of books or hidden in the files of old newspapers and sporting journals. When the AEE was in its infancy, Clarke would doubtless have had to take the initiative in arranging the matches. Once the Eleven was established as a going concern, popular and in demand throughout the country, he could spend the winter building up his list of fixtures, as would-be promoters of local teams approached him. Clarke, it follows, was not the only party with an eye to the profits. Some individuals would be satisfied with nothing beyond the honour and glory of playing against the Eleven, but behind them stood a group whose primary concern was financial speculation. It was not merely a question of the number of sixpences collected at the gate. Local businessmen could look forward to the opportunity of making a welcome addition to their annual income—the printers, the dealers in cricketing goods, the suppliers of tents, marquees, and in some instances massive canvas screens erected around the perimeter of the playing area to prevent spectators from watching the match without paying for admission. Above all, there were the caterers, anticipating a temporary boom in the sale of food and drink, and it comes as no surprise to find that matches often took place in a field adjacent to an hotel. Cricket played for profit rather than for its own sake was regarded as highly undesirable in some quarters, and throughout the existence of the AEE and other itinerant elevens, this aspect formed part of the rising chorus of adverse criticism voiced against them.

Broadly speaking, there seem to have been two forms of contract drawn up by the manager of an eleven and the local promoters. First, the services of the AEE could be engaged for a fixed sum of money—£65 is mentioned on one occasion, £80 on another—and the takings at the gate would belong to the promoters, to say nothing of the profits gained by the local businessmen, especially the caterers. This type of contract had one distinct advantage for the Eleven: whatever the weather, whatever the receipts, Clarke was assured of receiving a stated amount, enabling him to pay his players' wages and collect his own fee. It was an acceptable arrangement for the backers as well, provided the weather was favourable, but prudent promoters took precautions in the months and weeks preceding the match by opening subscription lists and engaging the interests of local businessmen.

The other form of contract was a reversal of the first: the backers yielded the gate receipts to Clarke, who would pay the expenses of staging the game and hand over an agreed sum for the rental of the ground during the period of the match. This arrangement relieved the promoters of any financial anxiety and could be hazardous for the Eleven on rainy days. Given good weather, however, it could prove an advantageous speculation, yielding more for Clarke than a fixed payment. In certain conditions, moreover, it created the opportunity for making additional profits by giving him some control over such issues as the catering.

It is likely, on the whole, that Clarke and other managers preferred the security of the first form of contract, ensuring them of the payment of a guaranteed sum and sparing them any irksome side-issue that could arise.

So much for Clarke's arrangements with local promoters, but what about the wages he paid to his employees, the members of the Eleven? These varied according to the players' status and, in the case of youngsters and newcomers, their performance in individual matches. William Caffyn said that, in his first full season with the AEE (1851), the match fee was £4, meaning probably that he received £4 himself and larger or smaller sums were paid to others, according to their seniority. Looking back over the years, George Anderson recollected that "We got £5 a game, and sometimes when we had a long journey we would get a little more, but never more than £6 a match in all". By the standards of the time, the wages seem fairly adequate, until it is remembered that players usually had to pay their own expenses. Returning from Scotland after assisting one of the itinerant elevens in the 1860s, Edward Pooley and William Mortlock found themselves arriving at *The Elephant and Castle* with no more than 1s. 4d. between them and the prospect of having to dine with Duke Humphrey!

Clarke was certainly accustomed to driving a hard bargain with his employees. To the end of his days, it is said, George Parr bore a grudge against the veteran for persuading him to accept low wages at the outset of his career with the AEE. A graphic description of the old man's dealings with his players was recorded by Tom Sherman. Well-to-do spectators often showed tangible evidence of their appreciation of a fine performance on the field by tipping the fortunate professional with a present, sometimes as much as a golden sovereign. Whenever this occurred, the lucky recipient was rarely left in sole possession of his windfall: Clarke, as manager, captain, and secretary of the AEE, always insisted on taking a share of the "present" for himself. The player rarely resisted this rapacious claim for long, allowing himself to be mulcted by his employer, who enforced his demands by threatening to omit his victim from the side in later fixtures, under the principle of 'no play, no pay'.

Sherman also remembered how the Eleven received their wages at the conclusion of a match. There was a distinct resemblance to an old-fashioned army pay parade: Clarke sitting at the table with a heap of gold and silver coins in front of him, the rest of the team standing in a group, waiting to be called forward in turn. Young Sherman, who was last, was a fascinated witness of the whole transaction. As each man approached the table, the paymaster doled out the wages, saying "Four pounds for you", or "Three pounds for you", or "Fifty shillings for you", assessing the amount according to the player's fame, seniority, and performance in the current match. Finally, it was Sherman's turn, and Clarke, looking up, said "Fifty shillings for you". Then, with a smile of profound satisfaction, the manager shovelled the remaining coins into his trouser pockets, adding *"and thirty-seven pounds for me!"*

It is difficult to determine the accuracy of this description, since Sherman assisted the AEE only twice during Clarke's managership, which suggests they did not get on well together. The veteran, it may be argued, was entitled to a handsome share of the profits in recompense for the burden of all the arduous administrative duties he performed throughout the year. As described by Sherman, the scene nevertheless aptly illustrates the unenviable reputation acquired by Clarke over the years—a dictatorial manner, a blatant tactlessness in dealing with players and their wages in public, and an overt display of his own greed. Small wonder, then, that players like Old Lillywhite, Dean, and Wisden, and newcomers like John Lillywhite, Lockyer, and Sherman, chose to sacrifice the opportunity of earning regular summer wages with the Eleven rather than swallow their pride and endure the humiliation of serving under Clarke.

The Eleven played fewer matches in 1852, yet a list of twenty-six fixtures was still ample for the continuance of Clarke's operations, but the year proved disastrous for the ageing manager of the AEE. He suffered physical disablement by injuring one of his arms, but this was of little account compared with an event that shattered his monopoly in the world of cricket. During the early part of the year, Wisden and Dean had been laying their heads together and negotiating behind the scenes with other disgruntled professionals harbouring real or imagined grievances against Clarke.

The gathering storm broke towards the end of the season. On August 26, 1852, the AEE were playing against 22 of Hereford. Picture Clarke's horrified rage on learning that a rival itinerant team, the United All England

Eleven, had been created and was contending against 22 Gentlemen of Hampshire on the same date! Both teams were engaged with twenty-twos on August 30, the AEE at Ilkeston, the UAEE at Newmarket. Determined to beard the lions in their den, Clarke delegated the captaincy to George Parr and travelled to Newmarket to try and arrange terms with Wisden and his allies. However unpleasant Clarke may have been, one cannot help but admire his courage in sallying forth alone to confront such hostile opposition. Exactly what transpired at this meeting was never recorded, but one can easily imagine the scene with all its rancour and recriminations, its accusations and counter-charges, leading to the inevitable defeat of Clarke, who nevertheless succeeded in expressing the depth of his outraged feelings.

After playing against 18 of Gravesend on September 2, the UAEE made their way north again for the final match of their first season, against 15 of Sheffield. The members of the United had evidently been discussing their grievances and Clarke's behaviour at the recent confrontation, and now they issued the following manifesto, couched in the pompous terms of a formal declaration of war:

At a meeting held at the Adelphi Hotel, Sheffield, this 7th day of September, 1852, by the members of the United Eleven of England, it was unanimously resolved,—That neither the members of the above Eleven shall at any time play in a match of cricket, for or against, wherein William Clarke may have the management or control (county matches excepted), in consequence of the treatment they have received from him at Newmarket and elsewhere.

JOHN WISDEN	GEORGE PICKNELL
JAMES DEAN	SAMUEL DAKIN
THOMAS ADAMS	GEORGE CHATTERTON
THOMAS HUNT	THOMAS LOCKYER
GEORGE GRAINGER BROWN	JAMES GRUNDY
JOHN LILLYWHITE	THOMAS SHERMAN
THOMAS NIXON	HENRY WRIGHT

It has sometimes been inferred that the United All England Eleven was established by a wholesale secession of members of the AEE, but nothing could be further from the truth. Of the fourteen signatories to the manifesto, less than half had actually played for Clarke in 1852, and some hardly at all in previous years. Only two could really be considered as true seceders—Tom Adams, who assisted the Eleven in the five fixtures before August 26, on which date he appeared against them as a Given Man for 22 of Hereford, and Jemmy Grundy, who had seven appearances in all, including the match at Hereford and the following one at Ilkeston, when Clarke was at

Newmarket. Grundy then deserted the AEE to play for the United in their final match at Sheffield. One name omitted from the list of signatories was Henry Sampson (landlord for many years of *The Adelphi Hotel*) who had appeared once for the AEE in 1852 and on rare occasions previously, and who assisted the United in their first three matches, playing for 15 of Sheffield against them in the fourth. On the other hand, Tom Sherman, who added his name to the manifesto, did not begin his playing career with the UAEE until 1853, dropping out after 1856, having participated in about one-third of their matches.

The establishment of the United Eleven was a *fait accompli*, but arguments continued to rumble throughout the autumn, becoming more strident towards the end of the year in the columns of *Bell's Life*. First came a lengthy contribution signed by "A Lover of Cricket". Its title implied that readers were being presented with a series of comments and reflections on cricket in 1852. In reality, it was a full-blown attack on the AEE, beginning with the by now hackneyed complaint that the name assumed by the team smacked of unjustified arrogance. The AEE were sailing under false colours, alleged the writer, for some of the members were no longer worthy of inclusion in a side purporting to represent the cream of English cricket. As was only to be expected, Clarke was the target for the principal shafts of criticism. He was assailed on the grounds of his dictatorial methods, high-handed behaviour, meanness, and profiteering. By way of illustration, the correspondent quoted the payments made to Clarke by local promoters, ranging from £66 to £75. Taking the lower figure as an example, "A Lover of Cricket" then estimated the actual match fee earned by each named member of the Eleven, leaving Clarke's share at £11 10s., or more if the gross sum were £70 or £75. Moreover, contrary to Sherman's description of the "pay parade", the writer claimed that the niggardly manager of the AEE often settled accounts with his players several months in arrears.

This "long, sickly, childish prattle", as Fuller Pilch call it, brought forth spirited replies from some of Clarke's supporters, among them Felix, the President and PR man of the AEE, who wrote in defence of the team's title. Clarke himself entered the lists with a counter-attack of blistering sarcasm, dealing blow for blow and stripe for stripe. Stating most of the estimates of wages were wrong, he asserted he was justified in taking higher payments as recompense for his administrative duties and left no doubt he was aware of the identity of "A Lover of Cricket". Another extensive contribution from Clarke's enemy appeared, supported by letters from Dean and Martingell, the latter thus declaring his secession from the AEE after having played in many of their matches in 1852 (he joined the United Eleven the following year). The editor of *Bell's Life* terminated the correspondence in January 1853.

Who could "A Lover of Cricket" have been? Of him Clarke wrote: "I know his name to be *not Sorrywether*, but something like it, a portly *barrister*, *noted* for his *old Dando qualifications* and his expensive professionals, old Dean and old Lilly, who cost about two penny postage stamps". 'Old Dean,' it may be noted, was nearly seventeen years younger than Old Clarke! In one sense, the latter was sailing pretty close to the wind, particularly since his adversary was a man of the law: *Dando* was current slang, signifying a 'seedy swell', a heavy eater, who made a practice of failing to settle his bills at restaurants.

In his book, *Alfred Mynn and the Cricketers of His Time* (1963), Patrick Morrah gives a detailed digest of the whole affair, stating that "Clarke clearly knew who his assailant was, but in spite of these allusive hints nobody since that time, so far as I am aware, has identified him. One can only conclude that he was some backer of the United England Eleven, probably of the name of Merrywether".

It is almost certain that "A Lover of Cricket" was Charles George Merewether, QC (born 1823), Recorder of Leicester from 1868 until his death, and Conservative MP for Northampton (1874–80). In all charity, one must attribute the somewhat chaotic passages of his letters in *Bell's Life* to the passion of the moment, or to the unfortunate activities of the editor and printer, for Mr Merewether was a man of intellectual and professional attainments. He is credited with being the author of the legal opinion relating to the vexed problem of heirlooms, incorporated by Anthony Trollope in his novel, *The Eustace Diamonds*, and subsequently recognized as an authority on the subject. A member of the Marylebone and Surrey Clubs, Mr Merewether was a keen supporter of cricket, whose assistance is acknowledged by the Rev James Pycroft in the Preface to the first edition of *The Cricket-field* (1851). He died suddenly on June 26, 1884, but a few months after John Wisden, whose United Eleven he had favoured from its foundation.

Clarke was responsible in more ways than one for the birth of the UAEE. His tyrannical behaviour and treatment of some of his players were obvious reasons, but there were others, not at first so obvious. By travelling round the country and stimulating the interest in cricket, he created a demand which no single itinerant eleven could possibly satisfy, even by playing two matches a week from April to October. At the same time, his policy of perpetually recruiting new players produced a pool of talented cricketers eager to capitalize on their skills. Clarke could not include them all in his Eleven, and so the need for a second team was born. Manning the AEE was no problem, for a strong cadre remained, and there was no shortage of youngsters aspiring to a place in the ranks. The greatest blow to Clarke was the termination of his monopoly—the realization that his enemies would be seizing a share of the rich pickings.

CHAPTER FOUR

Interlude—Against Heavy Odds

CONTESTS in which the AEE and other itinerant elevens encountered sides comprising eleven, fourteen, and occasionally sixteen players hold more interest for to-day's enthusiasts and statisticians, rather than fixtures with as many as twenty-two opponents. Matches now classified as "important" or "first-class" were, however, comparatively rare events: the majority in any one season were played against "odds", involving many tedious and exhausting journeys. Although secretaries attempted to organize their programmes for the maximum of convenience, players sometimes found themselves finishing a game one evening and travelling by an overnight train to distant town to fulfil an engagement with a twenty-two the following day. Inevitably, they were known to fall asleep in the dressing-tent or even doze off on their feet in the field. Wet weather was secretly welcomed, provided their wages were guaranteed, for the jaded professional could then enjoy a day of unexpected rest and relaxation.

In the early days of the AEE, it was still occasionally necessary to make these nocturnal journeys by stage-coach, and George Anderson recalled one such awesome experience in the depths of rural Lincolnshire. After much aimless wandering along dark, forbidding lanes, the driver confessed he had lost his way, whereupon the weary All Englanders were compelled to get off the coach and search for a sign-post in the vicinity. Finding one at last, one of Anderson's team-mates had to clamber up it and strike a match to read the directions.

Some years later, in June 1859, the AEE had an even worse journey travelling from Redruth in Cornwall across a wild, deserted district towards Launceston. On either side of the road lay a deep ditch, and as the coach rumbled on through the darkness, the team were beset by the additional hazard of a violent thunderstorm. Playing for the Eleven on this occasion was an army officer, Captain Handley, a Crimean War veteran who participated in the famous cavalry charge at Balaclava—perhaps the same man once reduced to a state of abject fear by "Cris" Tinley's under-hand twisters. The captain confessed later that the violence of the storm had frightened him far more than the Russian guns, but in true army fashion he concealed his terror under a volley of sonorous oaths, roundly cursing the

27

weather, the road, and the general situation. This only increased the nervousness of George Parr, who was frightened to death by the thunder and lightning and feared Captain Handley's ceaseless blasphemies would bring down the wrath of the heavens upon the whole team. The coach came eventually to an isolated cottage, where they hoped to obtain food and temporary shelter. Their cries and knocking went unanswered for some time, then suddenly a night-capped ancient appeared at an upper window clutching an old blunderbuss. This formidable weapon he aimed straight at Parr's head, which did nothing to calm poor George's nerves. A tragedy was averted, but it took some time for the team to explain their requirements, since the owner of the blunderbuss "was as deaf as an adder". Bread, cheese, and beer were produced, paid for, and speedily consumed, and the Eleven prepared to continue their journey, only to discover that their fast bowler, John Jackson, was missing. When he finally appeared, his team-mates were convinced he was in the middle of having a shave, as his chin seemed in the dim light to be covered with lather. In this they were mistaken, for the "lather" turned out to be clotted cream, which he had discovered in a large bowl in the dairy. Alas! such was Jackson's gluttony that little cream was left for the rest of the Eleven to enjoy.

Many of the fields on which the itinerant elevens were expected to play, especially in Clarke's time, left much to be desired, even by the less exacting standards of the day. Some consisted of a pitch surrounded by long grass reaching to the shins, and once, at Truro, in Cornwall, a deep-fielder chasing after the ball put up a whole covey of partridges. It is only fair to say, however, that such conditions—minus the partridges usually—could still be found many years later on the grounds of more remote villages. Indeed, the present writer can remember once playing in his boyhood as an "emergency" and taking a catch at long-on while standing in knee-high grass. In the early period of the AEE, some of the pitches themselves required urgent attention. Once, at Glasgow, play could not begin until Fuller Pilch has borrowed a scythe to mow the wicket. "It was," said George Anderson, "like playing in a meadow."

The exhaustion resulting from constant travelling and the necessity of playing on rough pitches were not the only problems confronting itinerant elevens. Why, one may ask, were they sometimes dismissed for comparatively low totals by mediocre local sides? The answer lies not only in the assistance provided for the opposition by one or more professional bowlers specially engaged for the occasion, but also in the daunting presence of twenty-two fielders—an absolute mob surrounding the pitch. There were precious few gaps in the field, and all hits had to be run out. A stroke perfectly safe in an eleven-a-side contest was often fraught with danger when playing against "odds"—even though the standard of fielding was not of the best—and the scoring rate was consequently painfully slow.

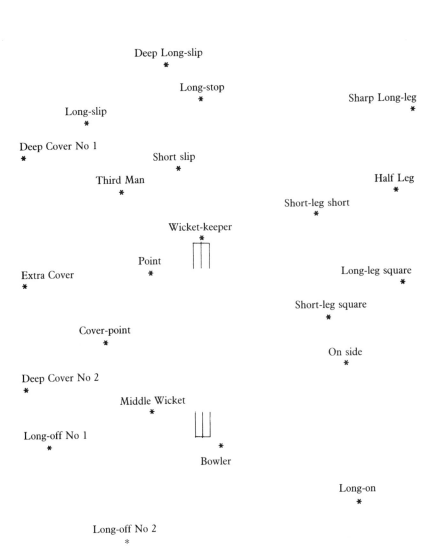

How Twenty-two Should be Placed in the Field for a Right-handed Batsman facing a Fast, Right-handed Bowler at the Commencement of a Match.

Although members of the elevens soon realized different styles of play were required for the two types of matches, they experienced some problems in switching from one technique to the other. An analogy may be seen in the difficulties encountered by twentieth-century cricketers in adapting themselves to the different conditions of three-day and one-day matches, when the limited-overs competitions were introduced.

For experienced professionals, a match between an eleven and a local team provided a means of earning wages for work much more palatable than toiling at the mundane occupations by which, at other times, they were obliged to earn their daily bread. The inhabitants often lionized them, and the adulation bestowed upon them as national celebrities and the various "presents" they received were some compensation for the discomfort of perpetual journeys and the sometimes primitive playing conditions. But what of the locals themselves? Some individual members of a twenty-two viewed an encounter with the AEE with a mixture of apprehension and delight, plus the added bonus of the chance of achieving enough success to attract Old Clarke's attention. Perhaps, even, the ultimate mark of recognition—an invitation to play as a guest member of the AEE itself! The match, moreover, was not regarded merely as a game of cricket: it was magnified into a social event of outstanding importance in the whole year. Richard Daft, who played during the golden age of the itinerant elevens and saw them dwindle and die, looked back with nostalgia on his years of service with the AEE, when people seemed to enjoy cricket much more:

> Certainly one never sees such holiday-making and high jinks as we used to in the old All England days, especially at those matches played in small country towns. The All England match was the topic of conversation months before the event took place. Special committees were formed to get up entertainments in the evening, and when the great day arrived the excitement was often intense.

There was also, as mentioned previously, the attraction of a successful financial speculation for the promoters and the local businessmen. Another of Daft's anecdotes relates the tale of a Leicester man responsible for getting up several All England matches. After one of them, played before a large attendance over three full days, the promoter was heard to declare he had lost £100 over his speculation, which seemed strange. In fact, he had cleared £150 but had been calculating on making a profit of £250!

In some ways, one match against "odds" was very like another, and the cricket itself often not remarkably outstanding, though occasionally there were other interesting matters connected with the administrative arrangements. A fixture on July 5, 6, and 7, 1855, when the AEE were engaged to play against 22 of Reading and District, reveals something of those arrangements and presents a telling picture of Old Clarke—his bowling, his high-handed, dictatorial behaviour, and even his relations with the other members of the Eleven. The same opponents had met in September of the previous year, and both matches were played on the Reading Ground, a field behind Radley's Hotel near the cattle market on Caversham Road, a short distance west of the main railway station. For the contest of 1854, the local press published an announcement giving the time of starting (11.00 a.m.), the price of entry ("Admission, 6d.; Saddle Horses, 1s.; Carriages, 2s. 6d."), and the information that there would be a printing tent on the ground for the sale of score cards. Refreshments would be provided by Mr Walley Cross, landlord of Radley's Hotel ("*An ordinary each day at half-past Two o'clock. Tickets*, 2s. 6d., each."), and marquees were erected on the ground for the accommodation of visitors. The home side made 38 and 62, the AEE 64 and 37 for 8.

The announcement for the match of 1855 gave the venue and dates of play, and the names of the players from whom the teams would be selected, twelve for the AEE and twenty-five for the home side. The list for the AEE, in its original spelling, was as follows:

A. Mynn, Esq, Willsher, C. R. Tinley, A. Clark, G. Parr, Stephenson, S. Parr, Anderson, Caesar, Box, Bickley, W. Clark.

In the event, A. Mynn, Esq, R. C. Tinley, Box, and Bickley did not play, and there were also some changes in the list for 22 of Reading and District. Admission was again 6d. each—the details about saddle horses and carriages were omitted—there would be commodious tents, and refreshments would be provided on the ground. As to who would be providing them the notice was silent, perhaps for a good reason.

The match was covered by *Bell's Life*, and accounts also appeared in local journals, *The Berkshire Chronicle* and *The Reading Mercury*, the *Chronicle* being more enthusiastic and informative. Dwelling on the prowess of the AEE in all departments of the game, the reporter asserted that "George Parr has averaged about 60 runs in each match" and praised the play of his "compeers". Consequently, the local managers were resolved to assemble as strong a twenty-two as possible to do battle with their redoubtable adversaries. The reporter of the *Mercury* delivered a more splenetic comment, saying, "The numerical strength of the parties seems to us out of all proportion, and we are, on the first mention of it, inclined to think the eleven somewhat overweening and too ready to 'bragg' [*sic*]". He grudgingly admitted, however, that the AEE were often too strong for many of their opponents, and then proceeded to give a fairly brief description of the play. Surprisingly enough, he omitted all mention of a *contretemps* that threatened to disrupt the whole match.

Not so the reporter of the *Chronicle*. The weather could not have been better for a grand cricket match, or, to borrow his own words, "The fifth of July was, indeed, clothed in her summer mantle", but eleven o'clock came and went without any sign of the commencement of play. Then it was noised abroad that there had been some misunderstanding with Old Clarke, "and there was a great probability the match would not take place". According to the *Chronicle*, the All England manager "had taken the ground on the same terms as last year", implying that this was one of those occasions, on which he was paying a rental fee to the local club, taking all the gate receipts himself. So far, so good, but Clarke interpreted the contract as giving him control over all other matters connected with the match. The bone of contention was the arrangements for supplying refreshments. Clarke, it appears, "had let the ground"—doubtless in return for a sizeable fee—to a well known London caterer with the resounding name of Baron Nicholson, who had already erected a marquee for the sale of food and drink. But Nicholson soon found he had competition, for Mr Walley Cross, landlord of Radley's Hotel, had also set up a small booth for the sale of refreshments, "anticipating there would be no objection". Cross, who had after all organized the catering the previous year—and had probably made a handsome profit—said he had not received any communication on the matter from Clarke. The latter, however, insisted he had let the ground exclusively to Nicholson, and Cross must therefore give way and dismantle his booth.

Cross's claims were, of course, supported by the club committee, who urged the All England manager to withdraw his objections, but Clarke dug in his toes and maintained his stance in the teeth of all opposition. Bitter words were exchanged, and the prolonged, acrimonious dispute delayed the start of play, "greatly to the annoyance of the players and the public who had assembled to witness the game". Baron Nicholson tried to pour oil on the troubled waters by expressing his regrets that such unpleasantness should have arisen, adding that he was quite willing for Cross to take a share in the catering. This, surely, ought to have stifled any further argument, but Clarke would have none of it and stormed off, declaring he would not play the match at all. A grave lack of judgement. By adopting this attitude, he found himself in a position of splendid isolation, faced with a threat of rebellion by his team, whom the club committee persuaded to go on with the match without Clarke's assistance. Their gesture of going out onto the field evidently brought their captain to his senses. Clarke appeared, and play began shortly after one o'clock, which indicates the amount of time consumed by the dispute.

The account in the *Chronicle* says, "the differences were adjusted", meaning the All England manager gave way, and the reporter continued, "There is no doubt that Clarke exercised a very wise discretion in waving [*sic*] the point, otherwise, it might have led to serious results in the cricketing world, as it was generally thought on the ground it would be the breaking up of the eleven". A slight exaggeration, perhaps? Who knows? The whole unsavoury incident is a perfect illustration of Clarke's sheer cussedness and determination to impose his own views on others, whatever the consequences might be. His failure to enforce his demands on this occasion may possibly be attributed to the fact that he was approaching the end of his career and was no longer quite so formidable as he had once been.

Playing for the AEE were Clarke and his son Alfred, Edgar Willsher, H. H. Stephenson (wicket-keeper), George Anderson, George Parr and his elder brother Sam, and Julius Caesar, whose names had appeared in the original list published in the press. The team was completed with the addition of bibulous Billy Buttress of Cambridgeshire, a genuine leg-breaker almost unplayable when sober, and two amateurs, Mr H. Wyatt, who had assisted Oxford twice against Cambridge (1850–51), and Mr C. H. Ridding, another Oxford man, with five appearances in the varsity match (1845–49) and five for the Gentlemen against the Players (1848–53).

The home side included seven individuals accorded notices in *Scores and Biographies*. These were the two professionals, Henry Paine (wicket-keeper), and David Burrin, a renowned bowler of the district, and five amateurs, A. H. Faber, an accomplished batsman (Free Foresters); H. T. Frere, a fast bowler (Gentlemen *v* Players, 1858–59); the Hon W. S. T.-W. Fiennes, a bowler (Oxford, 1856–58), and the Hon C. B. T.-W. Fiennes; and another talented fast bowler, G. E. Yonge, who, like C. H. Ridding, played five times for Oxford (1844–48) and five times for the Gentlemen (1847–52).

Reading took first innings, opening with Messrs R. Iremonger and A. H. Faber, who faced a perplexing contrast of bowling. At one end, Old Clarke himself with his insidious "slows"; at the other, Edgar Willsher, of Kent, "a tall, lanky, cadaverous-looking man", a fast left-hander delivering round the wicket with a suspiciously high action. As the years passed, Ned Willsher became the target for a swelling tide of complaint, his critics alleging that he infringed Law X by bowling above the level of the shoulder.

Bamboozled by Clarke, Mr Iremonger soon departed scoreless, but Mr Faber, in fine form, delighted the spectators with some mighty leg-hitting. He defied the attack for a long time, making 24, before also succumbing to "that tiresome bowling", caught off an impatient, ballooning hit at square leg. Only one other batsman got into double figures, and the whole side were dismissed for 77, with Willsher claiming 13 victims and Clarke 7.

The opening pair for the AEE were Alfred Clarke and Mr Wyatt. The latter, "more remarkable for his fine fielding than his batting", was soon bowled for 2 by Burrin. Young Clarke, who had already survived a chance at long-leg, was joined by Anderson, who immediately assaulted the bowling with some brutal drives. When stumps were drawn, both batsmen were undefeated, with Anderson on 14 and Clarke on 10.

The partnership was resumed the next morning before a large crowd, and the proceedings throughout the day were enlivened by the band of the Royal Berks Militia, "in attendance, by the kind permission of the officers". Neither batsman had time to play himself in. Clarke, without adding to his overnight score, was trapped lbw by the Hon W. S. Fiennes, who also disposed of Anderson for 15 with "a ripper" in the first two overs. George Parr and Mr Ridding stayed together for some time, trying to master the bowling, but their efforts to penetrate the closely packed field met with indifferent success, apart from a few of George's famous leg-hits. His partner was snapped up by a smart catch at short-slip, and George, to his dismay, watched the All England batting collapse. He was also taken in the slip, and the innings closed for 76.

The jubilation of the spectators was soon silenced, when five or six wickets fell for hardly any runs to Willsher and Old Clarke, who bowled unchanged throughout the match. Especially devastating were the captain's "slows", for Clarke was "bowling marvellously well, and as true as clock-work". Eleven wickets went for 29 runs, but the home side overcame these early set-backs with some resolute batting, four of them reaching double figures. Perhaps Clarke ought to have called for Billy Buttress's crafty spinners, but he persisted with his well tried bowling combination to the end of the day. On their second hands, 22 of Reading and District ran up a total of 91, Clarke capturing 13 wickets and Willsher 8. Only a few minutes remained for play, so the stumps were drawn, leaving All England a target of 93 for victory.

Saturday brought another large attendance, agog with wide-spread speculation. Could the AEE rub off the required runs against the bowling they had failed to dominate so far? Such a task, ran the general opinion, would take them all day and test their skills to the utmost. Clarke changed his order for the second innings, sending Sam Parr and the out-of-form Julius Caesar to the wickets. "Julie" managed to manipulate 3, but Sam was bowled for a cipher, and Messrs Wyatt and Ridding suffered an identical fate. The same sorry tale of the previous day was repeated with another collapse of the All England batting. Stalwart George Parr, the mainstay of the side, was bowled for 6, and this, as it turned out, was the second highest score from the bat (Extras totalled 9). Minor resistance to the tune of 5 each came from Willsher and Stephenson, the latter playing on after a circumspect innings, and only George Anderson gave a worthy exhibition of All England form. The indomitable "Old Scotchman" stood steadfast in the breach, his stumps inviolate, relishing the battle and putting loose deliveries to the sword. Eventually, he also had to yield, and All England were tumbled out for 66, with Burrin taking five of the wickets. Anderson's contribution was 32, the top score of the match, far surpassing the combined efforts of his ten team-mates, who could only manage a total of 25 runs between them.

So a match begun in an atmosphere of rancour and dissension ended in a woeful defeat for the AEE, who retired crestfallen and entrained for their next engagement at Enville Hall, in Staffordshire. Their fate here was even worse, losing by an innings to the Earl of Stamford's 22, which included some of his lordship's engaged professional bowlers and several first-class amateurs. The trauma was too much for Old Clarke, who succumbed to a severe inflammation of the eyes and was unable to play again for a month.

The score card for the match was as follows:

On the Reading Cricket Ground, behind Radley's Hotel, Caversham Road, July 5, 6, and 7, 1855

22 of Reading and District, with David Burrin, sen.

1st Innings		2nd Innings	
Mr R. Iremonger, b W. Clarke	0	b Willsher	0
Mr A. H. Faber, c S. Parr, b W. Clarke	24	b W. Clarke	0
Mr J. Parsons, b Willsher	2	b W. Clarke	2
Mr T. N. Smith, run out	0	c Anderson, b W. Clarke	0
Mr A. Barker, b Willsher	0	b W. Clarke	8
Capt Bowles, b Willsher	0	b W. Clarke	11
H. Paine (wk), b Willsher	1	c Buttress, b Willsher	1
Mr E. Knipe, c Stephenson, b Willsher	5	b W. Clarke	1
Mr H. T. Frere, b Willsher	3	st Stephenson, b W. Clarke	2
Mr J. L. Randall, b Willsher	0	b Willsher	6
Hon C. B. T.-W. Fiennes, b W. Clarke	3	b Willsher	3
Hon W. S. T.-W. Fiennes, c Caesar, b Willsher	4	b Willsher	13
Capt C. Slocock, c Buttress, b W. Clarke	4	c Stephenson, b Willsher	12
Rev R. Morres, b Willsher	0	c Ridding, b W. Clarke	16
Mr C. Stephens, b Willsher	11	st Stephenson, b W. Clarke	0
Lt Col Wallington, b W. Clarke	4	b Willsher	0
Mr G. E. Yonge, b Willsher	0	b W. Clarke	1
Mr J. Bourn, b Willsher	7	b W. Clarke	2
Mr A. C. Rawlinson, c G. Parr, b W. Clarke	0	not out	1
Mr J. Addison, b W. Clarke	0	b W. Clarke	3
Mr E. Y. Nepean, b Willsher	3	c Stephenson, b W. Clarke	2
D. Burrin, sen., not out	0	c W. Clarke, b Willsher	2
B 2, l b 2, n b 2	6	B 2, n b 3	5
Total	77	Total	91

All England Bowling

	Runs	Wickets		Runs	Wickets
Willsher	26	13	Willsher	28	8
W. Clarke	45	7	W. Clarke	58	13

The All England Eleven

1st Innings		2nd Innings	
Mr H. Wyatt, b Burrin	2	b W. S. T-W. Fiennes	0
A. Clarke, lbw, b W. S. T-W. Fiennes	10	c C. B. T-W. Fiennes, b Burrin	4
G. Anderson, b W. S. T-W. Fiennes	15	b Frere	32
G. Parr, c Yonge, b Frere	17	b Burrin	6
Mr C. H. Ridding, c Yonge, b Burrin	9	b W. S. T-W. Fiennes	0
S. Parr, b Frere	4	b Frere	0
Julius Caesar, b Frere	0	b Frere	3
E. Willsher, st Paine, b Burrin	1	b Burrin	5
H. H. Stephenson (wk), b Burrin	6	b Burrin	5
W. Buttress, not out	2	b Burrin	1
W. Clarke, b Frere	4	not out	1
B 5, w 1	6	B 6, w 3	9
Total	76	Total	66

22 of Reading and District Bowling

	Runs	Wickets		Runs	Wickets
Burrin	21	4	W. S. T-W. Fiennes	9	2
Frere	14	4	Frere	27	3
Yonge	27	0	Burrin	21	5
W. S. T-W. Fiennes	8	2			

Note.—The match is recorded in the three newspapers mentioned above and *Scores and Biographies*, V, 56. There are inevitably some variations in the initials and spelling of names in the Reading team, and one or two differences in the modes of dismissal. The local newspapers have been followed mainly in the matter of initials and names, and *Scores and Biographies* for the score.

CHAPTER FIVE

The All England and United All England Elevens, 1853–1856

So Old Clarke had sowed the wind and reaped the whirlwind, and the Two Elevens, at daggers drawn, went their separate ways. As far as possible, the All England manager excluded his enemies from any match under his complete control, and the United retaliated in kind. Though not immediately apparent, this first great schism in English cricket represented a polarization of North and South, which became more marked in the next decade. Each team in Clarke's time and for some years to come contained professionals from both halves of the country, but the AEE was primarily a northern concern, dominated by Nottinghamshire, whereas Sussex and Surrey provided the main driving force of the UAEE. There was, however, one noticeable difference between the two rivals: the AEE, superior in organization and management, always had a larger fixture list than the United.

Clarke's men won half of their twenty-four matches in 1853, losing seven and drawing five. In one of the unfinished contests, they met a combined team of Kent and Sussex, from which United men, such as Adams, Dean, John Lillywhite, and Wisden were excluded. Clarke had little difficulty in raising a strong side, since many of his regulars had remained loyal to him. There were three notable *débutants*, of whom two—Andrew Crossland, a Yorkshire all-rounder, and Frank Tinley (elder brother of "Cris"), a medium-pace bowler—had only slight connections with the AEE and were found more often playing for their opponents. The third, Samuel Parr, a regular member of the Eleven from 1853 to 1855, was a useful batsman and a fine fielder, without ever approaching the excellence of his younger brother George. He is chiefly remembered now as the perpetrator of those excruciating practical jokes, which created so much amusement in those days, provided you were not the victim. It was Sam who cruelly persuaded the naïve barber to crop Tom Box's carefully cultivated locks, and it was Sam who once early in the week placed a dead, decomposing mouse in Caffyn's best silk hat. The trick was not discovered until the Sunday, when Caffyn removed the stinking hat from its box, and the abominable Sam fled to give vent to his mirth in private.

The United played fifteen matches in their first full season, losing six, drawing six, and winning only three. Two of their victories, however, were achieved in "important" fixtures, against 14 of Yorkshire, and 14 Gentlemen of England (with three players). Tom Sherman and Billy Martingell joined the UAEE this year, and the team was assisted three times by Ned Willsher, the fast left-hander from Kent, who transferred his allegiance to the AEE the following season.

All the twenty-three contests in All England's programme of 1854 were played against "odds", resulting in sixteen victories, six defeats, and one draw. Willsher, of the dubious bowling action, appeared frequently for Clarke and was a regular member of the AEE in 1855–56 and 1860–64. Professional engagements with well-to-do employers often prevented him from assisting the Eleven in the intervening years.

Another famous player joining Clarke this season was Heathfield Harman Stephenson, who, like George Anderson, was socially superior to many other professionals but could not afford to adopt amateur status. H.H., as he was usually known, captained the first team to tour Australia (1861–62), acted as huntsman for the Duc d'Aumale in Worcestershire and was for many years the coach at Uppingham, achieving even more fame than "Ducky" Diver at Rugby. A tall, bearded man, a star of the Surrey eleven for nearly twenty years, H.H. was one of the all-round "cracks" of his time. Second only to Lockyer, his Surrey team-mate, as a wicket-keeper, he was Tom Box's successor as the All England stumper. Always ready in his younger days to doff pads and gloves and take a turn with the ball, he was in demand as a fast bowler with a vicious break-back from the off—a difficult accomplishment with a round-arm delivery. His action proved his undoing, causing him to lose the sensitiveness in his fingers' ends, and his accuracy suffered. A punishing batsman with an upright stance, Stephenson's favourite strokes were on drives and square leg-hits, but he was rather weak on the off side. He habitually wore a long, black frock-coat, which gave him an ecclesiastical appearance, and George Parr nicknamed him "Spurgeon" after a popular preacher of those days.

Billy Buttress, the "father of break-bowling", assisted the AEE once in 1854, ten times the following year, but only rarely afterwards. He had an easy, deceptive action, with the ability to turn the ball both ways, but was chiefly a leg-spinner. A boon companion and an amateur ventriloquist, Billy was on his best days the arch-tormentor of all batsmen, whatever their skills. His best days became depressingly few and far between: Billy, one of the great "might-have-beens", deprived himself of a long and honourable career by his failing for "pints".

Of a different calibre was Roger Iddison, who had a single engagement with Clarke in 1854, appeared very occasionally in subsequent years, but was more closely identified with the UAEE. An ex-butcher from Bedale, in

Roger Iddison, Yorkshire, United All England, United North of England, and Yorkshire United Elevens. Also played for Lancashire. Toured Australia, 1861–62. Captain of Yorkshire, and one of the 'rebels' of the mid-1860s.

Yorkshire, Roger became a popular figure, a "genial, thick-set man", rich of accent, scrupulously neat in attire, and growing more portly with the passing years. Like "Cris" Tinley, he came to the fore as a fast, round-arm bowler, but soon converted himself into a purveyor of the "slows". He developed into an excellent batsman, combining stubbornness in defence with a vigorous attack, being particularly fond of the off drive. Some critics asserted that he did not always play with a straight bat and left his ground too readily. Iddison eliminated the first fault, but not the second—he was the victim of a fair number of run outs—and he never lost his liking for playing forward to the first ball he received. His position at the crease was unusual for those days: he stood with both feet almost parallel to each other, his toes aligned in the direction of point. For several years from 1863 onwards, he held the Yorkshire captaincy and led the team with commendable shrewdness. During the 1860s, he resided in the Manchester district, fulfilling various professional engagements, and when not required by Yorkshire, Roger appeared—tell it not in Gath—in the Lancashire side. Providence was surely merciful in reserving Emmott Robinson for a future generation and sparing him the shock of witnessing such wicked apostasy. One of the most prominent characters in the era of the itinerant elevens, Roger achieved great success as a player, coach, team manager, and getter-up of matches. Equally versatile in business matters, he followed the vocations of dealer in cricket goods, commission agent, and auctioneer.

The United again played fifteen matches in 1854, but were much more successful this season. With only two defeats and one draw, their twelve victories included two in "important" matches, against 15 Young Players of Kent and 16 of Sussex. They travelled up and down the country, ranging from Kent and Sussex through the Midlands to Scotland and crossing the water for an encounter with 22 of the Phoenix Park Club at Dublin.

Billy Buttress made two of his five appearances for the UAEE in 1854, but Wisden engaged two other professionals, who played much more regularly in the 1860s. The first, a resident of Cambridge, was Frederick William Bell, a fair batsman, a reliable change bowler, and above all a splendid though flamboyant fielder in the deep with a predilection for dashing in at the ball and making a dramatic return to the wicket-keeper. Engaged for several seasons at Eton, he was a good practice bowler but barely adequate as a coach. Bell, who was nicknamed "The Count", was summoned occasionally to Windsor Castle to teach the rudiments of cricket to some of the Royal Princes, but he came away shaking his head and complaining he "couldn't make a job of 'em at all".

The other outstanding recruit of 1854 was William Mortlock, of Surrey, who spent most of his life in his native Kennington. A staunch batsman, concentrating at first almost exclusively on perfecting his defence to the neglect of punishing half-volleys, he later developed an array of scoring

Indoor Cricket at Lambeth Baths.

strokes, especially on the leg side. In the 1860s, when the Surrey bowling had become a spent force, he was sometimes given a turn with the ball. His achievements in this department were not world-shattering, but there were a few occasions when wickets were captured by what Haygarth termed "Mortlock's slow underhand 'rubbish' ". He was worth his place in any side as a long-stop, the equal of "Ducky" Diver of the AEE, and his impregnability as a batsman and fielder earned him the nickname of "Stonewall". A dealer in cricket goods with a shop near Waterloo Station, Mortlock tried to extend his operations in the winter of 1868 by renting the Lambeth Baths for cricket practice on a fitted floor, but the venture was not a success. His name appears regularly in the United team in 1856–57 and 1859–64.

All England began the 1855 season by narrowly defeating Surrey in an eleven-a-side contest at the Oval. More than one United adherent assisted the home team, but Clarke could do nothing about that. Twenty-four matches, all against "odds", were played, mainly in the North and Midlands. Fifteen victories and only five defeats gave Clarke some grounds for satisfaction, but he was doubtless disturbed by the memory of his incapacitating eye disease and the disastrous quarrel at Reading. On the credit side was the first appearance of John Jackson, who assisted the AEE regularly from 1856 to 1867 and played for them as late as 1871. Born in Suffolk, but residing in Nottinghamshire from his infancy, "The Demon Bowler" was one of the greatest fast men of his own or any other age. In height and weight, he looked rather like a young, beardless W. G. Grace. Somewhat clumsy in his movements off the field, his splendid physique lacked no co-ordination when attacking batsmen. Seemingly tireless, he could bowl for long periods, using a fairly long run and delivering the ball with the precision of a well oiled machine (in later years, he is reputed to have been to "well oiled"). His sustained accuracy was legendary, his pace on rough pitches awesome, and his armoury included the "yorker", the "beamer", and a fast full toss aimed at the top of the stumps. As a batsman, he favoured using the long handle and enjoyed some success, but he was first and foremost a shock bowler. He was, unfortunately, over-bowled to the point of exhaustion by the mid-1860s, and his decline was hastened by a leg injury. Jackson was nicknamed "The Fog-horn" on account of his strange habit of blowing his nose with an ear-splitting report immediately after taking a wicket. There were many such occasions: "The Fog-horn" accounted for well over 600 victims in first-class matches and countless others in contests against "odds".

Far less successful than their rivals in 1855, the United won only six matches and lost five of the fifteen they played. They fared little better the following season, with seven victories, six defeats, and three draws. Little George Wells, of Sussex and Middlesex, made his *début* for the UAEE in

1855 and assisted them frequently from 1858 to 1860. "Tiny" Wells was one of the smallest cricketers in the game, and though his diminutive stature was a marked disadvantage for a batsman, he had plenty of pluck. His manner of receiving the ball was curious: taking guard about two inches in front of the stumps, he raised his bat over his shoulder and stepped forward to the popping crease only when the bowler began his run-up. "Tiny" was once dismissed hit wicket, when the ball splintered his bat, and a flying fragment dislodged one of the bails. Rumour later magnified the fragment into the whole blade of the bat, but this story was denied by the bowler, William Caffyn. "Tiny" had his ups and downs in life. He planned to settle in Australia, was disappointed in his prospects, and returned the next year. Not long afterwards, his attempts to earn a living as a tobacconist and dealer in cricketing goods landed him in the Court of Bankruptcy, where he attributed his failure to "scarcity of business, and the expenses thereof exceeding my profits". When his playing days were over, he managed to secure several appointments as a coach at public schools.

William Caffyn missed few of the All England matches from 1851 to 1854, but his relationship with Old Clarke became so strained that he defected to the United in 1855 and played for them on a regular basis up to the end of 1863.

Edwin Stephenson made his *début* for *both* Elevens in 1856, and subsequently he took his wages wherever they were offered. Identified first with the AEE, he went over to the United, only to re-join the older team around 1863. A well built man of medium height, a native of Sheffield, Ned had one of those lugubrious Yorkshire faces and a steady flow of dry, straight-faced witticisms. He served his county and the North as wicket-keeper for several seasons, but was never chosen to represent the Players against the Gentlemen, being regarded as inferior to Lockyer and his namesake, H. H. "Surrey" Stephenson. Yet Ned was worth his place in most sides for his batting alone. His long reach enabled him to play forward with confident ease, and his strong physique was ideal for punishing loose bowling. As befitted his place of origin, however, he was a notoriously dour defender of his wicket, and his batting tactics sometimes dismayed the pundits.

The AEE played twenty-one matches in 1856, winning twelve—including one against Nottinghamshire—and losing six, but this season marked the end of the team's first phase. Their founder, manager, captain, secretary, and paymaster had reached the age of fifty-seven, and the resilience of spirit that had enabled him to overcome the shock caused by the establishment of the UAEE and endure all the quarrels and vicissitudes was beginning to desert him. Old Clarke's health was failing fast, and he played only three times for the Eleven. His final match was the fixture against 22 of Whitehaven, on June 16, 17, and 18. Towards the end of the opponents' first innings, Clarke, weak and frail as he was, put himself on and returned an analysis of 2–13. Fate smiled upon him, ordaining that this veteran of forty-one seasons should take a wicket with the last ball he ever bowled. A few weeks later, on July 10, 11, and 12, he stood as umpire when the Eleven met 22 of Melton Mowbray, and this was his final appearance on a cricket field in any capacity. He died in London, on August 25, 1856.

If Clarke could have been projected forward in time to a modern psychiatric clinic and tested on his faculty for human relationships, his rating would have been lamentably low. All his defects of character—arrogance, egoism, cupidity—militated against the establishment of an easy association with his fellow men. Yet these failings, deplorable though they be, were far outweighed in the balance by the incalculable benefits he rendered to the cause of cricket. He became—by accident, as it were—the apostle of the game, preaching the gospel in all corners of the land and winning many converts to his creed, yet there was little or nothing disinterested in his motivation. Clarke was no idealist, no philosopher, but a cool, hard-headed speculator with the perspicacity to recognize his opportunities for exploiting a situation favourable for financial gain. And, in his pursuit of wealth, he automatically stimulated a hunger for the national game.

Notwithstanding his misanthropic nature, Clarke made a notable contribution to the welfare of others associated with cricket, who in some instances enjoyed what might be called fringe benefits. Take the conversation, real or partly fictitious, between Clarke and Mr J. H. Dark, the proprietor of Lord's at that time and one of the leading dealers in bats and balls. As recorded by Pycroft, the exchange took place in the early days of the AEE. Dark was twitting his companion for arranging fixtures with piteously weak opponents, but he soon changed his tune when Clarke explained that the AEE would play against "odds", adding, "It is a-going to be, Sir, from one end of the land to the other, you may depend upon that; and what is more, it will make good for cricket—it will make good for you as well as me: mark my words, you'll sell cart-loads of your balls where you used to sell dozens". Pycroft could not vouchsafe for a boom in the sale of balls, but could point to the ever expanding stacks of willow laid out for seasoning year by year outside the proprietor's shop in the south-east corner of Lord's, or Dark's, as it was often called in those days. But cricketers would need not only bats and balls to play the game seriously: they would wish to purchase hats, shirts, trousers, boots, and, if they were wise, gloves and leg-guards as well. So more and more people became involved in the manufacture and marketing of cricketing equipment, among them Fred Lillywhite, who augmented his income from journalism and the sale of score cards, and with the spread of cricket came a growing demand for more reporters and sporting journals, for the printing of more score cards, more score-books,

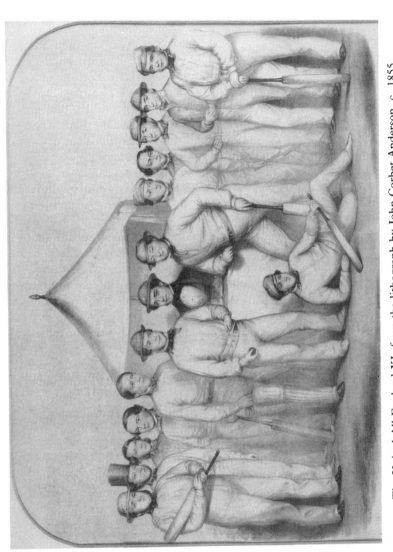

The United All England XI, from the lithograph by John Corbet Anderson, c. 1855.
Standing: T. Hunt, G. H. Wright, T. M. Adams, W. Mortlock, T. Lockyer, J. Wisden, J. Dean, W. Caffyn, J. Grundy, W. Martingell,
T. Sherman, H. Sampson.
In tent: F. Lillywhite.   On ground: John Lillywhite.   *Courtesy Burlington Gallery.*

and eventually cricket annuals. Nor should one forget the local businessmen all over the country, who always welcomed the extra trade created by the visit of an itinerant eleven.

So one might continue adding to the swelling list of the recipients of fringe benefits, thanks to Clarke's operations. Above all, however, it was the professional who derived the greatest advantages from the foundation of the AEE. Usually a member of the working classes, he was, say, a gardener, bricklayer, or labourer, and only a part-time cricketer, earning occasional fees for appearing in a few matches of varying importance, including the comparatively rare county fixtures and representative contests, such as Gentlemen v Players and North v South. The advent of Clarke and his imitators brought a new sense of security to the professional: provided he maintained his form, his health, and a workable relationship with his employer, he was assured of a regular income throughout the summer. There was, of course, no question of winter wages in those days, and in the off season the paid performer was thrown upon his own resources and compelled to return to less exciting trades, such as lamplighting, barbering, baking, cobbling shoes, and the like. Yet he developed a new feeling of independence and self-respect, and, with his name before the public, he had the opportunity to acquire fame and the offer of lucrative coaching appointments from wealthy employers. Professional engagements of this type sometimes had their disadvantages, however, since some patrons—as was after all their right—would refuse permission for their employees to play not only for an itinerant eleven—which was understandable—but for their counties as well.

The established "cracks" owed much of their continued success to the existence of the AEE, but they were not alone in deriving benefit from Clarke's enterprise. In travelling round the country, the All England manager occupied the unique position of an expert talent scout. Without Clarke and his team, many a promising player, like George Anderson, of Bedale, would have languished in the obscurity of districts remote from London. There was finally another category of professional who came to the fore—the "Given Man".

In the original, limited sense of the expression, a Given Man was a player whose services, for one particular match, were transferred from his own side to strengthen the opposition. This sort of transaction could back-fire on a team manager, as happened once in 1858, when the AEE were playing against 22 of Eastwell, in Leicestershire. One of the local team had as a house guest Mr J. Makinson, a well known amateur, who in his time assisted Cambridge University, Lancashire, and the Gentlemen. Mr Makinson was easily persuaded to turn out for Eastwell, but the All England manager, mindful that the 22 already included four professionals and some talented gentlemen, would have none of this. The amateur "crack", he insisted, would play for the AEE, and he would give Eastwell any one of his own men. This proposal was accepted after some discussion, and Alfred Diver was drafted into the home side. The arrangement went sadly astray for the red-faced All England captain: Mr Makinson made only 12, but "Ducky" Diver was the top scorer of the match with 60.

To all intents and purposes, however, a Given Man was the term applied to any cricketer engaged to play in a particular match for a side of which he was not a *bona fide* member. It was expected that the opposing team would agree to this arrangement, but occasionally objections were raised by one of the itinerant elevens. Many cricketers of the period, even the most illustrious, appeared at one time or another as Given Men. On June 24, 25, and 26, 1872, one of the itinerant elevens was matched against 16 of Grantham, with Mr W. G. Grace and Richard Daft—which means 16 of Grantham *including* the two Given Men. W.G. made only 3 and 1, but Daft, one of the Champion's rivals at this time, performed splendidly, carrying off "the leger" in each innings with 14 and 77, i.e., he was top scorer both times. This unfinished game had another remarkable feature: George Howitt, a fast left-hander assisting the eleven, accomplished the hat-trick twice.

Some professionals, such as Ned Stephenson, of Yorkshire, came to prominence by playing for local sides against itinerant elevens and, having proved their mettle, obtained an engagement as a member of the eleven. When their skills were on the wane, and they could no longer hold down a regular place in an eleven, some reverted to the role of Given Men and continued to collect the occasional match fee. Though appearing from time to time in the ranks of the elevens, several players, usually bowlers, obviously preferred accepting engagements with local sides, becoming in effect "professional" Given Men and earning good wages. The compiler of *Scores and Biographies* usually indicates the Given Men, but probably not all of them, for sometimes a local 22 includes the names of professionals with little or no apparent connection with the team. A "professional" Given Man sometimes played for his own club, but it becomes impossible to decide in every instance whether some individuals are genuine members of a team or Given Men.

The names of some "professional" Given Men have already been mentioned. Most notable in the early days were Edmund Hinkly (31 appearances, 1854–59), A. Crossland (44, 1846–60), Frank Tinley (72, 1849–61), and Billy Buttress (36, 1850–56). On his good days, Buttress was for several seasons a thorn in All England's flesh, once taking 7 of their wickets for 5 runs in 18 overs, of which 14 were maidens. One could not, however, always rely on Billy, who might turn up drunk, or not at all! There was the occasion when he failed in his promise to assist 22 of Coventry against the UAEE on July 9 and 10, 1855. *Bell's Life* tells the tale: "The two professionals given were Hinkly and Frank Tinley, the former being substituted for Buttress, who, although some time previously engaged, disappointed Coventry at the last moment, in favour of playing in another match. Such conduct of a professional cricketer cannot be too severely criticised". Perhaps Clarke had outbid the Coventry managers, since Buttress played on those dates for the AEE against the Earl of Stamford's 22, at Enville Hall, Staffordshire. The home side won by an innings, but Billy Buttress took 15 wickets for 78 runs (he must have abstained from too many "pints" for this match).

In later days, Tom Emmett, of Yorkshire, the famous left-handed all-rounder, played in over thirty matches against various elevens from 1867 to 1876, though sometimes he could claim an authentic connection with the team he assisted. Of all the "professional" Given Men, however, three more scions of the broad acres towered head and shoulders above the rest, each performing in his chosen role even more often than Frank Tinley. The first was Isaac Hodgson, a quiet, honest, good-natured individual, highly respected in his native town of Bradford. Though rather frail in build and constitution, Ikey was an active man, excelling at the northern game of Knurr and Spell, and was the first of that famous line of slow-medium, left-handed bowlers produced by Yorkshire. He assisted his county from 1852 to 1866, but was above all the most famous Given Man. His name is found slightly over a hundred times in opposition to three of the principal elevens, and on the majority of these occasions his services had been specially engaged by a local club. Ikey was of little account as a batsman, but some of his feats with "the leathern sphere" were legendary. Early in September 1860, he played for 22 of Bishop Auckland against the UAEE and captured 9 wickets for 22 runs in the first innings. All England's turn came later at Glasgow, when Hodgson, assisting 22 of the Caledonian Club, gave good measure for his wages by taking 6–37 and 7–8 (out of a total of 20, including 2 byes). He accomplished still more in September 1863 as a Given Man for 22 of Alnwick and District against the UAEE: the analysis has not been preserved, but Ikey claimed 9 of the 10 wickets in the first innings and 7 in the second. His trail of destruction would probably have lasted into the 1870s, but for failing health and mortal sickness.

The names of Hodgson and Slinn were often associated as partners against the AEE and UAEE, and this dreaded twosome appeared in opposition to them on some thirty occasions. William Slinn, a scissor-smith from Sheffield, was a tall, strong man with bushy mutton-chop whiskers. A poor fielder, a marginally feebler batsman than Hodgson, with one of the worst averages on record, he concentrated exclusively on the arts of bowling. Fast, round-armed, with an easy, controlled action, he made the ball rise steeply off the pitch and was famous for sending down many maiden overs in succession. In July 1867, he appeared for 22 of Bolton against the AEE, taking 7 wickets in the first innings and 6 in the second, and at one time delivering 14 overs without conceding a run. All England were also the victims when, playing for 22 of Scarborough, in September 1862, he performed his greatest feat as a Given Man. Bowling unchanged throughout the match in partnership with Ikey Hodgson, his figures were 6 for 23 and all 10 for 23. Slinn assisted Yorkshire for only a short period (1860–64) and played in comparatively few other first-class matches, preferring the steady wages to be earned as a coach and Given Man. He notched in all some eighty apperances against itinerant elevens, many of them on special engagement.

The name of the third "professional" Given Man is rarely remembered in this connection, probably because he had a lengthy career in first-class cricket, assisting Yorkshire from 1861 to 1874 and playing for other representative teams. Yet his total appearances against various itinerant elevens surpassed Slinn's and fell not far short of Hodgson's, and evidence of his contemporary fame as a Given Man is perpetuated in some of the earlier issues of *John Lillywhite's Cricketers' Companion*. This annual published diagrams of the fielding position for different types of bowlers, including one entitled "How Twenty-two Should be Placed in the Field to a Right-handed Bowler, like Luke Greenwood, at the Commencement of a Match". Luke, a product of the famous Lascelles Hall district near Huddersfield, was above medium height and weighed around 13st. He was the ideal Given Man. Whereas Hodgson, Slinn, and most of the others were primarily bowlers, Luke was an all-rounder. His fast bowling, though not quite so deadly as Slinn's, was its equal in accuracy, and he was also a good, forcing batsman. He was well worthy of his hire to any side in either role. His character of being "as honest and sterling a cricketer as Yorkshire has even produced" brought him employment as a first-class umpire once his playing days were over. Luke was one of the officials at the Oval, on August 28 and 29, 1882, when Australia defeated England by 7 runs (the birth of the Ashes), and afterwards expressed his indignant horror at one of his colleague's decisions. S. P. Jones, believing the ball to be dead, left his ground to do some gardening, whereupon W.G. coolly picked up the ball, dislodged the bails, and appealed successfully for "run out". It was, thought honest Luke, very sharp practice.

CHAPTER SIX

The All England and United All England Elevens, 1857–1862

THE tidings of William Clarke's demise reached the All England Eleven, and on the evening of September 26, during their final match of the 1856 season, the players held a meeting to discuss their future. If nothing decisive were done, the Eleven would be in danger of disintegrating, and they would be deprived of the summer wages they had earned over the last few years. Coming quickly to the conclusion "that the Eleven should be carried on as formerly when they were 'piloted' by the late William Clarke", they established a committee, consisting of Julius Caesar, Ned Willsher, George Anderson, H. H. Stephenson, and Alfred Clarke, to oversee the management of the team. While accepting the responsibility of general supervision, this body was incapable of looking after the day-to-day tasks of organization and administration, and a replacement for Old Clarke had to be found. The committee did not have far to look for his natural successor: George Parr was elected to the position of secretary, giving him automatically the captaincy as well. How far he was answerable to the Committee of Management is a moot point, for in his own way George seems to have exercised a regimen as absolute as Old Clarke's. He was, however, more of a benevolent dictator than his predecessor. Equally autocratic by nature and just as intolerant of fools, he nevertheless exercised his authority more successfully than Clarke. There were no accusations of profiteering or stinginess over wages, no stories of bitter, permanent ruptures with members of the Eleven. George's pugnaciousness spread beyond the confines of the AEE. Even more quarrelsome in some respects than Clarke, he was one of the principal actors in a drama of tragic proportions, one of the chief creators of an atmosphere of discontent and hostility in the world of cricket, that festered like an angry sore, until the poison was discharged in the 1860s. For the time being, however, Parr and others felt the time had come for establishing a better relationship with the Two Elevens.

With Old Clarke gone, circumstances were more favourable for the declaration of an armistice between the AEE and the UAEE. There was no

The All England XI *v* The United All England XI, Lord's, June 1, 2, & 3, 1857.
The first match between the Two Elevens.

particular antagonism between the two secretaries, since Parr and Wisden had become joint proprietors of a cricket ground at Leamington in 1849, a partnership that lasted for some fifteen years (what Old Clarke thought of this arrangement has not been recorded). From time to time, there had been muted suggestions that the Two Elevens should play against each other, but such a contest had never been countenanced by Clarke, who maintained his animosity to the end. Now, in 1857, the project was revived. Jemmy Dean of Sussex, one of the founders of the UAEE and a ground bowler at Lord's, had been playing before the public for some twenty years, and his friends were eager to arrange a suitable benefit match for him. What better than a fixture between the Two Elevens of England? The challenge, conveyed to George Parr, was accepted with one stipulation: the rivals should first play a match for the benefit of the Cricketers' Fund Friendly Society, which had recently been revived with a more efficient organization to provide financial assistance to professionals fallen upon evil days. This Society had an impressive list of officers and a committee comprising Tom Box (chairman), George Parr, Caesar, John Lillywhite, Anderson, Willsher, and Diver. The hon treasurer was Mr J. H. Dark of Lord's, the hon secretary Fred Lillywhite, who preened himself on the importance of his position. Unfortunately, poor Fred proved less than competent at his task and was removed from office a few years later. Great was his indignation on finding that his successor was Wisden, his erstwhile partner in "a cricket and cigar depot", and greater still when it transpired that Wisden was to receive an honorarium for his services.

Parr's proposal was favourably received, and Mr Dark agreed to place Lord's at the disposal of the Two Elevens. One difficulty arose, to be smoothed over after some negotiation. The UAEE wished to include in their side Messrs F. P. Miller and F. Burbidge, two gentlemen of the powerful Surrey team, who had both assisted the United occasionally in "odds" matches. To this the AEE objected on the grounds that they were amateurs, presumably because the fixture was to be played for the benefit of professionals. Cynics might also have concluded that Parr and his committee felt the presence of Messrs Miller and Burbidge would make the opposition too formidable for their liking. The UAEE consented to field an all-professional team, and this set the pattern for the whole series, no amateur ever appearing in any of the matches between the Two Elevens.

So, on Whit-Monday, June 1, 1857, history was made, with Lord's the scene for the first encounter in a sequence of representative matches more attractive than Gentlemen v Players, since the former at that time provided but weak opposition and were regularly defeated. Fine weather and the prospect of seeing an exhibition by the cream of the professional talent drew a large crowd, estimated at nearly 10,000 on the first day. Those attending included members of the nobility and gentry—among them subscribers to

H. H. Stephenson, Surrey, All England, and United South of England Elevens. Toured North America, 1859, and captain of first tour of Australia, 1861–62.

the Cricketers' Fund—as well as more humble folk. Anxious to obtain a good position for the day, some of the spectators began arriving at 9:30 a.m., two and a-half hours before the commencement of play. The warning bell rang shortly after midday, and many of the onlookers formed a ring, four or five deep round the ground. While employees from the tavern circulated among the crowd, dispensing pots of ale, the umpires (T. Barker and T. Sewell, sen., two old professionals) selected the pitch. Fine weather over the last few days had made the area between the wickets firm and hard, and it played well though at times favoured the fast bowlers. With the out-field, notoriously bad at Lord's, it was a different story, and some of the players complained—with justice, since instances of poor fielding occurred throughout the match.

George Parr tossed with a two-shilling piece, Wisden called correctly and decided to bat. The United opening pair, Tom Hunt and Jemmy Dean, came out to face the bowling of Ned Willsher and John Bickley. Hunt failed to score, and Jemmy Grundy, his successor, was bowled by Bickley for 9. Shortly afterwards, Bickley, suffering from a damaged thumb, surrendered the ball to "Fog-horn" Jackson, who carried all before him, capturing six of the remaining wickets. The last man was dismissed at 3:25 p.m., total 143, to which Dean had contributed 36 and Caffyn 38.

On this day and the other two, both sides were served with dinner at Mr Dark's residence, "where they partook of the old English fare of roast beef and plum pudding". It was this substantial meal, perhaps, which caused the inordinately long interval, since play was not resumed until 4:45, when the AEE began their first innings, and odds of 5 and 6 to 4 on the United were offered.

When stumps were drawn, All England had scored 136 for 7, the not outs being Parr (20) and Willsher (10). Having distinguished himself with a fine attacking innings of 51, H. H. Stephenson was justifiably proud of his performance. After close of play, he boarded a horse-drawn omnibus and climbed up to the "knife-board", where he found some of the passengers discussing the match. To his delight, he heard one of them say, "A rare young cricketer is that young Stephenson", and H.H. preened himself and tried to attract their attention. Failing to do so, he revealed his identity, anticipating further eulogies in his honour, but they refused to believe him. "*You* Stephenson?" they said. "Why, you young rascal, we've been to Lord's and seen him." Their jeers were suceeded by threats to eject him from the bus, but fortunately they got off themselves near Baker Street. The driver, on his high seat, had been listening to the conversation, and he too added his reproof, saying, "It's a very bad thing for a young fellow like you to do a thing of this sort—very bad indeed". (Surely the vocabulary throughout was more colourful?). The crest-fallen hero got down from the bus and continued his journey on foot, pondering over the injustice of the world.

John Lillywhite, Sussex, Middlesex, United All England, and United South of England Elevens. Toured North America, 1859. Sold cricket goods and published 'Green Lilly'=*Lillywhite's Cricketers' Companion*.

Parr and Willsher pushed the score along the next morning, and the bowlers were changed, but with little immediate result. Unable to perform himself because of a sprained ankle, Wisden gave the ball to Fred Bell and unwisely kept him on for eight overs. These cost twenty runs, since "The Count" persisted in feeding Parr's leg-hits. The innings closed at 1:30, total 206, Parr 56 not out, Caffyn 7–69, and the odds had shifted to 5 and 6 to 4 on the AEE.

The United lost three quick wickets for 19 (2 to 1 on the AEE), including Caffyn's. "The Surrey Pet" was glad to go, for he never forgot how he "received a terrible smack in the ribs from Jackson in my second innings, which made me feel very queer". Stubborn resistance came from Grundy (27), Bell (33), and Wright (21), who had a sprained thigh, but Willsher claimed five of the wickets, and the United were dismissed for 140. All England had just time to score 7 before stumps were drawn.

Several showers of rain on the Wednesday favoured the bowlers for a time, but at 2:00 p.m. the AEE achieved their target of 78 for the loss of 5 wickets. Not a great match by some standards, since some of the players seemed below their best, the fielding left much to be desired, and there were no less than three cripples (Bickley, Wisden, and Wright). Financially, however, the game was a notable success: after expenses had been paid, the Cricketers' Fund was enriched to the amount of £160 9s.

The second match, played at Lord's on July 27, 28, and 29, should have been a joyous occasion in honour of Jemmy Dean, but it was almost ruined by some unnecessary bickering, which threatened to disrupt the recent reconciliation between the Two Elevens. It had been expected that the AEE would field an unchanged side, while the United would substitute either Tom Adams or Henry Royston for Dean, permitting Jemmy to be present at the gate to receive "presents" from his admirers. In the second week of July, George Anderson fell ill, came back too soon to play in an "odds" match, and had a relapse. On the first day of Dean's benefit, "The Old Scotchman" was clearly not fit to participate in such an important contest. One of the engaged players at Lord's that year was Ned Stephenson, and the AEE proposed that he should be allowed to take Anderson's place. The United objected, on the grounds that "Yorkshire" Stephenson was not a regular All England man—and one wonders, incidentally, why a similar argument had not developed over the inclusion of Andrew Crossland. Since Anderson had been ill for several days, the UAEE felt an acceptable replacement could and should have been selected in good time. Now came All England's turn to behave nastily, by opposing the inclusion of Adams in the United team, though they had raised no objection previously.

This dispute lasted some time, delaying the start of play, and was still not settled after Parr had won the toss and chosen first knock for the AEE. It lasted, in fact, throughout much of the innings, until a curious compromise

R. P. Carpenter, Cambridgeshire, All England and United All England Elevens.
Toured North America, 1859, and Australia, 1863–64.

was reached: Adams had been an All England man in earlier days, so for this match he was "transferred" back to the AEE, and Jemmy Dean was called away from the gate to fill the vacancy in the United Side.

The weather was fine, the betting (evens) brisk, the crowd large and enthusiastic. Mindful of the well-being of the public, Mr Dark had arranged for the erection of a spacious refreshment marquee, which "was well patronised at different intervals". Was Wisden, normally an even-tempered man, enraged by the dispute over Adams and determined to work off his anger at the expense of the AEE? He performed his greatest feat of bowling—one of the greatest, indeed, by any bowler—in the whole series, operating unchanged with Caffyn to rout All England for 99. Eight wickets was Wisden's share of the plunder, and only George Parr (48) showed any real resistance. By the end of the day, the UAEE had scored 94 for 7, two of the wickets falling to H. H. Stephenson, who had removed pads and gloves to take a turn with the ball.

When play was resumed on the Tuesday, the not-out batsmen (Lockyer and Wisden) did not hold out for long, and the last wicket fell at 12:35 p.m. Total 126, a lead of 27 (5 to 4 on the UAEE). Unfortunately, Wisden and his team-mates relaxed their grip during All England's second innings. Encouraged by muffed catches and erratic deliveries, the AEE collared the bowling with some brilliant batting by Diver (46), Parr (36) and "Cris" Tinley (46). Stumps were drawn when the final wicket fell at 7:10 p.m. Total 214, a remarkable recovery aided by the United's indifferent performance in the field. Wisden's management of his bowlers, all eight of them, came in for some criticism, especially his failure to use Grundy until the very end of the innings.

The United made an early start to their second innings at 11:00 a.m. on the final day. They needed 188 runs to win, but this proved to be a task well beyond their capabilities. Once the favourites, they were now so demoralized that they surrendered meekly to the All England bowlers, particularly Willsher, who again took 5 wickets. The match ended at 1:20, with the AEE victorious by 133 runs. Grundy (15) was the only batsman to reach double figures in the puny total of 54, and "Extras 9" was the second highest score.

Dean made few runs and took no wickets, but his benefit match brought him the gratifying sum of "upwards of £400". He was not the only recipient of a gift. A small ceremony took place a few weeks later at Richmond, Yorkshire, when George Parr's fine batting (56 not out, 19 not out, 48, 36) was honoured with the presentation of a handsome gold watch. Paid for by subscriptions from his team-mates and well-wishers, it was handed to Parr by his friend George Anderson, "The Old Scotchman".

The series was continued for several years without any of those particular problems which threatened to strangle it at its birth, and the annual match or matches between the Two Elevens came to be regarded as *the* highlight of the season. Meanwhile, the bread-and-butter games against "odds" constituted the bulk of each itinerant eleven's annual programme. The number of engagements undertaken by the AEE was stabilized at an annual figure of about twenty, though this was increased to twenty-six in 1862. During the same period, the United had as always fewer fixtures, playing on an average some fifteen games each season. Some of the veterans dropped out of sight, surrendering their places to the rising generation, a few of whom successfully scaled the heights of fame in the years to come.

As far as the encounters between the Two Elevens were concerned, the pattern established in the first year—a match for the Cricketers' Fund, followed by a benefit—became the norm up to 1860, when the second fixture was played at the Oval. In 1861, there were three contests, one at Lord's for the Cricketers' Fund, the second at Old Trafford for the two teams themselves, and the third, a benefit, at the Oval. There was only one annual meeting subsequently, with five at Lord's (1862–1866) and one at Old Trafford (1867), all staged for the Cricketers' Fund. Single matches were arranged as individual benefits at Dewsbury in 1868 and 1869, when the series was terminated. There were nineteen contests in all, and the final table of results was remarkably even, with eight victories claimed by each team and three matches unfinished.*

Having suffered two defeats in 1857, the UAEE achieved their initial success in the first match played at Lord's in June 1858 before another good attendance. Some of the spectators were probably grateful for the opportunity to leave the City and the West End and travel out as far as Lord's, for this was the month and year when "The Great Stink" reached its climax in London. A combination of hot weather and a low rainfall created an unbearable stench arising from the effluvia of the Thames. Particularly obnoxious around Westminster, it caused considerable discomfort to the Members of Parliament, who were compelled to cover their mouths and noses with handkerchieves and sit in a chamber with the windows draped with curtains soaked in chloride of lime.

At Lord's, however, all was serene, and four United men made their *début* in the series. Three of them—R. P. Carpenter, T. Hearne, and G. Griffith—became famous over the next decade, especially the first. Robert Pearson Carpenter, of Cambridge, a strong man of medium height and build, was regarded as one of the finest professional batsmen in England for some fifteen years. Two or three others had their faithful supporters, who spoke admiringly of style and grace, but if you needed somebody to play for your life, and you would have chosen Bob Carpenter. He had a marvellously

---

*For details of the results in the series, see Appendix II, under The United All England Eleven—Summary of Results in Important and First-class Matches.

strong defence and, being primarily a back player, was an expert in the art of stopping a shooter—a common hazard for all batsmen in those days. Rarely would he play forward in the orthodox manner, preferring to step out of his ground and drive the bowling. His patience was exemplary, and he was capable of exercising great restraint, cannily nursing a bowler who gave him no discomfort. Cutting was as easy to him as driving, and he favoured a mighty hit to square leg, though he tended to loft the ball rather more than other renowned leg-hitters, such as George Parr. Carpenter made many runs throughout his long career, including two centuries for the Players against the Gentlemen, and he was famous for carrying out his bat, particularly against twenty-twos. He was the dominant figure for the United in their duels with the AEE and the most successful batsman of all in the whole series. From some of his Cambridge friends Carpenter acquired the nickname of "The Old Gardener", perhaps for his ability to dig out the shooters. Though not much of a bowler, he was a magnificent fielder at point, standing some distance from the wicket before craftily approaching an unwary batsman. When not required by the United, Carpenter often assisted the AEE, being a close ally of George Parr, whose shrewdness and knowledge of the game he shared. He was a good skater, taking part in one or two matches played on ice, and he enjoyed relaxing with a game of cribbage.

Carpenter was making his first apperance at Lord's, and he played a superb innings against the expresses of Willsher and Jackson, calmly quelling the shooters and scoring all round the wicket. Shortly after his dismissal for 45, he was called to the Pavilion, where he was "presented by the M.C.C. with a memorial of their approval in the shape of a bat"—high praise at Lord's, where such presentations were by no means common. An even higher score (54 not out) was made in the United second innings by another newcomer, Thomas Hearne. A tallish, spare man with whiskers, Tom was a good fielder anywhere and could keep wicket at a pinch. Not long after this match, he began to develop as an accurate, medium-pace bowler, in which capacity he was employed on the ground staff at Lord's from 1861 onwards for many years, succeeding Jemmy Grundy as head bowler in 1872. Tom is principally remembered for his batting. His style was not elegant, but he liked to move the score along with drives and leg-hits, and he resembled Wisden in his addiction to the draw stroke. By trade he was a tailor, with a shop in Ealing, where he could "make a cricketer a pair of flannel or any other trousers".

The third important reinforcement called up by the UAEE was George Griffith, of Surrey. As a boy, he was called "Ben" by his intimates, and this nickname clung to him throughout his career. Short in the neck and not very tall, he was nevertheless endowed with a mighty physique and powerful shoulders. A left-handed all-rounder, he bowled fast round-arm,

Richard Daft, Nottinghamshire and All England Eleven. Toured North America, 1879. Like Carpenter, one of the best professional batsmen of the period.

with a noticeable amount of break, later adding slow lobs to his repertoire and often employing both styles in the same match. Good in the slips, an occasional wicket-keeper, he was of most use in the deep and was renowned for his ability to throw the ball in from an immense distance. Griffith was regarded for several years as one of the best left-handed batsmen of the day. He could play "the goose game" if required, but dearly loved flogging the bowling with drives and huge leg-hits—though his bat, it must be admitted, was not always straight. When he toured Australia in 1861–62, the colonials were so impressed by his prowess that they dubbed him "The Lion Hitter". Playing once for the United against 22 of Hastings and St Leonards (1864), he smote each delivery of a four-ball over out of the ground for six. The unfortunate bowler, it may be added, was no mere local, but George Bennett, one of the mainstays of the Kent eleven. Like Jehu, "Ben" was a furious driver.

The return match at Lord's in 1858 was George Parr's benefit, and the AEE exacted a terrible vengeance, trouncing their opponents by an innings and 97 runs. "Yorkshire" Stephenson, making his *début* in the series, and Ned Willsher both made 33, while the beneficiary contributed 28 to the total of 254. "Fog-horn" Jackson was the All England star, carrying off "the leger" with a score of 45 and capturing 6 wickets in each of the United innings.

Wisden's men girded their loins for the contests of the following year, winning the first by a comfortable margin in a low-scoring match, even though Jackson was on the spot again with 14 wickets. The second resulted in a resounding United victory by 9 wickets, thanks to an opening stand of 149 by Hearne (62) and Carpenter, who went on to score 97. Mr Dark, for whose benefit the match was played, showed his appreciation by presenting "The Old Gardener" with another new bat.

Two newcomers assisted All England for the first time in the series in 1859. The first was Thomas Hayward—uncle of T. W. Hayward of later Surrey fame—one of the Cambridgeshire "cracks". Now in his early twenties, Hayward was of medium height, slightly built, and weighed less than 10st. His complexion was dark, his expression in repose rather gloomy, and he never enjoyed the robust health of his friend Carpenter, with whom his name is often linked. He did not last so long as Bob, for illness shortened his career, and he retired to devote himself to the management of the appropriately named All England Ale Stores at Cambridge. One of the leading all-rounders of his time, a specialist at cover-point and long-stop, Tom was also a good medium-pacer with a break-back from the off, and in Gentlemen *v* Players, at Lord's, in 1870, he achieved the hat-trick, all bowled, with W. G. and G. F. Grace as two of his victims. Above all, he was a superb batsman, dominating the 1860s in company with three other renowned professionals. One of the most

G. F. Tarrant, Cambridgeshire and All England Eleven. Toured Australia, 1863–64, and North America, 1868. One of the fastest bowlers of the period.

graceful, wristy performers in the game, he held his bat lightly near the top of the handle, and once he had taken guard, he fidgetted nervously with his feet, twirling the bat with a slight flourish and swinging it with a pendulum-like motion. When the ball came, however, he was rarely caught napping, having an excellent defence for coping with bumpers or shooters, playing forward or "half-forward"—whereas Carpenter was a back player. Unlike some batsmen who acquired most of their runs by one or two shots, Hayward hit the ball in all directions on and off, though he preferred the on side. He drove well, if sometimes uppishly, and excelled at forcing the ball between short-leg and mid-on. Tom had one fault in common with some famous batsmen of later generations: he was a very bad judge of a run and often ran out himself or his partner.

The second All England *débutant* was Richard Daft of Nottingham who, with Carpenter, Hayward, and Parr, formed the quartet of great professional batsmen of the age. He made an inauspicious beginning by collecting a pair and was dropped for the second match in 1859, but returned the next season to be ever present throughout the remainder of the series. Of a higher social class than most of the "professors", he played as an amateur at first, appearing for the Gentlemen in 1858, but found his financial resources too slender. Being a man of high principles, he turned professional, refusing to adopt the pseudo-amateur status assumed at times by Felix, Mynn, and the Grace brothers. After his retirement in 1880, he played in club cricket, though (as Mr Daft) he assisted Nottinghamshire twice in 1881 and was even recalled to the side for three matches as late as 1891. In the early part of his career, he dropped out of the All England fixtures against "odds" after a few seasons, having become a partner in a brewery at Radcliffe-on-Trent and the owner of a shop at Nottingham, selling tobacco, cigars, and sports equipment. He had a flair for business and for making money, but "unfortunately he had not the gift of keeping it". An enthusiast for other sports, his fanaticism for physical fitness always kept him in good shape. Quite tall and well proportioned, with a lithe, graceful form and fine features, he was considered to be one of the most handsome cricketers of his day. Though he occasionally bowled lobs, Daft is principally remembered as a splendid fielder away from the wicket and a magnificent batsman. After touching the block hole, he stood up to his full height to receive the ball, and he was adept at coming down on shooters or killing kicking deliveries. Holding the bat lightly, he scored all round the wicket with wristy elegance, timing his shots with scientific precision. His style would have guaranteed him success in more modern times, though present-day critics would not have applauded his favourite stroke for dealing with some of the deliveries around the line of the leg stump, when he raised his left leg and played the ball away hard under it. A natural leader and a successful captain of Nottinghamshire, he had a somewhat lordly,

The All England XI *v* 22 of the Lansdown Club, Bath, May 28, 29, & 30, 1863.
Standing: E. Willsher, T. Hayward, J. Jackson, G. Anderson, A. Clarke, H. H. Stephenson, R. C. Tinley, J. Rowbotham.
Seated: G. Parr, Julius Caesar, and (on ground) G. F. Tarrant.
W. G. Grace, aged 14, played for the Lansdown Club—and was dismissed for a pair by R. C. Tinley!   *Courtesy Roger Mann.*

outspoken manner and once achieved the near impossible by silencing the incessant chatter of Lord Harris fielding at point. Daft was a rather slow beginner at the wicket and often took time to settle down.

The United introduced a newcomer in George Robert Atkinson, a native of Ripon, well known throughout Yorkshire and the North. Quite a good fielder and a better batsman than some supposed, his chief talent lay in his fast-medium, round-arm bowling—extremely straight and accurate, pitching slightly short of a length, and very difficult to play. Those facing him for the first time were sometimes nonplussed by his peculiar action: he came "sailing up to the pitch with both arms swinging like a windmill", and there was some doubt as to whether the ball was being delivered from the right hand or the left. On his *début* in the series, he took 8 for 46, operating unchanged in both innings with Caffyn (11–63), and for several years he was one of the leading bowlers in many matches, but from 1866 to 1870 he was used more sparingly, when Yorkshire and the North acquired some capital fast men. Atkinson possessed a fine tenor voice and, with proper training, could have made his mark as a professional singer.

The year of 1859 saw an event of historic importance—the first complete tour overseas by an English team. At the conclusion of the season, a party of twelve leading professionals (plus Fred Lillywhite and his printing press) visited Canada and the USA to play against "odds". The side consisted of six members of the AEE (Julius Caesar, A. J. D. Diver, T. Hayward, J. Jackson, G. Parr, H. H. Stephenson) and six of the UAEE (W. Caffyn, R. P. Carpenter, J. Grundy, John Lillywhite, T. Lockyer, J. Wisden). Parr was captain, assisted by Wisden, all matches were won, and the financial results were good. So great was the interest shown in North America that the team's doings received front-page coverage in *The New York Times* until John Brown made his celebrated raid on Harpers Ferry.

Rheumatism and a sprained wrist incapacitated John Wisden for most of the following season, and "The Cardinal's" bowling replacement in the first fixture with the AEE was William Slinn, the "professional" Given Man. All England also introduced a new speed merchant, soon to be regarded as almost the equal of Jackson at his best. A native of Cambridge, George Frederick Tarrant, who later took the surname of Wood, was a strong, wiry, active man, one of the quickest bowlers of his time. For his first few overs he was even faster than Jackson but, lacking "The Fog-horn's" superior physique, was unable to maintain his terrifying speed for long periods. A bundle of nervous energy, Tarrant took a long run-up, delivered from both sides of the wicket and cut the ball back slightly from the off. He had the killer instinct, intimidating the opposition with bumpers, and one of his specialities was bowling a batsman off his legs. An excellent fielder anywhere, he was no stylish batsman but developed the ability to force the scoring rate. Like Julius Caesar, Tarrant was good with his fists, and his bowling action ("all over the place like flash of lightning, never sparing himself"), excitable nature, and irascibility earned him the nickname of "Tear'em". With Carpenter and Hayward he formed the great triumvirate that sustained Cambridgeshire as a first-class county for several seasons. "Tear'em" had a story-book *début*: though out of luck in the United second innings, he contributed his share to All England's victory with 6–28 in the first.

The Oval was the venue for the second contest of 1860, got up for the benefit of William Martingell. Good knocks were played for All England by Willsher, Hayward, and Parr, while Carpenter and John Lillywhite scored well for the UAEE. The most successful United bowler was Jemmy Grundy, marking 8–42 in the first innings and 2–47 in the second, and on the other side Jackson also accounted for ten opponents. As a display of first-class cricket, the match was a rather lack-lustre affair, ending in a tame draw. The United fielding was "to say the least, very indifferent", but the AEE threw away their opportunities for victory by an even worse performance. On their second hands, the United batsmen, especially Carpenter, were let off repeatedly, when catch after catch went to ground through carelessness or excess of confidence. Two of the chances were put down by the usually safe Diver at long-stop. One, a particularly soft dolly, was evidently too simple, "for had he opened his mouth it would certainly have lodged there with perfect ease, and he would scarcely have felt the weight of the 5½ ounces of leather."

Three newcomers assisted the United at the Oval, the first being "Yorkshire" Stephenson, formerly of the AEE. Second was George Bennett, a bricklayer from Kent, nicknamed "Farmer Bennett" because of his bucolic appearance. According to one story, he was imprisoned for burglary in his youth, but he was a respectable citizen these days. A stiff, ungainly, but competent batsman, he was a comparative rarity as a bowler, delivering his "slows" with a round-arm action instead of under-hand, and giving the ball a lot of air. Bennett was the unfortunate bowler whom "Ben" Griffith smote for four successive sixes at Hastings, in 1864.

The third was Thomas Sewell, junior, a Surrey man, whose father played for the AEE in 1846. "A little tub of a man", Tom was short of stature, broad in the shoulders and beam, and very active in the field in spite of his girth. His slightly comical appearance and merry disposition endeared him to spectators. A useful batsman but not much given to defence, he was a fast run-getter if given the chance. As a bowler, he was fast round-arm, with a slinging action, and though never in the same class as Jackson, Willsher, or Tarrant, he rendered good service and was always ready to chance his arm. "Busy Tom" turned out for Kent at times as well as for his native county.

The Two Elevens were pitted against each other three times in the following season. Played as usual at Lord's in aid of the Cricketers' Fund, the first match was one of the most exciting contests in the whole series, ending in a hard-fought victory by only 5 runs for the AEE. Finding themselves short of a bowler, the United engaged the services of Billy Buttress at the eleventh hour. The rules for qualification were evidently nothing like so rigid as they had been in 1857, when the UAEE had objected to the inclusion of "Yorkshire" Stephenson on the grounds that he was not a regular member of the AEE. By no stretch of the imagination could Buttress be considered as holding authentic membership of the United at this time, since he had assisted them only twice as far back as 1854. Evil tales were told of the Cambridge leg-breaker and his failing for "pints", but on this occasion he belied his reputation. Bowling unchanged with Caffyn, he tormented the opposition, and All England were sent packing for 74. The United's elation was short-lived: crumbling before the onslaught of Jackson and Willsher, they suffered an ignominious collapse (total 61, top score 8). Both teams performed better on second hands, and though Buttress was less economical in All England's second innings, he took 5 wickets (match figures 9–95) and gave an exhibition of his legendary skills by dismissing Hayward and Parr in one over. Unfortunately, "the father of break-bowling" succumbed to temptation a few weeks later when playing for Cambridgeshire against Surrey and appeared no more for either his county or the UAEE. The wayward Billy achieved a kind of literary distinction, being immortalized in the verses of an acquaintance, the minor poet Charles Stuart Calverley ("I have stood serene on Fenner's // Ground, indifferent to blisters, // While the Buttress of the period // Bowled me his peculiar twisters").

Rain interfered with play in the second match, an extra contest got up at Old Trafford for the benefit of the two teams, and the inevitable result was a draw. Grundy's accurate bowling yielded 7 wickets for the United, but Jackson led the All England counter-attack to capture 5, though his thunderbolts were treated with scant respect by "Ben" Griffith. In All England's second innings, Richard Daft made 66, his highest score so far in the series, mastering the bowling with the assistance of the two Georges, Parr (36) and Anderson (54 not out).

Kennington Oval was the venue for the third encounter of 1861, played for the benefit of Thomas Barker. Old Tom's career as a fast bowler for Nottinghamshire and MCC was interrupted when he broke a leg in an accident in 1843. Returning briefly two years later, he soon retired to take up umpiring, becoming one of the leading arbiters of the game and officiating in the first eight matches between the Two Elevens. Some of the Nottinghamshire members of the AEE were not at first anxious to participate in the match, which is rather surprising, considering Barker came from the same county. Perhaps their attitude reflected a growing hostility towards Surrey and the Oval authorities, but the difficulties were adjusted for the time being, and the arrangements were satisfactorily concluded.

The UAEE batted first, and for some strange reason—unless the intention was to prolong the match for Barker's sake—Parr entrusted all the bowling to only three men: Hayward (medium) who took 5 wickets, Willsher (fast), and Tinley (the "slows"). This policy of leaving the pace of Jackson, Tarrant, and even H. H. Stephenson out of the reckoning was a tactical error, since the United ran up a total of 171, with good knocks from Griffith and Mortlock and a remarkable contribution of 72 by Grundy. Only Hayward (36) distinguished himself in All England's first innings, six of the wickets falling to "Ben" Griffith. With their tails, up, the United went to the wickets again to administer even more merciless punishment to the impotent All England attack. The heat was so intense that at one stage, "out came the welcome Surrey loving cup to the baked and tired All-Englanders". Tarrant, ignored during the two previous matches of the season, was the sixth and last bowler to be tried, but "Tear'em's" sterling effort (5-45) came too late in the proceedings. The UAEE attained the massive total of 260, with Caffyn, on his own stamping ground, making his highest score of the series (63). By close of play on the Tuesday, the AEE had lost one wicket and faced the gargantuan task of having to score over 300 on the morrow. They fell far short of their target, though Daft and H. H. Stephenson did well, and Julius Caesar, exploiting like Caffyn the more familiar conditions at the Oval, played a magnificent innings (72). The ever generous Surrey authorities—they had wined and dined both teams on the second day—made a habit of presenting sovereigns for distinguished performances with bat, ball, or the gloves, and several players were awarded "the talent sov." in an elaborate ceremony in front of the Pavilion. Old Tom Barker received a tidy sum to sweeten his retirement, with the players and officials claiming as their fees little more than enough to cover their expenses (£5 was the highest), and "Wisden charged nothing."

The year 1861 closed with an event of historic importance in the annals of cricket. Messrs Spiers and Pond, the Australian firm of refreshment contractors, sent an agent to England to arrange for a team to go on the first ever tour of Australia. Negotiations were prolonged, and some leading players, considering the remuneration inadequate, declined to join the side. Eventually, the agent secured the assistance of the Oval authorities, and a team of twelve professionals was selected, though it was far from being representative of England's full strength. No less than seven were Surrey men, including H. H. Stephenson as captain, and only two northerners (Ned Stephenson and Roger Iddison, both of Yorkshire) agreed to go. The preponderance of Surrey players in the side and the appointment of H. H. Stephenson to the captaincy caused some ill-feeling among the northern "cracks", who had perhaps been holding out in the hope of being offered a higher fee. Parr and his supporters saw in the whole affair an instance of Surrey seeking to dominate the world of cricket.

In the following year, early attempts were made to repeat the arrangements of 1861 with two extra meetings at Old Trafford and the Oval, but they proved abortive, both sides having previously accepted engagements to play against twenty-twos. There is the sneaking suspicion also that possibly some of the northerners wished to avoid appearing at the Oval again. Henceforth, there would be only one contest per season until the end of the series.

The solitary fixture of 1862 was played at Lord's in aid of the Cricketers' Fund. Assisted for the first time in the series by Roger Iddison, the UAEE were dismissed for 126, with the indomitable Bob Carpenter retiring unbeaten for 63. For this historic innings, his second highest against the AEE, the Cambridgeshire "crack" was lavished with praise and called to the Pavilion to be presented with a new bat by Lord Henry Paget, the president of the AEE, "a rare honour on this ground". Ned Willsher (5–46) was the most successful All England bowler, but the doubtful legality of his action came in for some adverse comments. A patient knock by Richard Daft (36) and a splendid innings by H. H. Stephenson (70 not out) enabled the AEE to establish a comfortable lead with a total of 203. Carpenter (39) obtained the "leger" again on second hands, but the United notched only 129. The odds were 3 and 4 to 1 on the AEE, requiring only 53 to win. In a courageous attempt to snatch a seemingly impossible victory, the United gave their opponents a horrible fright. Stark disaster stared All England in the face, when 6 wickets were surrendered for only 14 runs! Delays caused by rain and the dinner interval took the devil out of the pitch, and resolute batting by George Anderson and Alfred Clarke enabled the AEE to scrape home to a victory by four wickets.

All England tried a new opening partnership in this match with two Yorkshiremen, Joseph Rowbotham and John Thewlis. The former was a short, bulky man from Sheffield, whose dumpy figure eventually tipped the scales at around 15st. A good, forcing batsman, who rendered yeoman service to his county, Joe performed with only moderate success in the contests between the Two Elevens. He was an excellent long-stop— "Ducky" Diver's successor for the AEE—and a competent wicket-keeper.

Thewlis, a product of Lascelles Hall, was of about the same height and weight as Rowbotham, but he never ran to fat like Joe. Perhaps this was a legacy of the grinding poverty of his youth, and to poverty he was reduced again in old age, living only a few months after he was rescued from obscurity and want by the Yorkshire Club. A steady batsman and a reliable fielder, his greatest moment came at the Oval, in 1868, when he opened the batting with his nephew, Ephraim Lockwood. The latter, making his *début* for Yorkshire, blossomed under the watchful eye of "Uncle John", and the partnership was worth 176, when Lockwood was out for 91. Thewlis remained and went on to reach his highest ever score (108).

Two famous members of the UAEE made their final bow in the series in 1862. John Wisden, co-founder, secretary, and captain of the United Eleven, suffered another injury during the season and played little cricket of any consequence after 1863, though he continued to serve in an administrative capacity. A little plumper now, "The Cardinal's" whimsical expression had vanished behind a dense, bristling beard. He prospered in his business as a dealer in cricket equipment in London, and in 1864 he published the first edition of *John Wisden's Cricketers' Almanack*. Wisden died on April 5, 1884.

The second United stalwart to go was John Lillywhite, whose myopia was proving too great a handicap to withstand the best fast bowling of the day. He continued playing for Sussex for a while, making a few good scores, and was still appearing occasionally in various matches in the early 1870s. Like Wisden, he had established a thriving business for the sale of sporting goods in London, and in 1865, he issued the first edition of *John Lillywhite's Cricketers' Companion*. So, for a few years, Lilly lived in contentment, still wearing his hat at a jaunty angle, his face framed by those whiskers that were turning white. At the age of forty-seven, he suffered an acute "bilious attack" and died at his residence on October 27, 1874.

Since their foundation, the AEE had played several "odds" matches against Yorkshire (or Sheffield). In three of the fixtures, between 1850 and 1852, Yorkshire had fielded only fourteen players, and this "important" contest was revived at Barnsley, towards the end of August 1862. The dates chosen were unfortunate, since many of the "cracks" were appearing at the same time in a match at the Oval between Surrey and England. Although only two Yorkshiremen (Anderson and Iddison) were engaged, several All England regulars were also participating in the game. Consequently, the encounter at Barnsley saw a depleted side facing a strong 14, who could afford the luxury of allowing Joe Rowbotham to assist the AEE as an emergency stumper against his native county. Parr's men made a horrible hash of their first innings. Unable to withstand the famous combination of Isaac Hodgson and William Slinn, they meekly permitted themselves to be dismissed for 47. After a comfortable reply of 136 by the Yorkshire team, All England staged a remarkable recovery to amass a total of 205 and got rid of their shocked opponents for 86. Man of the Match was George Tarrant, who took 10 wickets in all and scored 60 on second hands. Ten wickets were bagged also by Ikey Hodgson, who surpassed himself with the bat, actually notching 10 and 5.

CHAPTER SEVEN

The All England and United All England Elevens, 1863–1864

THERE was a slight reduction in the number of engagements fulfilled by the AEE in 1863, but Parr still managed to compile an extensive fixture list: twenty-six matches were played, resulting in fifteen victories and only four defeats. The United's programme was larger than it had ever been—twenty contests, a total exceeded only once in a later season—but their performance compared very unfavourably with their rivals' record. Wisden's men found themselves on the losing side ten times and were victorious on only two occasions. Owing to circumstances prevailing in 1864, the activities of both Elevens were considerably reduced.

It was hoped in some quarters that the original pattern of playing two matches—one for the Cricketers' Fund, the other for the benefit of an individual—might be revived in 1863. Old Tom Sewell, one of Clarke's original All England team in 1846 and an umpire in the first three matches between the Two Elevens, deserved some recognition of his services to cricket. An active, lively player in his hey-day, the elder "Busy Tom" had been associated with Surrey from 1839 to 1849, and it was proposed that he should be honoured by a contest between the AEE and the UAEE at the Oval. This worthy cause foundered on the rock of northern hostility, and eventually a match between Surrey and Middlesex was substituted.

There was, however, no question of cancelling the annual Whitsuntide meeting for the Cricketers' Fund, and a grim struggle, with the bowlers in the ascendant, was played out on May 25 and 26. The match was also notable for a welcome innovation in the history of cricket reporting and, above all, for evidence of the adverse conditions prevailing at Lord's in those days. So deplorable was the state of the ground that a special committee meeting was held in the Pavilion on the Monday morning to decide if, in the future, umpires should be engaged several days in advance to ensure proper pitches were chosen. This served no purpose for the present fixture, and less than an hour before the start, the officials ruled that no play was possible on the area originally selected. Among various defects, it had "a large hole immediately in front of it". The wickets were moved

The All England XI *v* The United All England XI, Lord's, May 25 & 26, 1863.

some twenty yards nearer the Pavilion, but the parched ground, hard and fiery from a drought, was totally unprepared. Beaters were sent for and a roller—too light to be of any use. The pundits shook their heads, fearing the worst, and some of the players were filled with apprehension, especially the United, one imagines, since All England could call upon the services of four fast bowlers. Over 6,000 spectators attended the match on the first day. Some of them were incommoded by the telegraph board displaying the score, which also caused "a great annoyance" to Fred Lillywhite in his printing tent.

The hasty "preparation" of the new pitch delayed the start of play until 12:30, when Tom Lockyer, having won the toss, sent in Grundy and Hearne to open the United innings (6 to 4 on the AEE). The crowd, a prey to curiosity and impatience, were expecting a sensation. Towards the end of the previous season, Willsher had been no-balled for delivering above the level of the shoulder, and MCC had issued warnings that Law X would be strictly enforced at Lord's. Would Ned's action pass muster to-day? It was Jackson, however, who sent down the first ball from the Pavilion end. Tom Hearne took the strike and was caught and bowled off the second delivery. He was succeeded by Mortlock, who hit his first ball to square leg for three.

Now came Willsher's turn to bowl, and the crowd waited in breathless hush. Down came the first ball of the over, and those hoping for a moment of melodrama were sadly disappointed. It was obvious immediately that, in conformity with Law X, Willsher's action was low, "and no doubt lower than we shall see him again". Jackson, generating great pace, soon disposed of Mortlock with a shooter, and Carpenter emerged to do battle once more with his old adversaries. The next to go was Grundy, bowled by Willsher for a single. Two and three wickets down for 6 runs. Grundy had showed no relish for batting in this match: more than once he drew back from the line of fire, holding out his bat with one hand to defend the stumps. Also distinctly uncomfortable was Caffyn, who, like Grundy, had had his ample share of Jackson and Willsher over the years. Carpenter made a fine drive for four to the Pavilion off Jackson, but even he was having problems with the ball coming through at different heights. Lord's was not Caffyn's favourite ground, and when he had made only 2, he received a shattering blow on the elbow, which, he confessed, "took all the play out of me". Lashing out in desperation, "The Surrey Pet" was caught by Tarrant at mid-on. Four for 12.

Number 6 was a newcomer, Charles Newman, of Cambridge, who played for his county for a few years but was not really first-class material. He was out of place at Lord's on this day and quite incapable of coping with the extraordinary conditions. The batsmen, however, were not alone in running the gauntlet: one of Jackson's expresses kicked terrifyingly from the pitch and pole-axed H. H. Stephenson behind the stumps. When he had recovered, the unfortunate wicket-keeper prudently retired with a throbbing head to a safer distance. Newman was bowled shortly afterwards by Willsher for 0. Five for 16.

The more experienced "Ben" Griffith joined Carpenter. Belligerent as ever, the sturdy left-hander attacked the bowling but soon surrendered his wicket to Jackson for 13. Six for 45. Burly Roger Iddison now appeared and signalled his arrival with a splendid on drive for four. Both batsmen received several painful bruises, with the ball still flying through at unpredictable heights, and this proved to be Carpenter's undoing. He completely misjudged one of Jackson's deliveries and, anticipating a head-high flyer, offered no stroke to a ball that kept low and smashed into the stumps. Frequently applauded throughout his courageous innings of 26, Carpenter smote three mighty drives (a five off Willsher and two fours off Jackson). Seven for 56.

George Atkinson joined his fellow Yorkshireman to add 30 to the total, most of them coming from Iddison, who was repeatedly cheered for his skilful play. Now Tarrant took up the bowling at Willsher's end, and in the next over Jackson disposed of Atkinson for 3. Tom Lockyer, who preferred the "fasts" to the "slows", opened his account at once, and the total soon rose to 101, when "Fog-horn" Jackson succeeded in beating Roger's broad bat to prostrate the leg-stump. Iddison's praiseworthy innings—deemed by some onlookers to be the finest exhibition of batting in the whole match—included three fours and provided some much needed ballast to the United's efforts. Last came Ikey Hodgson, who, in spite of his numerous engagements as a Given Man, contrived to make three rare appearances for the UAEE this season. Lockyer added a few more runs and then hit up a skyer to long-on, where Alfred Clarke, with plenty of time to spare, muffed the catch. It mattered little, since Hodgson was bowled for a cipher in Jackson's next over. Total 109, including 20 byes given away by some fumble-fingered long-stopping.

The pitch was at its worst (very "bumptious", according to *The Times*) during the United first innings, with the ball sometimes rearing head-high or rattling about the batsmen's ribs and hands, and sometimes shooting along the treacherous ground. More than once a batsman was struck, only to lose his wicket immediately afterwards. Willsher took 3 for 34 in 21 overs, and one shudders to think what might have been the consequences, had he not been compelled to lower his arm. Yet again, the most successful All England bowler was Jackson. Operating unchanged and taking full advantage of the playing conditions, he "victimised seven out of the ten", six clean bowled and the seventh dismissed by a catch off his own bowling.

The UAEE were all out at 2:20, and All England began their reply half-an-hour later. Perhaps George Parr cherished a fond hope of saving his best batsmen by sending in Jackson and Tarrant as openers. The United had no bowlers who quite matched the ferocity of Jackson and Tarrant, or the pace of Willsher, but on such a dangerous surface Atkinson and Griffith were fast enough to give the All Englanders a dose of their own bitter medicine. Tarrant received a sickening blow on the chest, and his partner soon succumbed to Atkinson for a single. One for 3. The Yorkshireman's windmill action may not have satisfied the purists, but, accurate as ever, he succeeded in extracting as much life from the fiery pitch as Jackson and Willsher, and many a ball bumped over the batsman's head. Equally dangerous was Griffith. In giving the ball to the fast left-hander rather than the medium-paced Caffyn, Lockyer showed great acumen: Griffith, bowling against the slope, found the conditions suited him to perfection.

First wicket down was "Surrey" Stephenson, who had little joy of his innings. Two or three times he was surprised into chopping the ball away from the stumps at the very last moment. Perhaps his timing was out, resulting from the blow he received on the head while keeping the wickets. H. H. was dismissed for 5 by a perfect "bailer" from Griffith. Two for 12, and glum-faced Tom Hayward took guard. He soon lost two partners, Tarrant caught in the slip by Grundy off Atkinson for 5 and Daft comprehensively bowled by Griffith for 2. (Betting even).

Surviving a stinging crack on the leg, George Parr was at first "anywhere but at home" and barely succeeded in keeping the ball out of his stumps. Hayward, with his slight form and sloping shoulders, looked little suited to withstand the persistent drumfire of Atkinson and Griffith. So light was his grip that it was a wonder the bat was not repeatedly dashed out of his hands. Skill, technique, and the straightest of blades enabled him to defend his wicket and punish any loose delivery. Hayward made 30, including three fours, and seemed well set when he was beaten by an unplayable ball from Griffith. Five for 52.

The Cambridge "crack" was replaced by Julius Caesar, another man of determination. Parr, facing Griffith, brought his score to 8 with a good drive for two, before fending off a ball in the direction of point, and Carpenter earned loud applause by taking the catch just clear of the turf. Six for 60. Alfred Clarke scraped 3 runs and came in for a nasty knock on the right hand. Caesar, a firm believer in the virtues of aggression, sprang his bat, and play was interrupted while another was procured. Immediately afterwards, Clarke and his successor Tinley were bowled by Atkinson. Seven for 65, eight for 69. Ned Willsher came to the crease, and now it was Caesar's turn to go, dismissed in the same manner as Parr. "Julie's" fighting 15 included two fours, and he and Hayward were the only All England batsmen to reach double figures. Nine for 75. A bright little stand by the two left-handers, Willsher and Wootton, took the total to 92, when the latter was bowled by Griffith at 5:40 p.m. Atkinson (4) and Griffith (6) shared the wickets between them.

Half-an-hour later, Mortlock and Hearne were at the crease, facing Jackson and Willsher. Mortlock marked 10 in as many minutes before putting his leg in the way of a straight one from "The Fog-horn". One for 18. Iddison, promoted in the order, joined the in-form Hearne, and no more wickets were lost by close of play. Total 47, Hearne 20, Iddison 10. The United, with a lead of 64, were now the favourites, with odds of 6 to 4.

This match was a red-letter day for journalists. Hitherto, no special arrangements had been made at Lord's for the gentlemen of the press. Whenever possible, they had tried to position themselves near the scorers where, jostled and impeded by spectators, they did their best to produce their reports, and sometimes they had to keep their own record of the score. Little wonder, then, that there are discrepancies in various surviving match accounts. In 1863, however, Mr Day "of the St. John's Wood Tavern . . . set apart a room for the exclusive use of the Press". Yet this special accommodation did not prevent at least two of the leading reporters from failing to observe that Grundy replaced Atkinson for one over at the end of the All England innings. Perhaps the proximity of the tavern had its disadvantages.

Jackson and Willsher continued bowling the next morning, but "The Fog-horn" was a mere shadow of his usual superb self, and when the total reached 60, he gave way to Hayward. Soon the latter terminated the threat posed by Iddison, who turned a ball into Parr's hands at short-slip and departed for 20. Two for 66. The field spread out on the appearance of "Ben" Griffith, and Willsher, who had enjoyed no more success than Jackson, was relieved by the newcomer Wootton.

George Wootton, a shy, unassuming man from Clifton (Nottinghamshire), was only 5ft. 6in. tall and weighed less than 11st., but he had plenty of stamina and made his mark as a fast-medium, left-handed bowler with a round-arm action. He was engaged at Lord's from 1862 to 1873, where he was well known for the remarkable straightness of his bowling, tutored perhaps by the apostle of accuracy, Jemmy Grundy, with whom he shared the MCC attack in many matches. Though sublimely ignorant of the principles of scientific batting, Wootton came off at times with some uninhibited hitting. Not quite so good a left-handed all-rounder as either Griffith or Willsher, being inferior as a batsman, he nevertheless achieved some great feats with the ball, once capturing all 10 wickets for the AEE in a first-class match.

"Ben" Griffith had time to unleash one of his favourite drives, a four off Hayward, before "his wicket was rent by Wootton" for 6. Three for 74. Carpenter joined Tom Hearne to push the score along briskly to 115, when the latter skied a ball from Wootton to Willsher at cover-point. Hearne's 44 was the highest individual figure in the match. (3 to 2 on the United). Next came Tom Lockyer to stay for a while with Carpenter. "The Old

Gardener's" preference for defensive back play stood him in good stead once more, and he played a meritorious innings of 24, scoring fours off both bowlers and a five off Wootton. Then the left-hander held a return catch, and five wickets had gone for 129.

Willsher replaced Hayward, and the United suffered a collapse. Caffyn came in, scored a single, and lost his middle stump to Willsher, whereupon Grundy deposited his first ball into the hands of Daft at mid-off. Six and seven wickets down for 130. It was almost eight, for the next batsman (Newman) barely escaped being run out in trying to steal a bye. He managed to notch a single before being bowled by Willsher. Eight for 136. Lockyer, meanwhile, was playing a captain's innings. Supported by Atkinson, he increased the total to 147, when Wootton struck once more, lowering Atkinson's middle stump. The end was close, for nobody could expect Hodgson to last very long. Ikey duly secured the inevitable pair, and the innings expired at 150. The most successful All England bowler was Wootton, who achieved his best performance (5–46) in the series. In spite of the United collapse, the AEE were left with the necessity of scoring 168 to win. (3 to 1 on the UAEE).

Since the last United wicket fell shortly after 2:30, dinner was taken, and the AEE did not begin their second innings until 3:45, when Caesar and Willsher went to the wickets. Lockyer opened his attack once more with Atkinson and Griffith. The Yorkshireman failed to recapture his venomous accuracy, but it was a different story with Griffith. Caesar, patently ill at ease, made 3 and was dismissed in "Ben's" third over. One for 8, and "Surrey" Stephenson joined Willsher, who lost his wicket for 5 in Griffith's next over. Two for 9.

Hayward, at number 4, seemed more confident, and on him and Stephenson reposed All England's best hopes. This pair prospered for a time, with H. H. playing the major role. Bravely they carried the attack into the enemy's camp, until Stephenson yielded his mastery by holing out to Newman at long-leg for 26. Three for 52. Could Richard Daft retrieve the situation? Caffyn replaced Atkinson at the Pavilion end, but it was Griffith who killed any threat of a Daft-Hayward partnership, which expired still-born, when the left-hander flattened Hayward's leg-stump. Four for 52. The appearance of George Parr brought a little comfort to the All England supporters. At first, it seemed, they were not grasping at straws, and a possible stand was in the making. Playing with less caution than usual, Daft gave a chance that went begging. Now Griffith, the spearhead of the United assault, was rested, and the wily Hodgson took the ball for the first time in the match.

The advent of Ikey was another nail in All England's coffin. Daft, flattering only to deceive, mistimed his stroke and was caught by Grundy at short-leg for 11. Five for 76, and two more hours of play. Tarrant joined

Parr, who had lapsed into a state of sluggish torpor, seemingly content to take singles off strokes worth at least two, and prompting one reporter to declare acidly that "Parr's running days are nearly over". Lingering but a short time at the crease after Daft's departure, the All England captain was dismissed for 9, caught by Mortlock at long-stop off Caffyn. Six for 76. Jackson's rash attempts at stealing singles were abortive. Run out for 4, seven for 81. Alfred Clarke survived a chance at short-leg, but Tarrant, who had been batting much more competently than some of his team-mates, lost his wicket in the same manner as Parr for 16. Eight for 96. Hodgson, whose crafty skill delighted the connoisseurs, then bowled Wootton and Tinley for ciphers, final total 97. So, at 5:45 p.m. on the second day, the UAEE were victorious by 70 runs. Apart from "Surrey" Stephenson's contribution, there was little to be said in praise of the All Englanders' performance in their second innings. "Ben" Griffith was again the most successful bowler with 4–29 (match figures 10–73), sharing the honours with Ikey Hodgson (3–15). Score:—

The United All England Eleven

1st Innings		2nd Innings	
T. Hearne, c & b Jackson	0	(2) c Willsher, b Wootton	44
J. Grundy, b Willsher	1	(8) c Daft, b Willsher	0
W. Mortlock, b Jackson	5	(1) l b w, b Jackson	10
R. P. Carpenter, b Jackson	26	(5) c & b Wootton	24
W. Caffyn, c Tarrant, b Willsher	2	(7) b Willsher	1
C. Newman, b Willsher	0	(9) b Willsher	1
G. Griffith, b Jackson	13	(4) b Wootton	6
R. Iddison, b Jackson	24	(3) c Parr, b Hayward	20
G. R. Atkinson, b Jackson	3	(10) b Wootton	2
*†T. Lockyer, not out	14	(6) not out	24
I. Hodgson, b Jackson	0	(11) c & b Wootton	0
B 20, 1b, 1	21	B 17, 1b 1	18
Total	109	Total	150

All England Bowling

	Runs	Wickets		Runs	Wickets
Jackson	48	7	Jackson	23	1
Willsher	34	3	Willsher	37	3
Tarrant	6	0	Hayward	26	1
			Wootton	46	5

The All England Eleven

1st Innings		2nd Innings	
J. Jackson, b Atkinson	1	(8) run out	4
G. F. Tarrant, c Grundy, b Atkinson	5	(7) c Mortlock, b Caffyn	16
†H. H. Stephenson, b Griffith	5	(3) c Newman, b Griffith	26

T. Hayward, b Griffith	30	(4) b Griffith	14
R. Daft, b Griffith	2	(5) c Grundy, b Hodgson	11
*G. Parr, c Carpenter, b Griffith	8	(6) c Mortlock, b Caffyn	9
Julius Caesar, c Carpenter, b Griffith	15	(1) b Griffith	3
A. Clarke, b Atkinson	3	(9) not out	3
R. C. Tinley, b Atkinson	0	(11) b Hodgson	0
E. Willsher, not out	9	(2) b Griffith	5
G. Wootton, b Griffith	6	(10) b Hodgson	0
B 5, lb 2, nb 1	8	B 1, lb 5	6
Total	92	Total	97

United All England Bowling

	Runs	Wickets		Runs	Wickets
Atkinson	37	4	Atkinson	35	0
Griffith	44	6	Griffith	29	4
Grundy	3	0	Caffyn	12	2
			Hodgson	15	3

NB. The analysis of the United bowling in the first innings contains errors in most accounts. It is believed that the above details, involving reconstruction from different sets of figures, are more correct, but it is one more example of the difficulties encountered in arriving at complete accuracy in the statistics at this time.

The takings at the gate in the two days amounted to £279, and this sum was augmented by subscriptions to the Cricketers' Fund, yielding a total of £303 12s. The expenses were £127.

Six players made their exit from the series. Newman, out of his class, appeared no more for the United. Nor, unfortunately, did Ikey Hodgson, who deserved better recognition. He continued to beguile batsmen with his left-arm spinners for a while, often as a Given Man, but his health broke down, and he succumbed to consumption on November 24, 1867.

Towards the end of 1863, George Parr took a team of eleven professionals and one gentleman (Mr E. M. Grace) to tour Australia and New Zealand. This side was much more representative of England's strength than H. H. Stephenson's party in 1861. They arrived back in England after the annual meeting of the Two Elevens had already taken place in 1864. Parr's team included four stalwarts who never played again in the great series. One was Alfred Clarke, the honest journeyman of the AEE, who was approaching the end of his career. Another was dashing Julius Caesar, increasingly hampered by gout in his feet, though this affliction was not the cause of his departure from the AEE. Tom Lockyer, the ever dependable wicket-keeper and latterly captain of the UAEE, would also be missing. So, too, William Caffyn, who as a batsman rarely came off at Lord's, but who was the most prolific taker of wickets for the United (73 in thirteen

William Mortlock, Surrey, United All England, and United South of England Elevens. Toured Australia, 1861–62. Known as "The Surrey Stonewall".

matches). "The Surrey Pet", who has the unique distinction of being the only man to participate in the first three tours abroad—Canada and the USA (1859), Australia (1861–62, 1863–64)—remained down under for several years, earning his living as a cricket coach and hairdresser. When he returned to England, the United Eleven had been disbanded.

The absence of Parr's touring team for part of the season of 1864 curtailed the activities of the Two Elevens, the AEE playing only 15 matches, and the United 11. With so many of the "cracks" unavailable, it was felt that some of the interest might be missing from the annual encounter for the benefit of the Cricketers' Fund. Not so. The fine weather and the prospect of seeing some new blood attracted a good attendance. Mr J. H. Dark had relinquished the management of Lord's to his nephew Sidney, who, with the support of the MCC secretary (Mr R. A. FitzGerald), took infinite pains in preparing a pitch vastly superior to the dangerous ground used the previous year. Nevertheless, one reporter was dismayed at the sight of the umpires following the antiquated custom of cutting the creases in the turf with a knife instead of employing the more reliable method of marking them with whitewash. Members of the press were again provided with special accommodation by Mr Day, who as usual made highly satisfactory arrangements in catering for the needs of the public. It is to be assumed he did a roaring trade, since the weather was intensely hot.

The teams were skippered on this occasion by Ned Willsher (AEE) and Jemmy Grundy (UAEE). Ned was not perhaps the best of professional captains, and in this match he relied to a certain extent on the advice of H. H. Stephenson. He was, however, considered good enough to lead the all-professional team touring North America in 1868.

Vacancies in the two sides were filled by a few veterans recalled to the colours and a leavening of new recruits. It was a high-scoring match by the standards of the day. Having won the toss, Willsher took first innings, and the AEE scored 218, with noteworthy performances from "Farmer" Bennett (39), Richard Daft (44), H. H. Stephenson (34), and C. Brampton (45). The United's early batsmen capitulated to Willsher (5–55) or ran themselves out, but there was a rally in the lower order with a fighting knock of 55 from little Tom Sewell and solid contributions from C. H. Ellis (31) and George Atkinson (32 not out). All England went to the wickets again with a lead of 37, and Willsher changed the order by opening with Brampton and George Wootton. The latter, as it turned out, achieved a personal triumph by notching 60, one of his highest scores in first-class matches, but his team-mates fared less well, and the final total was 166.

Faced by the Herculean labour of scoring 204 in the fourth innings of the match, the United began their uphill struggle on the third day. Grundy, overcome by the persistent sweltering heat, was too unwell to open the batting, and odds of 2 to 1 were freely offered against the UAEE. With two wickets gone and only 10 runs on the telegraph board, the odds shifted to 6 to 1. Griffith and Mortlock took the total to 40, when the former was bowled by Wootton, and Roger Iddison joined Mortlock. Their partnership, famous in the records of the series, put an entirely different complexion on the game. Moving from obdurate defence to devastating attack, they launched a murderous assault on the innocuous All England bowling, until finally Mortlock got a top edge, lobbing a simple catch to short-leg. Three for 126. "The Surrey Stonewall's" 65 included one stroke for 7, all run out, a "mammoth" leg-hit dispatching the ball out of the ground through the gates, which had just been opened to admit a carriage. His partner Iddison was run out for 44 (six for 156), and the UAEE lost two more wickets with 9 runs still to get. Number 10 (Frank Silcock) was virtually the United's last hope, since the ailing Grundy was in poor shape to handle a bat. His services were not required, for Silcock and Sewell confronted the pace of Slinn and Wootton with confident ease. The appearance of 200 on the telegraph was greeted with enthusiastic applause, and not long afterwards Silcock struck the ball beyond cover-point's reach, whereupon the scorers, according to the custom of the day, stood up to indicate that the game was a tie. To Silcock fell the honour of making the winning hit, and the United were home by two wickets at 4:50 p.m. on the final day.

The expenses for the match were £125, leaving the Cricketers' Fund with a clear profit of £102 11s 6d, which was augmented by additional subscriptions to the amount of 9 guineas.

Fourteen matches had been played so far in the series, and the honours were even, with six victories to each side and two games unfinished. There was every reason to suppose the series would continue to be played unchanged in subsequent seasons, but 1864 was a momentous year, bringing a time of crisis in the history of cricket, and nothing would be quite the same again.

CHAPTER EIGHT

The Troubles

It was a quarrelsome, bad-tempered age of for cricketers. The first twenty years of the All England Eleven's existence were marred by a succession of incidents that shook the even tenor of the noblest game. During Clarke's reign, the most outstanding example was the swelling dissension culminating in the foundation of the United All England Eleven in 1852, but there were many instances of bickering, beginning with the argument over alleged unfair bowling in the match between the AEE and 18 of Yorkshire in 1846. To this may be added the question of conflict of interests. Clarke arrogated to himself the exclusive right to dictate where and when the members of his team should play. According to his lights, the demands of the AEE took precedence over all other arrangements. Notable absentees from the Nottinghamshire team contending against Sussex at Nottingham, in 1848, were Clarke himself, George Parr, and Guy, who were all assisting the AEE against 20 of Leeds on the same dates. A similar situation arose over Gentlemen *v* Players at Lord's, in 1854, when there was a dispute between Clarke and MCC over the constitution of the Players' team. As a result, Clarke, Caffyn, Julius Caesar, and George Parr were omitted from the side, which consisted largely of United men. The absentees did not suffer financially, however, since they were all playing for the AEE against 18 of Maidstone. This conflict of interests would become one of the principal causes of complaints levelled against the itinerant elevens by those who lamented the continuation of their operations, when the number of first-class matches began increasing season by season.

It would be unfair to maintain that Clarke, cantankerous and cross-grained as he was, should be held responsible for all the nastiness pervading the world of cricket. Without doubt, he left a legacy of uncompromising hostility, but others could be just as bloody-minded as he. From the end of his career until well on into the 1860s, a succession of disputes, varying in magnitude, arose between individuals, between individuals and employers, between clubs, and—most disastrous of all—between North and South.

The enmity between the Two Elevens was much in evidence in 1855. Clarke, it seems, tried to persuade some of the UAEE to play for a representative England team against Surrey, at the Oval. His overtures were roundly rejected by the non-Surrey United men, who refused to appear in any match under his management, thereby conforming to the declaration made in their manifesto at the foundation of the UAEE in 1852. Later, Wisden's men turned the knife in the wound by deliberately excluding the All Englanders from the fixture they got up between South and North at Tunbridge Wells. Clarke retaliated by omitting, as far as possible, United players from a match he arranged between Nottingham-shire and Six of Kent and Five of England.

The same year saw a rift between individuals and employers. Julius Caesar and H. H. Stephenson fell foul of the Oval authorities by demanding an increase in their wages and, as a consequence, they were dropped from the Surrey team for the remainder of the season. The two offenders were doubtless piqued by this cavalier treatment, but they were far from being reduced to the breadline: "Julie" and H. H. played for Clarke in twenty-four of the twenty-five All England fixtures in 1855.

Comparative quiet reigned throughout 1856, apart from one or two blemishes. George Parr and Bickley became involved in an obscure argument, and most of the United men were once again excluded from the fixture got up by Clarke between Nottinghamshire and England. All was not honey and roses either for the UAEE, who incurred adverse publicity over their match with 20 of Bradford in September. Wisden's side, still needing 19 for victory, were 38 for 6 when stumps were drawn on the final day, and they accused the Bradford team of preventing them from winning the game by lengthy, unnecessary delays in consultations and other hallowed, time-wasting ploys. This alleged skulduggery was denied by their opponents in a letter published in *Bell's Life*, adding that the United would probably have lost the match anyhow, since all their best batsmen were already out . . .

The 7th Earl of Stamford (President of MCC, 1851) was an ardent patron of cricket. Many games were played at Enville Hall, his residence in Staffordshire, and the earl, who dearly loved to win, was in the habit of selecting powerful teams of talented amateurs with a stiffening of "crack" professionals, particularly when the opponents were one of the itinerant elevens. In 1857 and 1858, Lord Stamford employed as engaged bowlers Bickley, Brampton, R. C. Tinley, and Willsher, and his lordship, behaving even more harshly than William Clarke had done previously with his All England men, refused to allow his employees to take part in other matches on numerous occasions, even to the extent of telegraphing for them to return immediately to their duties at Enville Hall. Lord Stamford can hardly be blamed for denying them permission to play in many of the All England fixtures against "odds"—he was after all paying their wages for the season—but his ban went far beyond this, affecting in particular Tinley and

Willsher, who were often required to appear in minor affairs at Enville Hall, rather than playing in county matches, Gentlemen *v* Players, and other representative contests. His lordship was perfectly entitled to crack the whip, according to the letter of the law, but one might have expected a more enlightened attitude to be adopted by a so-called lover of cricket.

The UAEE had their *contretemps* with their Bradford opponents in 1856, and in the following year came All England's turn to suffer at the hands of a local team in Yorkshire. Parr's men were overwhelmed by 22 of Leeds, who dismissed the Eleven for 29 and 49 to win by 121 runs. Smarting at this humiliation, the AEE were moved to register a protest in *Bell's Life*, recommending Leeds "to keep the selection of their side more confined to their own club, as they (the England side) were not 'superhuman', and it would be more honourable to win by playing men of their own district". It had often been the practice for local teams to call upon the services of outsiders for contests against one of the itinerant elevens, but on this occasion the Leeds managers had engaged several imports, including Roger Iddison, George Atkinson (who took 6 wickets), and Ikey Hodgson. The chief architect of All England's downfall, however, was Harry Lee, a genuine Leeds man, who captured 11 wickets. There would have been some justice if Leeds had issued a counter-claim, objecting to the somewhat surprising inclusion in the All England team of two regular United men, "Ben" Griffith (who took 12 wickets) and Tom Lockyer. A remarkable oddity was featured in this match: George Parr, who had taken to bowling lobs a while back, was the most successful All England trundler, taking 9 wickets in the first innings and 11 in the second.

Nothing particularly untoward occurred in 1858, but there were two noteworthy incidents in 1859. The first concerned the jealous rivalry existing at this time between MCC and the Surrey Club. In an eleven-a-side match at Lord's the former easily defeated their opponents, who were assisted by three professionals (Caffyn, Lockyer, and H. H. Stephenson). The fixture and return were dropped for several years (until 1865) on the initiative of the visitors, who asserted that the ground at Lord's was "so rough, that it was quite dangerous to play on, and also that the match at the Oval did not pay".

Of much greater importance was an unfortunate event in the match between the North and Surrey, at Manchester, at the end of August 1859. Around this time, an atmosphere of blatant hostility between the North, master-minded mainly by George Parr, and Surrey began to develop. The origins of this situation can at best be described as rather crepuscular. Perhaps it was triggered off by the Manchester incident, but it was destined to have far-reaching consequences, when teams and clubs were enveloped by a whirlwind of enmity, and individuals were driven to acting with hasty malice rather than prudent forethought. Surrey batted first at Manchester, and the North's wicket-keeper (Ned Stephenson) received a painful injury to one of his fingers. His place behind the stumps was filled by "Cris" Tinley, and "Yorkshire" Stephenson fielded out for the remainder of the innings. Struggling on first hands, the North lost several wickets, and George Parr approached his opposite number with a request that a substitute should be allowed to bat in place of Stephenson. The laws for substitutes were rather more nebulous than they are today, but the Surrey skipper, Mr F. P. Miller, refused to countenance such a move and flatly rejected Parr's request. Tempers flared as a heated discussion ensued, but Parr failed to carry his point. When the ninth wicket fell, the crowd cheered at the sight of "Yorkshire" Stephenson going to the wickets, intending to bat with one hand. Before he could receive a ball, his furious captain stormed out of the pavilion "and peremptorily ordered him to come back". The North batted with only ten men in each innings and were defeated by 34 runs. Mr Miller had justice on his side. In many respects an excellent captain, he believed in playing a hard, uncompromising game and always imbued his team with the desire for nothing short of victory. In view of future developments during the next few years, however, it would have been more politic for Mr Miller to have forgotten the letter of the law and behaved more magnanimously in what might be regarded in some lights as a sort of exhibition match. From now onwards, the North nurtured a feeling of resentment against Surrey, which eventually encompassed the whole of the South. For the time being, though, the ill-feeling slept fitfully, and the seasons of 1860 and 1861 were undisturbed by any overt hostility. Surrey and Nottinghamshire played home and away fixtures, the former had contests with England and the North, and there were several engagements between North and South. George Parr turned out in all these matches except three in 1860 (he was ill), and the unhappy dispute arising out of "Yorkshire" Stephenson's injury at Manchester seemed to have been forgotten.

Yet Parr had evidently neither forgotten nor forgiven, and in 1862 he began a personal vendetta against the targets of his animosity. Though still prepared to appear for his county against Surrey at Trent Bridge, for the North against the South at Lord's and against Surrey at Manchester, he declined to take part in any fixture at the Oval. Thus, on August 25, 26, and 27, he chose to assist the AEE against 14 of Yorkshire, at Barnsley, and was absent from the encounter between Surrey and England at the Oval, on the same dates. The England side comprised two amateurs and nine professionals, of whom eight were northerners. It was, in more respects than one, an historic contest. Batting first, England were not dismissed until late in the afternoon of the second day for the colossal total of 503, including one century, two nineties, and only three batsmen in single figures. Surrey began their innings about 6:00 p.m., with Ned Willsher bowling from the Pavilion end, where John Lillywhite was standing as umpire. A wide-spread belief prevailed at this time that Willsher frequently infringed Law X with a high action at the moment of delivery, and some critics even maintained that he threw the ball. Lilly had had many opportunities as a player to observe Willsher's bowling, and now, as umpire, he watched the left-hander's action closely and warned him he was breaking the law.

The first Surrey wicket fell for 4 runs, and Willsher, apparently heedless of Lilly's admonition, bowled in his usual manner to the new batsman . . . He was no-balled six times and, in a fit of high dudgeon, threw down the ball and strode off the field. The other professionals, all eight of them, followed Willsher, leaving the centre of the field occupied by six lonely men—the umpires, the batsmen, and the two amateurs playing for England.

Lillywhite, of course, had his supporters, who admired his courage for enforcing a law continually broken in the past with precious little intervention from more complaisant umpires. Willsher, however, was a pet with the public, and much of the popular opinion was on his side. His action was the same as it had always been, so why pick on him now as the victim of such flagrant humiliation? Turmoil reigned, and a hasty meeting was held in the Pavilion, with a now penitent Willsher tendering to the committee an apology for his bad-tempered behaviour. The Oval authorities devised a curiously pusillanimous solution. Instead of supporting the umpire's decision, they attempted to persuade Lillywhite to permit Willsher to continue bowling without let or hindrance *in this particular match*! All praise to Lilly for refusing to officiate under such conditions and maintaining his right to call Willsher every time Law X was infringed. Rather than abandon the match—and lose the gate money on the third day—the authorities replaced Lillywhite with another umpire. No more no-balls were credited to Willsher's analysis, and the match ended in a draw, with Surrey following on and holding out successfully in their second innings.

There was a twofold outcome to this memorable scene. Less than two years later, on June 10, 1864, Law X was amended to abolish the restriction on the height of the hand at delivery, and over-arm bowling became legal. Of more immediate importance was the attitude of the northerners. Some, harbouring black suspicions against the Oval authorities, professed to believe that John Lillywhite had been instructed to no-ball Willsher in the hope of saving Surrey from a humiliating defeat! This interpretation of events served to place an even greater strain on relations between Surrey and the North.

The ill-starred season of 1863 achieved dubious notoriety for a series of unsavoury incidents. Even at this early date, there was internal strife in Yorkshire. In July, George Atkinson failed to turn out for his county against Nottinghamshire. Yorkshire were defeated by a narrow margin, and eight

E. Willsher, Kent, All England, and United South of England Elevens (first captain and secretary of USEE). Toured North America, 1868 (captain). His unfair bowling action—raising the arm above the shoulder—resulted in the change in the Laws of Cricket, making the present-day overarm delivery legal (1864).

of their professionals signed a petition, declaring they would not play against Surrey later in the month, if Atkinson were included in the team. The selection committee yielded to this ultimatum. Atkinson always maintained he had not promised to participate in the Nottinghamshire match, and happily for all concerned he played for Yorkshire again in the future, "the matter being smoothed over".

All was not well in the South, either. Henceforth, Sussex—like the Surrey Club in 1859—would refuse to meet MCC, complaining among other things of "the roughness of Lord's Ground". At the end of August, "queer-tempered" Tom Lockyer was sent to play for the Surrey Club against Southgate, whose team was got up by the famous Walker brothers. On arriving at the ground, Lockyer made an objection ("for some private reasons of his own") to one of the umpires, called David Jordan. Mr John Walker, the head of the Southgate clan, refused to replace Jordan, so Lockyer withdrew from the Surrey Club side.

More serious events in 1863 gave rise to comments that the hostility of the North towards the Oval authorities was becoming more obvious, thanks to the baleful influence of George Parr and his "clique". In June and July, Cambridgeshire, for whom three of Parr's staunchest adherents played (Carpenter, Hayward, and Tarrant), withdrew from engagements to meet Surrey at the Oval. Parr and some of his associates turned out for the Players against the Gentlemen at Lord's, but none appeared in the same fixture at the Oval shortly afterwards. They had no qualms about assisting the North against the South at Manchester, Lord's, and Liverpool, but Surrey and the Oval were anathema to them. There was no fixture between Nottinghamshire and Surrey, and Parr's "lot" were conspicuous by their absence from Surrey's matches with England and the North at the Oval, and even North v Surrey at Manchester. Finally, there was the previously mentioned affair of the benefit match in honour of Tom Sewell, senior. It had originally been expected that the teams for this contest at the Oval would be the AEE and the UAEE, but the arrangements fell through, because some members of the Elevens—their identity is easy to guess—declined to play, and a match between Surrey and Middlesex was substituted.

Parr and his cronies may certainly have welcomed opportunities to express their displeasure with Surrey and the Oval, but it is only fair to recall that on most of the occasions they were absent, one or both of the Elevens had fixtures against local teams, for which advance arrangements had probably already been made. In one instance, the boot was on the other foot: not a single Surrey professional took part in Gentlemen v Players at Lord's, because their county required them to play at the Oval against 18 of Rugby, Cheltenham, and Marlborough Schools!

A similar pattern of behaviour occurred the following season. Parr, who was very injury-prone around this time, returned late from his tour of Australia to captain the Players at Lord's—but not the Oval—and Nottinghamshire against Yorkshire, only to suffer a badly damaged hand in the county fixture, which prevented him from playing again in 1864. His example of boycotting Surrey was followed in part by his closest supporters, who at this time were largely confined to some of the leading professionals of his own county and Cambridgeshire. Somewhat surprisingly, the home and away fixtures between Nottinghamshire and Surrey were resumed, but once more there were no meetings of Surrey and Cambridgeshire. A challenge was forwarded from the Oval to the northern county, with an offer to bear the entire expenses of the match. This generous gesture was regretfully declined by the Cambridgeshire secretary (H. Perkins, later secretary of MCC) with the explanation that "R. Carpenter, T. Hayward, and G. Tarrant positively decline to play at the Oval at present". Surrey, it may be added, abandoned any idea of playing the North at the Oval, contending instead against the South.

George Parr's most zealous disciples were at first the three Cambridgeshire professionals named above, George Anderson of Yorkshire, and "Fog-horn" Jackson and "Cris" Tinley of Nottinghamshire. To this group may be added Richard Daft to a certain extent. A friend and admirer of Parr, Daft adopted a curiously ambivalent attitude by declining invitations to take part in some matches while accepting others—for instance, he assisted England against Surrey. It is probable that some of his absences were caused not by sheer bloody-mindedness, but by business commitments that occupied much of his time in the early 1860s and often prevented him from playing cricket. With the exception of George Anderson, the leading Yorkshire professionals held aloof from Parr and made no bones about playing at the Oval or against Surrey on other grounds. All that would be radically changed within the next twelve months, for 1864 was above all a Year of Decision.

There were three contests between North and South, but there should have been four. Sleaford was the venue for the first, at the end of June, at the same time as the Lord's fixture of Gentlemen v Players, the latter containing the hard core of Parr's "clique". The second was played at Old Trafford, in August, with eight Surrey men assisting the South and most of Parr's adherents appearing for the North. The third meeting was arranged for September 5, 6, and 7, on the (then) Middlesex County ground near the Cattle Market at Islington. John Wisden selected a strong side for the South, and the task of getting up the North team was entrusted to Roger Iddison, the Yorkshire captain, who experienced considerable difficulties, since many of the principal northern professionals were not available. Moreover, Roger was at that time engaged by the Whalley Club in Lancashire, who had arranged a twenty-two match against the AEE on

September 8, 9, and 10. As the club professional, Roger was required to be present at the Whalley ground immediately prior to the forthcoming match. He therefore wrote to Wisden, saying he could not play himself and enclosing the list of players for the North. One of the names was W. H. Iddison, Roger's younger brother, a cricketer of moderate ability, who never played for his native county but assisted Lancashire on a few occasions.

Unfortunately, W. H. failed to appear at Islington, and the vacancy had to be filled very late by an amateur to make up the eleven. On the first day of the match, it was widely believed that Roger had defaulted after having promised to play—evidently the substitution of W. H. for R. Iddison was not known, since Wisden did not put in an appearance on the ground. Burning with indignation at the absence of Roger and other first-class northerners, and at the weakness of the opposition—the South won in two days by an innings and 29 runs—the southern professionals held a meeting on the evening of the 5th and passed the following resolution:

"We, the South of England, decline playing at Newmarket on the 6th, 7th, and 8th of October, as they, the North of England, refused to play in London". Signed T. Lockyer, W. Mortlock, E. Pooley, James Lillywhite, junior, G. Griffith, T. Humphrey, H. Jupp, C. H. Ellis, T. Hearne, T. Sewell, junior, G. Bennett, John Lillywhite, and Julius Caesar [the whole South team, plus John Lillywhite and Caesar].

As a result of this declaration, the return fixture at Newmarket was cancelled and replaced by a makeshift match, Cambridgeshire and Yorkshire v Kent and Nottinghamshire, with G. Wells (the Sussex player!).

In fairness to the northerners, it must not be forgotten that the AEE were engaged to play against 22 of Scarborough—a club with whom they had good relations—on the same dates as North v South at Islington. Moreover, Ned Willsher, a first choice for any side representing the South, elected to assist the AEE at Scarborough and took part in the match at Whalley, the two remaining All England fixtures of the season, both against twenty-twos in the north, and the stop-gap affair at Newmarket. No adverse criticism was aimed at Willsher for not assisting the South at Islington.

The spirit of contention smouldered throughout the remainder of the long season, and though a few southerners played in the Two Elevens' matches against "odds", more chose to participate in other fixtures. Finally, in November, came the crunch with yet another form of manifesto, when seven disgruntled southern professionals—John Lillywhite, Lockyer, Hearne, Mortlock, Sewell, Griffith, and Jupp—officially resigned their membership of the United Eleven. More was to come. Ned Willsher, abandoning his continued adherence to the AEE, now attended a meeting with the deserters from the UAEE and five others (Bennett, James Lillywhite, junior, T. Humphrey, E. Pooley, and Julius Caesar)—an ominous total of thirteen. The purpose of the meeting was to discuss the foundation of yet another itinerant eleven, and the newly elected officers were Willsher (secretary and captain) and John Lillywhite (treasurer). Two more names were added to the roll of members—C. H. Ellis, a signatory to the Islington declaration, and H. H. Stephenson—and the United South of England Eleven was born. Initially an all-professional team, the USEE was destined to flourish for years to come, though in somewhat changed circumstances.

John Lillywhite and Tom Lockyer shared the somewhat dubious distinction of being associated with all the declarations of secession from 1852 onwards, when the United All England Eleven was founded in opposition to Clarke.

So the great schism between North and South finally became a reality, enduring for several years. The UAEE, more seriously affected by the secessions than the AEE, rallied and reorganized their forces, with the more dynamic Robert Carpenter taking over some of the secretarial duties and the captaincy from John Wisden, who had retired as a player. Henceforth, the annual contest between the Two Elevens would be to all intents and purposes the North v the Rest of the North. There were some advantages: the AEE would acquire a worthy replacement for Willsher, while the UAEE would at last field bowlers whose pace and accuracy matched those of Jackson, Willsher, and Tarrant.

CHAPTER NINE
Responsibility and the Status of the Professional

THE prolonged ostracism of Surrey and the Oval practised by George Parr and his "clique" furnished a considerable contribution to the deplorable schism between North and South in 1864. Their overt hostility was clearly regarded as deliberate provocation by the southern professionals, in whose eyes the fiasco of the North v South match at Islington was merely the culmination of a succession of malevolent manoeuvres calculated to impair southern morale. Yet the South was far from blameless in the whole affair, and the two schisms of 1852 and 1864 were the result of hasty, petulant gestures by factions consisting largely or entirely of southern professionals. Belated claims that their refusal to play in North v South at Newmarket applied to *that match only* are belied by their speedy organization of the United South of England Eleven in the autumn of 1864. The whole sorry business was discussed *ad nauseam* in the press from time to time, but in the more permanent literature of cricket the most prominent critiques show a marked bias in favour of the South.

One of the writers most bitterly hostile to the North was Fred Lillywhite, a southerner enjoying close connections with the Oval. Parr and his associates had sometimes behaved towards Fred with an ill-disguised display of amused contempt, regarding his humourless fussiness with his match reports, score cards, and printing press as an unmitigated nuisance. Fully aware of this attitude and further embittered by the way in which he was edged out of the administration of the Cricketers' Fund, Fred seized the opportunity to work off some old scores in the 1865 edition of his *Guide to Cricketers*. His sentiments in the "Review of the Season" of 1864 were comparatively mild, but he failed to exercise a modicum of restraint in some of his remarks on the "Professionals of England". He criticized Carpenter and Tarrant, and upbraided Roger Iddison over his alleged mishandling of the arrangements for the infamous Islington match. Tom Hayward was the recipient of much more unpleasant strictures, but the main outpouring of Fred's vials of wrath was reserved for John Wisden and George Parr. The former, once Fred's partner in a business for the sale of cricketing gear, was

UNITED SOUTH OF ENGLAND ELEVEN

The United South of England XI *v* 20 of Lewes, Lewes, September 7, 8, & 9, 1865   *Courtesy Roger Mann.*

trounced for his connection with the Cricketers' Fund and his secretaryship of the UAEE. Even worse was the castigation of Parr. Heavy irony was the weapon used by Fred, who began with several lines of character assassination ("his well-known good temper, easy and quiet disposition, void of jealousy, and never interfering with other people's business"). An accusation of exerting a powerful influence over the affairs of the United Eleven as well as his own AEE was followed by an oblique reference to one of George's less endearing personal habits, his fondness for imbibing gin ("Was the able manager (when out of his bedroom) in America"). In conclusion came a final sentence relating to Parr's activities with the Cricketers' Fund. Fred paid the penalty for indulging in this unbalanced vituperation, when MCC withdrew their patronage of the *Guide*.

On a different level were the criticisms of the Rev James Pycroft and Arthur Haygarth. Both expressed a general concern that the continued activities of the itinerant elevens were detrimental to the development of eleven-a-side cricket. In principle, there was much justice in this point of view, and the critics deplored the increasing tendency of northern professionals to absent themselves from county matches and other representatives contests in favour of playing against local twenty-twos, usually in the North. Like a tongue prodding at a sore tooth, Haygarth pursues this theme with relentless persistency in the pages of *Scores and Biographies*, reserving most of his animadversions for George Parr and his "lot", especially for their refusal to play at the Oval or even to meet Surrey and sometimes the South on other grounds as well. Criticisms of the conduct of the southern professionals are muted in contrast to his frequent attacks on Parr and his supporters, and his remarks are interlarded with gibes at their preference for engagements with local twenty-twos "as being more convenient and profitable".

In propounding his opinions, Haygarth assumed the role of spokesman for the leisured classes, for whom cricket was a pleasant pastime played "for fun" (*pace* Wilfred Rhodes!) as and when the spirit moved them. It was alien to their nature to regard cricket as a game to be played regularly throughout the summer months purely for financial reasons, and they were unable or unwilling to comprehend the attitude of professionals preferring to meet twenty-twos rather than choosing the honour of appearing in a grand match at Lord's or the Oval. Honour was all very well, but honour never paid the rent. It cannot be denied that hard-liners, such as Parr, Carpenter, Hayward, and Tarrant, welcomed the opportunity to prolong their boycott of Surrey, but this was not their sole motive. The cost of travel, accommodation, and incidental expenses made a large hole in the wages received by a northern professional accepting engagements to play in the South. By limiting the bulk of their activities to matches against twenty-twos in the northern counties, individuals could still earn good wages and incur less in the way of expenses. It was a question of economics and hard-headed common sense, but Haygarth and other censorious critics could not or would not acknowledge this simple concept of the stern facts of life.

There were other reasons lying behind the proliferation of the hostility towards the paid fraternity. Thanks to Clarke and the existence of the itinerant elevens, a first-class professional with moderate habits could, as mentioned previously, look forward to regular payments throughout the season. Improvidence created straitened circumstances during the dark, winter months, but many individuals had the chance to earn some sort of income from other sources. For some there were also fringe benefits in the shape of temporary coaching appointments at the public schools and universities, while a number of professionals exploited their reputation by becoming mine host of an inn—a form of employment not to be recommended for a landlord too weak-willed to resist demands made upon his popularity. Yet few indeed were those who managed to earn their living solely from the game and still live in reasonable comfort. An exception was George Parr, who came from farming stock, and who never took up any other profession but cricket. He attributed this good fortune to a lucky charm he received in exchange for kissing the heavily tattooed Queen of the Maoris while touring Australia and New Zealand in 1863–64. On presenting George with this talisman, a piece of green malachite, the queen informed him it would bring him luck as long as he carried it about in his pocket, and he would never have to do a day's hard work. "And I never have", George would add, producing the stone whenever he recounted the story. George married late and died without issue, leaving a personal estate of £356. The charm eventually passed into the possession of one of Richard Daft's daughters, but—tantalizingly—there is no record as to whether it retained its magic properties.

In the Hambledon days and after, wealthy and aristocratic patrons of the game often obtained the services of talented players by employing them as gardeners, grooms, and the like. Treated as servants or members of the household staff, in a temporary or more permanent appointment, these employees were naturally at the beck and call of their masters, and this situation still existed in the era of the itinerant elevens—witness the case of Lord Stamford and his engaged bowlers. Professionals characterized as "civil and obliging" were regarded with approval, while those displaying a greater independence of spirit and bluntness of speech were considered less reliable.

In the more rarefied atmosphere of social stratification prevailing in the Victorian age, it was considered natural in the order of things that the gentleman cricketer should claim as his inherent right the romantic role of batsman, while the more menial tasks—for so they were regarded—of

bowling and even fielding were allotted to the professional. The writer of
one surviving description of a country-house match tells of two noblemen
lounging in chairs in the company of admiring ladies, while their places in
the field were filled by substitutes! On another occasion, a much more
ludicrous situation arose, resulting in an altercation between a nobleman's
steward and two professional bowlers from Nottingham. The nobleman in
question was a poor batsman, but he always wanted to make the top score on
his side. In order to satisfy his employer's desires, the steward offered the
professionals a bribe of half a sovereign to bowl loose balls off the wicket
whenever his lordship had the strike. All went well at the beginning of the
nobleman's innings. His partner (a young tailor), so far the top scorer, was
also privy to the plot and obeyed his instructions "to stop run-getting and let
the Marquis score". But fate intervened: just as the marquis was about to
overtake the tailor, he played an inept stroke and dragged a wide delivery
into his stumps. When the professionals demanded their half-sovereigns,
the steward refused to pay up on the grounds that one of them had failed in
his obligation by dismissing the marquis before he achieved the top score.
The indignant professional retorted that the ball had pitched three feet off
the stumps, declaring forcibly—he was a northerner, remember—that if his
lordship was so clumsy as to play the ball onto his wicket, that wasn't the
fault of the bowler, who should not therefore be penalized. Eventually, an
English compromise was reached: the two bowlers were persuaded to settle
for the lower sum of five shillings each!

Most of the professionals at this time came from the working class, with a
small number, such as Parr, Anderson, Richard Daft, and H. H.
Stephenson, belonging to a slightly higher stratum. Expressed in feudal
terms, the emergence of the itinerant elevens represented for many
professionals a sort of deliverance from thraldom, though the old
forelock-knuckling days remained in a modified form for many years to
come. One can appreciate the dismay of the more leisured classes, when the
world of cricket was dismembered by the schism of 1864. Whatever the
rights and grievances of either North and South, it was in the widest
possible sense detrimental to the welfare of the national game. So far, so
good, but there was an additional cause of resentment. The limited type of
liberation achieved by the professionals was regarded in some quarters as a
threat to the established social order. They were developing ideas above
their station, even to the extent of expecting to be addressed as "Mister" in
public houses! Some of the criticisms were, however, much more savage
than this semi-humorous dig at the professors' social climbing. None more
so, perhaps, than the fulminations of a journalist signing himself *Land and
Water*, who published an article on "Professional Cricket" and another on
"Amateur Cricket" early in 1866. The gentlemen were not exempted from
all censure, and the failure of many to cultivate the arts of bowling and

George Parr, Nottinghamshire, captain and secretary of the All England Eleven.
Toured as captain North America, 1859, and Australia, 1863–64. For years the
premier batsman of England.

fielding is condemned, but the lash is applied with much more vigour to
those playing cricket as a means of obtaining a living. *Land and Water* began
his first piece by establishing what was, in his opinion, the proper
relationship between gentlemen and players:

> Just so we employ grooms, because we do not care to rub down our own
> horses, and gamekeepers because we do not care to feed our own
> pheasants; but we have no intention of letting the former go out
> fox-hunting on the cream of our stud, or of putting the latter in the warm
> corner of our best cover. In a word, then, professionals are necessary as an
> accommodation to amateurs, and their position ought to be a secondary
> and subsidiary one.

Warming to his theme, the writer then posed the question: ". . . what *is*
their actual position at the present day?" Comparing them to the Praetorian
cohorts of the Roman Empire, *Land and Water* asserted that the
professionals had been spoiled by success, flattery, and public adulation,
becoming "puffed up with self-importance". As individuals, he conceded,
"many, very many, are invariably civil and respectful"—the standard
epithets—but as an organized body they were obnoxious. By way of
explanation, *Land and Water* referred to the schism, the boycotting of
certain grounds, the professionals' unpunctuality, and their drinking habits
in certain matches ("they leave the ground during the day to 'liquor up' (as
their vocabulary has it) as often as they please, without asking or obtaining
permission"). Whereas discipline was maintained at Lord's, it did not
prevail at all grounds. Indeed, part of the responsibility for the
professionals' present attitude rested with the Oval authorities, who were
far too lavish in their distribution of talent money and much too ostentatious
in their elaborate ceremonies of presentation, at which the recipient was the
cynosure of all eyes.

Land and Water could not, of course, refrain from dragging in the
obligatory sneer at "those gate-money speculations", the matches against
local twenty-twos. "They are", he said, "happily falling into well-deserved
contempt. Few gentlemen will play in them; few cricketers will go to see
such a burlesque". Events, as it turned out, were to prove him wrong.
Finally, he moved to his ponderous peroration, summing up his thesis as
follows:

> Professionals are auxiliary to the cricketing world, and in that position
> they may do good service; but about their quarrels and disputes, their
> grievances and their claims, the great body of cricketers on whom they
> depend, the members of the Public Schools, the Universities, and the
> Army, know nothing and care nothing. They entirely ignore them, and

are so heartily sick of having them forced season after season on their notice, that they are very likely before long to decline paying any more a heavy price for unserviceable servants.

As a reflection of the views on the social order at that time, *Land and Water's* diatribe is the Heaven-sent answer to a sociologist's prayer. The gloomy gravity pervading his article is happily lightened by a rare touch of unexpected comedy. One can only marvel at the wry sense of humour or extreme naivety of the sub-editor responsible for designing the lay-out of the page: enclosed within the columns of *Land and Water's* tirade against professional cricketers is a wood engraving of George Parr, the Demon King of cricket in the 1860s.

CHAPTER TEN

The Troubles (continued), 1865–1870

THE pattern prevailing in recent seasons was repeated in the representative matches of 1865. Richard Daft, Carpenter, Tarrant, Atkinson, and "Cris" Tinley all assisted the North against the South at Lord's, and, but for injury, Tom Hayward would also have played. "Fog-horn" Jackson, no longer so formidable as of yore, was probably not selected, but it is not known whether Parr was invited to participate or not. Perhaps he declined the offer, since the opposition consisted entirely of members of the newly established United South of England Eleven. At any rate, Parr and Jackson turned out for the AEE in a twenty-two match on the same dates. A slightly amusing event occurred on the evening of the second day at Lord's, when North and South sat down together in solemn conclave for the Annual General Meeting of the Cricketers' Fund, though Tom Lockyer, as hard a man in his own way as George Parr, was a non-attender. Minutes were read and approved, Richard Daft succeeded old Tom Box as chairman, the committee of management—three northerners and three southerners—was re-elected, and proposals for new members of the society were tabled. The adversaries were evidently on their best behaviour within the hallowed precincts of Lord's.

Only two northern professionals, neither a hard-liner, assisted the Players against the Gentlemen at the Oval: Parr and his favourite companions were engaged in a match between the AEE and a twenty-two. The positions were reversed in the equivalent match at Lord's, with seven northerners (including Parr, Carpenter, and Hayward) and only four southerners, possibly because the United South were playing against 22 of the Hertford Town Club. George Parr, who had first represented the Players as far back as 1846, made his final bow in the series, striving in vain to ward off defeat with a battling 60 in his second innings. Carpenter, Hayward, Tarrant, Jackson, and Tinley all appeared for the North against the South at Canterbury, but George was skippering the AEE against 22 of Trentham Park. None of his "clique", of course, participated in the contest Surrey v England at the Oval, when the AEE and UAEE both had fixtures.

The programme of county matches was not without its blemishes. On June 1 and 2, Middlesex achieved an easy victory over Hampshire at Islington. Arrangements had been made for the return fixture to be played at Southampton on July 13 and 14, but at the eleventh hour the Middlesex secretary wrote to his opposite number, stating he "could not collect an eleven together owing to the Eton and Harrow match at Lord's, which *everyone* was anxious to see". An announcement that the county fixture had been postponed appeared in *Bell's Life*, provoking an indignant retort from the Hampshire secretary. Complaining at the tardiness of the Middlesex secretary's letter to him, he stated he had sent a reply to the effect that Hampshire refused to permit the postponement of the match "on such frivolous grounds", adding that it would not be played at all unless some more satisfactory reason were forthcoming, "the fixture having been made previous to the alteration of the Eton *v* Harrow fixture". There was no return match in 1865, nor did the two countries meet again for many years.

Home and away matches were played by Nottinghamshire and Surrey. The first, at Trent Bridge, resulted in a comfortable victory for the home side, assisted by Richard Daft, Jackson, and Tinley, but not George Parr, who preferred to play for the AEE against 22 of Brackley. Things went differently in the return at the Oval—when Parr again refused to appear, giving precedence once more to an AEE match—and a close, hard-fought contest ended in Surrey winning by 1 wicket. The 14 runs required were all obtained by the last man (Tom Sewell, junior), but the Nottinghamshire team and their supporters were outraged by an umpiring decision. Sewell was once run out "most palpably"—by as much as a yard and a half, according to one of the fielders—but the appeal was rejected. To the visitors this seemed like one more instance of blatant favouritism to save Surrey from defeat on their home ground, and the old grievance flared up once more. The Nottinghamshire committee and team were unanimous in their belief that "if the match could not be played pleasantly it were better not played at all", and there were no more fixtures until 1868.

The secession of the southern professionals from the AEE and UAEE to form the United South Eleven automatically guaranteed their absence from the annual match in aid of the Cricketers' Fund, and all but one of the players participating in the contest were drawn from Cambridgeshire (5), Nottinghamshire (9), and Yorkshire (7). There is no doubt that the recent manoeuvres culminating in the formation of the USEE were interpreted by the northerners as a deliberate attempt to destroy the Two Elevens, the source of the lion's share of their summer wages. Now Parr gained new adherents to his cause, when the world of cricket was presented with a spectacle become all too familiar in future times—internal strife in Yorkshire, with players and a committee in headlong collision. The principal control of affairs resided at this period with the Sheffield authorities, and the first shot fired in the internecine warfare was the refusal of five professionals to play against Surrey at Bramall Lane, in the third week of June. This was a serious blow to the selection committee, since the five "secessionists" (Haygarth's term) formed the backbone of the side—George Anderson, George Atkinson, Roger Iddison, Joe Rowbotham, and Ned Stephenson, all members of the AEE or UAEE.

When an explanation for their conduct was demanded, the five were not backward in declaring their sentiments. Anderson, "The Old Scotchman", outlined his position in no uncertain terms with the following statement:

> The players of the South have made a dead set against the North. The Surrey men have declined to play in a match which is for the benefit of cricketers who are members of the Cricketers' Fund. I uphold the North and will not play against those who have combined to sweep us from the cricket field altogether if they could.

Roger Iddison, the Yorkshire captain, expressed the case in more succinct terms ("I consider that by trying to break the United England XI up, they are taking the bread out of our mouths"), while Stephenson referred to "the players who have been most cruelly ill-treated by the Surrey men". Their views were whole-heartedly supported by Atkinson and Rowbotham. It was, all five felt, a question of economics rather than hostility for its own sake.

The opinions of Anderson and his companions were ignored. One influential member of the Sheffield Club asserted that he would do his utmost to prevent the five malcontents from ever appearing at Bramall Lane again, and as an immediate punishment they were excluded from the team in *all* matches under the jurisdiction of the Sheffield committee. Yorkshire had a disastrous season, losing seven matches and drawing two, of which five were got up by the Sheffield authorities. One of these was an eleven-a-side contest with the AEE at Bramall Lane, and the five were not permitted to assist either the county or the Eleven. Jealousy, resentment of the dictatorial attitude emanating from Sheffield, and sympathy for the victims resulted in the issue of invitations to Anderson and the others to appear in home and away matches with Nottinghamshire and Cambridgeshire, which came under the management of other authorities, such as the Bradford committee.

In spite of their forebodings, the "secessionists" were able to earn their living after all. Rowbotham and Stephenson assisted the AEE in almost all, and Anderson in over two-thirds, of the fixtures. Atkinson and Iddison played in most of the United matches—though there were not many in 1865—and appeared several times for All England. At the end of the season, a match was got up for the benefit of the five on the Hyde Park Ground,

Sheffield, the teams being 18 Gentlemen of the North (with several professionals given) and the AEE (with Anderson, Atkinson, Iddison, Rowbotham, and Stephenson). Captious critics might have asserted that George Parr was rewarding recruits to his banner, but at least he provided some security to those who stood by their principles and believed themselves to be the victims of the machinations of the South.

The general situation deteriorated still further in 1866. While the Two Elevens, consisting entirely of northerners, were engaged in their annual match for the benefit of the Cricketers' Fund in May, Mr R. A. FitzGerald (secretary of MCC) was occupied with plans for the North v South contest scheduled for the beginning of July. He requested Bob Carpenter to assist the North, but, to his consternation, Carpenter declined the invitation, and the leading northern "cracks"—except those who were ground men at Lord's—followed suit, nor would they appear in Gentlemen v Players at Lord's, at the end of June. With the ban on Kennington Oval now extended to St. John's Wood, Parr's supporters withdrew to the isolation of their northern fastnesses. The exact cause of their quarrel with headquarters is obscure. A question of payments and expenses, perhaps, but it must be added that around this time the management of affairs at Lord's created misgivings in the hearts of some people in no way connected with Parr's "clique".

MCC counter-attacked by cancelling future patronage of the match played for the benefit of the Cricketers' Fund and establishing the Marylebone Professional Fund, for which a benefit fixture would be arranged the following year. While declining to become involved in the dispute between North and South, the authorities at Lord's announced that henceforth they would select teams "from those who are willing to play together in a friendly manner in the matches on that ground". In a somewhat meaningless gesture, the Surrey secretary wrote to Mr FitzGerald, stating that nobody who had refused to play in North v South at Lord's would be permitted to appear at the Oval. There was a curious exception to this embargo. In those more free-and-easy days, there were instances of individuals assisting more than one county in the same season (example, James Southerton, who appeared for Hampshire, Surrey, and Sussex in 1867). Since Yorkshire had few fixtures in 1866, Roger Iddison, who had a professional engagement in Lancashire, played for his adopted county several times, even against Surrey at the Oval, where he achieved a personal triumph by scoring 49 and 106.

So, many of the northern "cracks" eschewed most of the grand matches of 1866 in favour of All England or United fixtures with twenty-twos, finding it "*just now* more profitable to confine their performances entirely in the North" (Haygarth). The ill-fated meeting between North and South at Lord's ("a farce of a match") resulted in the abysmal defeat of the former, who were represented by a very weak team. There would be no more authentic North *v* South contests in the next few years: they were replaced by a milk-and-water affair, North of the Thames *v* South of the Thames, a fixture ignored by Parr's men.

Only Middlesex, still playing at Islington, were exempt from the excommunication of the South and were able to arrange home and away fixtures with Cambridgeshire and Nottinghamshire, with Parr and his "clique" assisting their native counties. The return match with Cambridgeshire at Fenner's Ground was marred by an extraordinary incident, furnishing Haygarth and other critics with fresh ammunition to fire at northern professionals. Taking first knock, Middlesex scored the comfortable total of 248, and during this innings Bob Carpenter suffered an injury to one of his hands, while George Tarrant probably received a dent in his pride, since his 4 wickets cost 120 runs. When Cambridgeshire took their first hands, it was obvious that Carpenter could not hold a bat, and the Middlesex captain magnanimously agreed to the introduction of a substitute—Charles Newman, who had played once (1863) for the United against All England. Perhaps there was bad blood between Newman and Tarrant, for the latter committed an act of crass folly. "Tear'em", reacting in a most irrational manner, declared he would take no further part in the match if Newman came into the side. His objection was overruled, Newman played, and Cambridgeshire batted twice with only ten men, losing the contest by an innings and 4 runs. The enormity of his behaviour dawned on "Tear'em" before the game was over, but his offer to bat in the second innings was firmly rejected. His conduct was condemned in the sporting press, and he tendered a formal apology some months later at a meeting of the Cambridgeshire CCC.

Yorkshire remained in the doldrums in 1866, with the Sheffield committee apparently sulking in their tents and refusing to participate in the administration of county cricket. The local authorities got up two matches at Bradford against Cambridgeshire and Nottinghamshire, and a third came off at Trent Bridge, resulting in two defeats and one draw. Four of the five "seccessionists" assisted Yorkshire in all three games, and the fifth (George Atkinson) missed the last one only because his employer in Middlesbrough claimed his services.

Two minor storms in a teacup during the season illustrated some of the irritants arising out of the conduct of twenty-two matches and the behaviour of professionals, to which such critics as Haygarth and *Land and Water* took exception. The first occurred when 22 of Redcar met the UAEE at Redcar, Yorkshire, in July. Several well known northern cricketers, a few of first- or nearly first-class status, were engaged to appear for the home side. But for some misunderstandings and arguments there would have been two more. The Redcar managers were convinced *they* had secured the services of

George Anderson, who lived not far away, but the United were equally sure he had been booked to appear for *them*. Eventually, after a prolonged dispute before the match began, it was decided that he would play for neither team! Yet another difficulty arose over George Atkinson, who also resided a few miles distant. Engaged to assist Redcar for a fee of £5, he wrote shortly before the match to demand £7. The Redcar managers ruled this to be unacceptable, and, in addition, they would not permit him to turn out for the United!

The second affair, containing a touch of farce, occurred shortly afterwards, when the AEE encountered 18 of Bishop's Stortford, whose captain was Mr W. F. Maitland, a current Oxford Blue and a member of the Gentlemen's team against the Players. All England distinguished themselves by employing no less than three umpires. The first and authentic official, since he was not playing, was George Parr, who relinquished his duties during the match and left the field. Whether illness was the cause, or the demands of administration, or even, as *Land and Water* might have opined, a desire "to liquor up", is not recorded. His place was taken by Joe Rowbotham, one of the All England team. Joe also stepped down later, and his replacement was another player, Tom Hayward. During Rowbotham's tenure of office, one of the All England batsmen, none other than George Anderson, made a long hit for which the batsmen ran two. "The Old Scotchman", who seemed fated to attract trouble these days, was convinced the ball had reached the boundary line. After he was out, he confronted the scorers, requesting them to mark 4 for his hit. They refused to make the alteration without the sanction of the umpire officiating at the appropriate time, but Rowbotham was nowhere to be found. The argument waxed fast and furious as All England wickets fell, the last going for a total of 132—2 runs short of Bishop's Stortford's score. Consternation reigned. The final court of appeal was Mr Maitland, a future MP and a good-natured individual, who agreed to Anderson's representations, and consequently the match was declared to be a tie!

The season of 1867, apart from one or two exceptions, was very much the mixture as before. Having now abandoned or been excluded from Lord's, the Two Elevens chose Old Trafford as the venue for their contest in aid of the Cricketers' Fund. Shortly afterwards, the inaugural match for the benefit of the newly established Marylebone Professional Cricketers' Fund came off at Lord's, having as its object "the support of those professional players, who, during their career, shall have conducted themselves to the entire satisfaction of the Committee of the M.C.C." The opposing sides were England and Middlesex, the former assisted by three southern professionals and five northerners, of whom four were ground bowlers. Most of the "cracks" were engaged elsewhere, since the All England, United, and United South Elevens were all playing in "odds" matches.

Parr's supporters continued to boycott Gentlemen v Players and North of the Thames v South of the Thames, and, in one instance, a fixture between Cambridgeshire and Yorkshire was arranged to coincide with Gentlemen v Players at the Oval. Nottinghamshire maintained their contests with Middlesex, and Lancashire (largely untouched by George Parr's influence) with Surrey. Otherwise, little connection existed between North and South on the county level, apart from one exception, which showed a glimmer in the Stygian gloom of the tunnel.

There was some fence-mending in Yorkshire, when a partial success was achieved in generating a reconcilation between the Sheffield committee and the "secessionists". Two of the black sheep, Roger Iddison and Joe Rowbotham, made their peace with Bramall Lane and returned to the fold, consenting to assist Yorkshire against Surrey at the Oval and Sheffield. Unfortunately, Anderson, Atkinson, and Stephenson were still marching to a different drummer and persisted in their refusal to play against Surrey, though they were willing to participate in fixtures with other counties. They were not alone in expressing disapproval of Sheffield's well-intentioned decision to revive relations with the old enemy. A match between Cambridgeshire and Yorkshire at Bramall Lane had to be cancelled, because certain professionals—Carpenter, Hayward, and Tarrant, without a doubt—refused ("out of spite") to have dealings with a committee guilty of promoting a contest with Surrey! Arrangements for the fixtures between the two northern counties were altered, the first being played at Wisbech and the second at Dewsbury, where the authorities lent a more sympathetic ear to the views of the northern "cracks".

In spite of all prognostications, matches played by itinerant elevens against "odds" were by no means a dead letter. On July 18, 19, and 20, a strongly represented All England side encountered 22 of Bolton, assisted by several professionals. The AEE were evidently not strong enough, losing by almost an innings to the bowling of two of the most renowned Given Men, William Slinn (13 wickets) and Luke Greenwood. An attendance of at least 10,000 persons, including 2,500 ladies, gave ample testimony to the popularity of the match, and the proceeds fell little short of £350. "Such being the case", said Haygarth sadly, "no wonder the 'Twenty-two matches' flourish, much, however, against the interest of true cricket, Eleven v. Eleven".

The northern "cracks" maintained their ostracism of Gentlemen v Players in 1868, and North of the Thames v South of the Thames was again substituted for a genuine North v South contest. Meetings took place, however, between northern and southern counties, the most important being the resumption of home and away fixtures for Nottinghamshire and Surrey. As might be expected, a notable absentee at both the Oval and Trent Bridge was George Parr, still showing no inclination to abjure his hostile attitude.

As far as Yorkshire were concerned, the improvement in relations was extended in 1868: Ned Stephenson and George Atkinson were reconciled with the Sheffield committee and made themselves available for selection. The former played against Surrey at Bramall Lane, and both joined Iddison and Rowbotham to assist their county at the Oval, where Yorkshire defeated their opponents by an innings and 142 runs. A notable contribution to the visitors' success was a stand of 176 for the first wicket by John Thewlis, who went on to mark 108, and his bucolic-looking nephew Ephraim Lockwood (91), a future stalwart making his *début* in first-class cricket. George Anderson, however, now in his twilight, was content to play for the AEE in twenty-two matches.

The most obvious indication of attempts to repair the schism between North and South occurred at the close of the season, when a party of twelve professionals went on a short tour of Canada and the USA. Seven of the team came from the South, including Ned Willsher as captain and "Ben" Griffith, survivors of the old days of strife, and five ardent members of the USEE. They were joined by five northerners, among them Joe Rowbotham, John Smith of Cambridge, a promising young batsman, who had been following his senior team-mates' example in boycotting southern grounds, and one of the most extreme hard-liners, George Tarrant. Perhaps "Tear'em" was anxious to demonstrate his willingness to make amends for his previous conduct.

Although the Yorkshire professionals had in the main deserted George Parr, the veteran and his closest associates showed no sign of renouncing their principles. At a meeting of the Cricketers' Fund Friendly Society in London, on the last day of 1868, approaches were made in turn to Parr, Carpenter, and Hayward to get up a team to represent the North against the South at Lord's, in 1869. All three refused, and they were absent from the North *v* South contests at the Oval and Bramall Lane, though six Yorkshiremen played in the first and seven in the second encounter, but none participated in a third meeting at Canterbury. Gentlemen *v* Players remained under the ban, though Richard Daft, never much of a rebel, made his reappearance in the fixture at Lord's. Parr and his "clique" were not out-of-pocket: All England engagements were arranged to coincide with the dates of several of the grand matches of the season.

Surrey had home and away matches with both Nottinghamshire and Yorkshire, and once again Parr declined to play against the southern county. George Anderson, one of his keenest supporters, actually agreed to turn out for Yorkshire in one match. The opponents were not Surrey, but Cambridgeshire, giving "The Old Scotchman" an opportunity to hob-nob with two of his like-minded friends, Bob Carpenter and Tom Hayward.

Two minor incidents of bickering, completely independent of the schism, occurred in 1869. On arriving to begin a match with 22 Gentlemen of Worcestershire, the United South found to their dismay that the home side had arranged to employ George Howitt as a Given Man. Howitt, a fast left-hander (Nottinghamshire and Middlesex), one of the star bowlers of the United All England Eleven, was notorious for his ability to exploit rough pitches and had scant respect for a batsman's person. The United South had recourse to that tradition hallowed since the days of Old Clarke: they raised objections, carried their point, and Howitt was omitted from the local team.

There was also some awkwardness between two southern counties. The energetic secretary of Hampshire was eager to arrange matches with Surrey, only to find his advances rejected on the grounds of "an old grievance and alleged indebtedness". Both counties rushed into print, and several letters on the subject were published in the press, with Surrey, it was felt, not appearing in a very attractive light.

The season of 1870 marked a turning-point in the affairs of cricket. A spirit of reconciliation reigned, and the breach between North and South was largely healed. Though still refusing to appear at the Oval, Parr assisted Nottinghamshire against Surrey at Trent Bridge, and the North against the South at Lord's! George had virtually arrived at the end of a long career, but others had not. Two of his staunchest supporters, Carpenter and Hayward, together with young John Smith—but not, alas, George Tarrant, who was on his deathbed—capitulated still further. At Lord's they represented Right-handed against Left-handed, the North against the South (also at Canterbury and Dewsbury), and the Players against the Gentlemen, though they were absent from the equivalent fixture at the Oval. This change of heart was not entirely disinterested. They welcomed the opportunity to continue putting jam on the bread by accepting any engagement offered to earn their wages. Carpenter in particular, and his team-mates, were facing the prospect of periods of unemployment. They could still play for the AEE in fixtures against "odds", but Cambridgeshire, once so formidable, had almost ceased to exist as a first-class county—one final match was got up in 1871—and, as far as Bob Carpenter was concerned, another source of income had also dried up. Above all, however, the reconciliation of North with South was symbolized by three matches played in 1870, of which details will be given subsequently.

So the great schism, which had threatened to inflict mortal wounds on the body of cricket, came to an end after several years of bickering, ostracism, and overt hostility. On both sides there were faults, but the unhappy situation was to a certain extent prolonged by the conduct of Parr and his "clique". Their attitude was of a certainty detrimental to cricket as a whole, and their self-imposed exile detracted from the interest of grand matches, depriving the southern spectators of the opportunity to see them displaying their skills. In palliation, let it be repeated that the northern "cracks" played cricket for their daily bread, and "odds" matches in the North provided the most convenient and economical means of earning their pay. Had they been offered the inducement of higher wages and something towards their expenses in return for playing in the South, perhaps matters might have been different.

Never again would cricket in England suffer to the extent it did in the 1860s. There would be, of course, disagreements and disputes in the years to come, and the potential threat of another disruption, with teams refusing to play against another county, was created by the throwing controversy of the 1880s. The difficulties were fortunately smoothed over, and the situation of the great schism was never repeated.

CHAPTER ELEVEN

The All England, United All England, and United South of England Elevens, 1865–1869

As a predominately northern organization, the All England Eleven were able to weather the storm and survive the wounds inflicted by the schism more easily than the UAEE. Three regular members, all stalwarts who had made their *début* during William Clarke's managership, had departed to sign up with the newly formed United South. The youngest (at thirty-two) was H. H. Stephenson, the first choice as wicket-keeper, but a replacement was available, his namesake Ned. Though almost as good a batsman, "Yorkshire" Stephenson was not quite so reliable behind the stumps and occasionally revealed a lack of big match temperament by muffing simple chances. The other two, in their middle thirties, were Julius Caesar and Ned Willsher. Less serious was the loss of the former: increasingly afflicted by crippling attacks of gout, "Julie's" years on the cricket field were numbered. The AEE still had the services of George Wootton, but the gap left by Willsher was filled by another fast left-hander, who soon proved himself to be a more than adequate substitute with the ball.

There was no danger of unemployment for the AEE in 1865. Out of a total of thirty-one engagements, they defeated their opponents nineteen times and lost only six matches. One of their victories was achieved against their old adversaries in the annual match at Lord's for the benefit of the Cricketers' Fund, when the UAEE were beaten by 66 runs. Since all but one of the professionals participating were northerners, there was a feeling in some quarters that the public's interest in the match would be limited. These Jeremiahs turned out to be false prophets: more spectators than ever were in attendance, and the accolade of royal patronage was bestowed by the presence of the Prince of Wales. "Yorkshire" Stephenson celebrated his birthday by obtaining the "leger" with a free-hitting innings of 59, his highest score in the series.

The AEE played another first-class fixture in 1865. Bramall Lane was the venue, and Yorkshire, in the throes of their own particular schism, were the opponents, fielding a team deprived of the assistance of the five "rebels" (Anderson, Atkinson, Iddison, Rowbotham, and Stephenson). The visitors had but one innings, running up the gigantic total of 524, to which Carpenter contributed 134, Hayward 112, Parr 78, and all the batsmen got into double figures. Yorkshire were defeated by an innings and 255 runs, and in their second hands George Wootton distinguished himself by taking all 10 wickets for 54 runs.

All England confined their operations in 1865 almost exclusively to the North and Midlands, as was to be expected, and were only seen in the South in the contest with the UAEE at Lord's and a couple of twenty-two matches.

Although a few of the members were northerners, the United All England Eleven had a strong southern contingent, and consequently many gaps appeared in the ranks after the schism. Most important was the departure of Griffith, Hearne, John Lillywhite, Lockyer, and Mortlock. Wisden had retired, Caffyn had settled in Australia, while promising youngsters, such as Henry Jupp of Surrey and James Lillywhite, jun., of Sussex, were no longer available. Grundy, now in his forties and showing signs of corpulence, Carpenter, Roger Iddison, and Atkinson remained as a nucleus, around which the team could be rebuilt. It looked at first as though the UAEE had suffered such irreparable harm that mere survival was in doubt. Never so well organized and administered as the AEE, the United had a depressingly small programme in 1865—only nine matches, less than one-third of All England's tally, all played in the North or Midlands, apart from the encounter with the AEE at Lord's and a fixture against "odds" at Bath. Towards the end of 1864, when the departure of the southern professionals and the foundation of the United South were acknowledged facts, the UAEE made some hasty moves to regroup their forces. Wisden was to be treasurer and would share the secretarial duties with Bob Carpenter, but the UAEE remained in a parlous state in 1865.

The United South of England Eleven played their inaugural match against 22 of Ireland, at Dublin, on May 11, 12, and 13, 1865. All the names were familiar—Ned Willsher (Kent), Hearne (Middlesex), John Lillywhite and his cousin James (Sussex), and seven from Surrey (Caesar, Griffith, T. Humphrey, Jupp, Lockyer, Mortlock, and Sewell). The Prince of Wales, visiting Ireland for the opening of the Dublin Exhibition, attended the match. Since he was also present at Lord's for the encounter between the AEE and UAEE some four weeks later, one can only admire the strict impartiality observed in HRH's patronage of all three principal itinerant elevens.

Most of the USEE's fixtures were played in the South of England, and their first season was not particularly successful. Some fifteen matches were got up, producing only four victories and five defeats. The composition of the team followed the traditional lines laid down by William Clarke: above all a concern manned and run by professionals, the USEE were not averse to including one or two amateurs in their side on occasions. It would not always be thus, for a strange metamorphosis lay in store for the USEE in the years to come.

Maintaining their momentum in 1866 with a programme of thirty matches, the AEE recorded sixteen victories, six defeats, and one tie. Only one fixture was first-class, the contest with the UAEE for the benefit of the Cricketers' Fund, played at Lord's for the last time, for this was the season when the northern "cracks" extended their boycott of the South. Comfortably victorious in the previous year, All England suffered a reverse in 1866, being defeated by almost the same margin. Two new bowlers were on show, making their *début* in the series. In J. C. Shaw, who had been given a brief trial in 1865, the AEE found the replacement for Willsher. Jemmy Shaw, a fast left-hander with a high action, made a modest beginning, taking 5 wickets in the match, but for several years he was acclaimed as one of the best bowlers in England. He was certainly one of the greatest characters in the history of cricket, the 'hero' or 'villain' of several anecdotes, and renowned as one of the most redoubtable of W. G. Grace's early adversaries. The other *débutant*, also a fast left-hander, was George Howitt, whose employment as a Given Man would be so strenuously opposed three years later by the USEE. Justice was doubtless on their side. Howitt's bowling system consisted of erratic deliveries, a hideously fast break-back from the off, and bumpers, and in this battle at Lord's he felled Richard Daft with a blow on the chin. The United owed much of their victory to Howitt, whose match figures were 13–129.

Another United recruit also had a turn with the ball, took no wickets, but conceded only 15 runs in 13 overs. He was described by a leading reporter as "a neat, fair, good pace and truthful bowler of the Grundy style, and one we should imagine could always be relied on as a good change in any match". The journalist was speaking of a man who, in the following season, took 66 wickets in 8 first-class matches at an average of slightly over 8 runs each—George Freeman, a native of Boroughbridge in Yorkshire and one of the handsomest cricketers in England. A dashing batsman and a good fielder, he is principally remembered for the magnificence of his bowling, and he made full use of his splendid physique to pulverize his opponents. His easy action, with the right arm slightly above shoulder level, was deceptive, for his deliveries came through at a great pace with a wicked spin. The Oval was his favourite ground, since its true pitches enabled him to control the spin to a nicety. Throughout the memoirs of his contemporaries, the praise of Freeman as *the* most difficult bowler of his day constitutes a veritable *leitmotif*. "Fog-horn" Jackson in his prime and "Tear'em" Tarrant may have been a little faster, but nobody was so formidable as Freeman. "His delivery was easy", said W. G., "and he could keep it up for a very long time; and when the ball hit you, you felt as if you had been cut with a knife or a piece of the skin had been snipped off". No exaggeration, witness Allen Hill, another Yorkshire fast man, who declared he had known "the inside of 'W.G.'s' thigh, above the pad, pounded into the appearance of a mutton-chop by balls from Freeman, which whipped in and struck the champion". Freeman's first-class career was short, and he was rarely seen after 1872, when he decided to devote most of his time to the business of auctioneering at Thirsk.

The match at Lord's against the UAEE was the only appearance of the All Englanders in the South, and their contests against "odds" were played in the North and Midlands. There was no such limitation on the activities of the United Eleven, who enjoyed a highly successful season. They had twenty-two engagements in all, winning fourteen and losing only two, and several came off in the South, one even as far afield as Guernsey. Perhaps Bob Carpenter, the captain and joint-secretary, was partly responsible for arranging such an extensive programme: never in all their history did the UAEE have so many fixtures in one season. It looked as though the second oldest travelling eleven were making a successful bid to survive the damage wrought by the schism.

The United South played seventeen matches—less than either of their rivals, though seemingly the largest number of fixtures in one season throughout their existence. None was first-class, and the results (four victories, seven defeats) were far from encouraging. Unlike the AEE, however, the southerners were prepared to go anywhere, encroaching on All England territory by meeting opponents in the North and Midlands on several occasions. A famous personality, whose long career was still in its lusty infancy, played once for the USEE in 1866. At the time, perhaps, it attracted little comment, but it marked the inception of W. G. Grace's connection with the United South—an association destined to exert an all-pervading influence over the fortunes of other travelling elevens.

With twenty-eight matches in 1867—two less than the previous season—the AEE still comfortably outdistanced their rivals. They hardly ventured beyond their chosen area, and six defeats were offset by seventeen victories. Banished from Lord's, they met the UAEE at Old Trafford in the last match they played for the benefit of the Cricketers' Fund, though it was not the final encounter of the Two Elevens. Haygarth, of course, disapproved of the venue as much as the behaviour of the northern "cracks", observing that "it 'paid' more to confine their efforts to the North". Sensible of the honour bestowed upon them, the authorities took the utmost pains to make a success of this special event, and the whole ground was in perfect order. The clerk of the weather, however, refused to co-operate, sending a bitter north-easter sweeping across Old Trafford and adversely affecting the attendance. This was unfortunate, since some of the best cricket of the whole series was displayed.

The UAEE won the toss and made 208, to which Carpenter contributed a solid 28 and Cornelius "Kerr" Coward of Preston 25, but the "leger" was obtained by Roger Iddison. With his usual judicious blend of cast-iron defence and rugged hitting, he occupied the crease for some three hours in scoring 63. Since Tarrant was absent injured, the main burden of the All England bowling was borne by Jemmy Shaw, who at one time sent down fifteen maidens in succession. Jemmy, who was afflicted with a disconcerting squint, delivered the ball with a late swing of his left arm from behind his back and was inordinately addicted to histrionics in the matter of appeals. Once he had taken a wicket, he calmed down, plunged his hands into his trouser pockets, and stared vacantly into space. Jemmy claimed seven victims in this innings.

No byes were conceded in either of the United's innings, a testimony to the expertise of All England's new wicket-keeper, who achieved front rank in the 1870s. Tall, brawny, long in the arms, George Pinder of Sheffield excelled at taking fast bowling and was a genius on the leg side. He was no mean batsman either and would occasionally condescend to bowl lobs without, however, removing his pads. On tour in North America in 1879, he derived much enjoyment from the ministrations of the local barbers, but was appalled at the prices they charged ("a man could 'ave 'is bloody 'ead coot off in England for that!"). A mere stripling in 1867 and anxious to make his mark, Pinder was not averse to a little exhibitionism. In a match against 16 of Trinity College, Cambridge, he performed well but was castigated for "the silly 'show off' of knocking down the wicket causelessly, as well as the nonsense of troubling the umpire with frequent and unnecessary questions". Since the same journalist even objected to the sound of nightingales singing in an orchard contiguous to the ground ("the only disturbing element"), perhaps his criticism of the youthful Pinder was a little jaundiced.

All England achieved a first-inning lead of 24, thanks to a free-hitting 34 from John Smith of Cambridge (employed in the locomotive department at Stratford, Essex, and always known as "The Stoker") and a chanceless 111 not out from Richard Daft, the only century in the series. Anxious to emulate the famous rituals at the Oval, the Old Trafford authorities summoned the gentlemanly Daft to the Pavilion and, on behalf of the Manchester Club, presented him "with a new bat as a memento of his splendid cricket". The more patently professional Roger Iddison had previously been rewarded with "the talent sov."

The United also had a wicket-keeper new to the series. About the same height and weight as Pinder, Thomas Plumb was a more competent batsman and also a change bowler. It would be difficult to decide which was the better stumper, Pinder or Plumb—or, for that matter, the other member of the great triumvirate of Ps, Ted Pooley of Surrey and the United South. Born in a second-class county (Buckinghamshire), Plumb had fewer opportunities to display his skills, and his neat, quiet efficiency and lack of panache attracted less of the recognition accorded to his more flamboyant rivals. Be that as it may, Plumb was certainly the equal of Pinder and superior to Pooley in keeping to fast bowling, and it is said that George Freeman rated Plumb higher than Pinder, his Yorkshire team-mate.

The UAEE collapsed in their second hands for 81, with only Coward (34) and Iddison (26) showing any resistance. As his bowling partner, Jemmy Shaw had John Jackson. The old war-horse, now in the eventide of his career, had not opened the All England bowling in the series since 1863. In length of service a veteran, though just thirty-four, "The Fog-horn" had been over-bowled for years, and in a county match in 1866 he ruptured a blood vessel in one of his legs. The terrifying speed was largely a mere memory, but Jackson answered the call to do battle for All England once again. It was his final appearance in first-class cricket, but his swan-song could hardly have been sweeter—6 wickets for 50 runs. There was, alas, no sweetness for him at the closing of his days. Reputedly a victim of heedless improvidence in more affluent times, Jackson's condition in his declining years was pitiful in the extreme. Homeless, often destitute and unable to obtain regular employment, perpetually faced by the looming spectre of the dreaded Victorian workhouse, he struggled to subsist on the meagre allowance of 5s. 6d. a week from the Cricketers' Friendly Society—the organization on whose behalf he had once laboured with unflagging zeal in the benefit matches between the Two Elevens.

Needing 58 to win, All England faced some ferocious bowling from Howitt and Freeman and lost 6 wickets in achieving their target. Only William Oscroft (20 not out) displayed any competence, surviving a confident appeal for a chance to the wicket-keeper, much to the disgust of Bob Carpenter, who was convinced that it was a fair catch.

Jackson was not the only veteran to make his final bow from the series. Also departing, after a record total of seventeen appearances, was Jemmy Grundy, who had assisted the United without a break since the first contest of 1857. This was his only match for the UAEE in 1867 and his last of all.

The United undertook fewer engagements in 1867. Only sixteen matches—as opposed to twenty-two in 1866—were played, all in the North or Midlands, apart from the last two in Guernsey and Essex. Their record for the season included eight victories and four defeats.

Very similar was the United South's programme, a total of sixteen matches, of which they won eight also, but they lost only twice. A variation crept into the pattern of their fixture list, almost all of their opponents being southern teams comprising fifteen to twenty-two players.

The AEE still led the field in 1868 with twenty-six fixtures—again a reduction of two—winning seventeen times and losing only five, venturing beyond their usual area of operations to play twice in Ireland and once at

Chelmsford. Dewsbury was the venue for the annual encounter with the UAEE, who had added another fast left-hander (Tom Emmett) to their attack. Played for the benefit of Bob Carpenter and Tom Hayward, it resulted in an easy victory for the UAEE by 8 wickets. Freeman returned match figures of 9 for 94, while Tarrant, restored to the AEE, captured 6 for 76 in the United first innings.

In spite of Carpenter's efforts to prolong the United's existence, the situation looked ominous in 1868. The programme consisted of the All England match and only six fixtures against "odds", one of which was played in the South. Undefeated, with six victories, their popularity was nevertheless on the wane. The United, a poor third, were falling far behind in the gruelling race for supremacy.

The United South, meanwhile, were in a healthy condition and outstripping their weaker competitor. Their list comprised fifteen matches, played in various parts of the country, but they could manage only six victories as opposed to five defeats.

The season of 1869 saw the AEE still enjoying a comfortable lead, even though there was yet another slight decline in the number of their engagements. Twenty-three matches (eight victories, six defeats) were played in Scotland, the North, and the Midlands. Dewsbury was chosen once more for the traditional fixture with the UAEE, arranged for the benefit of a long-serving All England veteran, George Anderson. "The Old Scotchman" received a daunting disappointment. Inclement weather interfered with play to such an extent that the match was abandoned as an inconclusive draw, when the UAEE had made 24 for 2 in reply in All England's total of 131 in their first innings.

Crushed by their failure to obtain an adequate total of fixtures in 1868, the UAEE had come to the end of the road. Recognizing they had lost the battle for survival and were doomed by the comparative success of their rivals and the competition created by the proliferation of first-class matches, the United managers were compelled to face reality. A side was got up for the encounter with the AEE, but no other matches were arranged, and the team was disbanded. The United All England Eleven could look back on a long and quite successful existence, affording employment for many professionals beyond the confines of the All England Eleven. In destroying Clarke's monopoly, they established a rivalry culminating in the great series of nineteen contests between the Two Elevens of England, originating in 1857 and terminating in 1869.

Untouched by the collapse of the UAEE, the United South played twelve matches in different quarters of the realm. There was nothing especially remarkable in their results (five wins, three losses), but the disappearance of one of their main rivals gave the promise of less competition in future seasons. They had, however, not bargained for the emergence of a new travelling eleven in 1870.

CHAPTER TWELVE
Minor Itinerant Elevens

THE All England, United All England, and United South of England Elevens were not the only itinerant sides contending against twenty-twos from the 1850s onwards. Prior to the foundation of the USEE in the autumn of 1864, various individuals endeavoured to follow the trail blazed by Clarke and Wisden in forming their own teams. Unable to compete with the established organizations on anything approaching level terms, they met with little or no success. Consisting largely of second-rate players or beginners unable to secure regular employment with the principal elevens, these mushroom growths lacked the potential to provide attractive opposition for local twenty-twos and failed to secure sufficient engagements to ensure financial gain. Some received little publicity, and there is scant possibility now of establishing a complete roll of all that ever existed. The titles of some and brief details of their activities have nevertheless survived, furnishing a modicum of information on various speculations of short-lived duration.

The first team of note to appear after the formation of the UAEE was the United Ireland Eleven. Founded in 1856, only to vanish in the 1860s, the UIE was much indebted to the determination of the enthusiastic secretary, Charles Lawrence, a professional connected briefly with Surrey. A member of H. H. Stephenson's party in 1861–62, Lawrence remained in Australia as a permanent resident, though he visited England in 1868 as the manager of a team of Aborigines.

No less than three organizations bore the imposing title of New All England Eleven. The first was the creation of Tom Sherman, who assisted the UAEE in the early days, and his associate, Frederick Chadband, an individual largely unknown to cricket except in his native district of Epsom. Little was achieved under their joint-secretaryship: one match was played in 1858 and five the following year. Revived in 1862 for a specific purpose, the First New All England Eleven then finally expired.

The Second New All England Eleven was formed in 1862 by Frederick Bowles Caesar, elder brother of the more famous Julius and an occasional player for Surrey. Six engagements were undertaken, including one of a special nature. Since the Sherman-Chadband organization had been the first to call themselves "The New All England Eleven", a dispute arose over nomenclature. Caesar replied to their objections by issuing a challenge, and the two teams met at the Oval on September 11 and 12, 1862, to decide which one had the right to bear the title. Sherman's eleven were defeated, but Caesar apparently derived little advantage from his victory. No evidence of any activity in 1863 is forthcoming, and the Second New All England Eleven "seems to have come to a premature end".

But the tale was not ended, and an attempt was made in 1864 to salvage something from the wreckage with the formation of the Third New All England Eleven. Seemingly an amalgamation of elements from Sherman's and Caesar's teams, with Ted Pooley as secretary, the new organization played two matches and gave up the ghost at the end of the year.

In the previous year, many miles away, another venture was launched, only to perish on its maiden voyage. A native of Stockton-on-Tees, Thomas Whitfield Hornby was a left-handed batsman with a fair reputation in the North. Though almost unknown in first-class cricket, he was selected to play for England against Surrey in 1864, when most of the northern "cracks" were refusing to appear at the Oval. In the previous year, Hornby got up a team entitled An Eleven of the North of England to contend against 22 of Crook. The eleven, assisted by several professionals who had turned out for Yorkshire, defeated their opponents easily. It is uncertain whether Hornby intended to limit his speculation to this one match, or whether he nourished wider ambitions, but no trace of a team operating under the name he chose has survived.

Since Parr's team did not return from their tour of Australia and New Zealand until mid-June 1864, their absence reduced the number of matches undertaken by the AEE and UAEE in the season. In order to fill the gap and provide wages for some of the professionals remaining in England, Ned Willsher and H. H. Stephenson formed the so-called English Eleven. The beginning was inauspicious. Arrangements for fixtures in Dublin and Belfast fell through at the last moment, and the first match was not played until May 19, the opposition being 22 of Accrington, with several Given Men, including Luke Greenwood and Ikey Hodgson. Two more contests came off in June, after which the operation was abandoned, and nothing more was heard of the English Eleven.

As previously mentioned, the United South of England Eleven was established as a going concern in 1864–65, but still others, of a more ephemeral character, made their appearance during the next few years. In the autumn of 1866, the United North and South of England Eleven was formed, with G. Baker of Kent as secretary. The impressive title was rather bogus. Like the various New All England Elevens, few of the personnel could claim a position of eminence among the "cracks" of the day. Two matches were played in 1867, only one in 1868, and then the team vanished beyond man's ken, collapsing "through (it is presumed) bad management or want of support".

Of even shorter duration was the existence of the North of England Eleven. The name of the founder has not survived, and though some of the players were of a much higher calibre than those of the United North and South of England team, the North of England Eleven was able to attract only one engagement in 1868 and was consequently disbanded.

Several more itinerant elevens were formed in the 1870s, some of them connected with Yorkshire, but there was one of southern origin bearing a marked resemblance to the three New All England Elevens and the United North and South of England Eleven. The founding secretaries were two veterans, William Caffyn, returned from residing in Australia, and the indefatigable Tom Sherman, who adopted the somewhat unoriginal title of the New United South of England Eleven. The players were none of the best, and, after playing one match in 1875 and two the following season, the New United South also ceased to exist.

CHAPTER THIRTEEN

The United North of England Eleven, Yorkshire United, and Others

WITH the collapse of the United All England Eleven in 1869, some of the regular members saw themselves once more facing the bleak prospect of a certain reduction in their earning powers. Bob Carpenter, the secretary and captain, suffered much less than some of his team-mates. Cambridgeshire, his county, had virtually ceased to exist but, having played over ten years for the AEE as well as the UAEE, he could count on obtaining employment with the All Englanders. Match fees were available also from other sources. Though approaching the end of his career, "The Old Gardener" was still rated as one of the best professional batsmen in England and, having made his peace with the authorities at Lord's and subsequently the Oval, he was automatically selected for two or three seasons in representative fixtures such as Gentlemen *v* Players.

Whereas other United members had reasonable expectations of being invited to assist their counties, there were still not enough fixtures at this level to provide regular wages throughout the season. Undaunted by the fate of the UAEE, optimists laid plans for the formation of a new organization. Much of the impetus came from Yorkshire, with some assistance from Lancashire, and a new team was created, entitled the United North of England Eleven. An original venture, the UNEE had no connection with those transitory sides bearing similar names that shrivelled in the bud in the 1860s. The first president was Lord Londesborough, a generous patron of Yorkshire cricket, and the vice-presidents were Messrs J. H. Wise of Malton and A. B. Rowley, the well known Lancashire amateur. Most of the credit for establishing the UNEE, however, lay with the joint secretaries, Roger Iddison and George Freeman of Yorkshire, former members of the defunct United All England Eleven. Business commitments soon compelled Freeman to relinquish his post, and throughout the team's existence Iddison's name is listed as the secretary, though his duties may have been rather nominal after a time.

There was little to distinguish the UNEE from other important travelling elevens. Beginning with a flourish in 1870, the secretaries drew up a full programme of nineteen fixtures for the first season, and the inaugural match was played against 16 Colts of England, at Dewsbury, on June 6, 7, and 8. Iddison and Freeman engaged a side of first-class professionals to represent the United North: all, with one exception, had at one time or another assisted the UAEE, and seven were regular members of the Yorkshire team. As might be expected, most of the games were played in the North and Midlands, but visits were made also to Hove and Truro. Ten victories and only four defeats testified to the success of the Eleven's first season in the field. To what extent it was successful in financial terms is a moot point, since the momentum of 1870 was not maintained throughout the United North's existence.

The difficulties in tracing details of *all* the United North's activities—indeed, those of any itinerant team from 1870 onwards—are only too apparent. Formerly, it was the rule rather than the exception for the sporting press to publish a report or at least a match score of any fixture between a travelling eleven and a local team. By the 1870s, with more and more first-class contests to whet the public appetite, the situation had changed. The visit of a travelling eleven still loomed large in the eyes of their opponents and the promoters, but wide-spread interest was on the wane, and some of the matches were deemed to be of only local rather than national importance. Records of the number of matches played by any itinerant eleven are unfortunately incomplete, because some of the fixtures were ignored by the sporting press and were probably only reported in provincial journals with a limited circulation.

Abundant evidence of this shortcoming appears in the later volumes of *Scores and Biographies*. Haygarth, the compiler, was the most conscientious of men, but his efforts to include details of every engagement undertaken by the travelling elevens were doomed to failure. Whenever possible, he attempted to consult an eleven's score-book, particularly when a match was ignored by *Bell's Life* and other sporting journals. Even in this endeavour he was not always successful: sometimes he obtained the information from a score card, but on other occasions he was reduced to inserting a bald announcement that a match, "it is believed"—a favourite phrase of Haygarth's for many eventualities—took place on such and such a date between one of the elevens and some local twenty-two, and even the result of the contest was not always available to him. Lacking the gift of hindsight and sublimely ignorant of the possible interest of future historians, the managers of the various elevens seem to have adopted a cavalier attitude towards the preservation of permanent records of their performances. The supreme example occurred when Haygarth wished to publish full details of a match between the United South and 22 of Alexandra Park, played on

June 16, 17, and 18, 1873. His failure to achieve his goal is expressed in the final sentence of his notice:

Many inquiries were made for this match, but a perfect score could not be obtained, and the United [South] scoring-books, even of this late date, were already destroyed in 1875, when asked for.

He returns subsequently to the theme of his difficulties several times, expatiating on his fears that he has omitted details of matches overlooked by the press, and delivers his apologia, a blend of venom and regret, in the following manner:

The compiler of these pages (A.H.) wished much to insert the whole series of each itinerant eleven, but he received but poor assistance to carry out that end.

One must of necessity draw conclusions from the information Haygarth *was* able to obtain. Even with the proviso that some matches may have escaped his notice, surviving details suggest that the popularity of the United North rapidly declined. Only eight matches are recorded for 1871, ten for the next season, tapering off to seven, four, two, and finally three in 1876, after which the organization's existence was terminated. The name was revived in November 1877, when fourteen professionals—from Derbyshire, Lancashire, Nottinghamshire, and Yorkshire—held a meeting at a Sheffield hotel. Assured of the support and assistance of other prominent cricketers, including amateurs, the Sheffield party passed a resolution to form a new northern team, the (second) United North of England Eleven. Apart from the title and some of the players, this fledgling organization was not connected with the original UNEE founded by Iddison and Freeman. Judging by the names of some of those involved, the desire to form the (second) UNEE might indicate that the old All England Eleven was coming to the end of the road, though some professionals at that time appeared to belong to more than one itinerant eleven—a far cry from the early days of Old Clarke! George Pinder, the Yorkshire wicket-keeper, was elected captain of the (second) UNEE. The deeds of his team received little publicity, apart from one first-class match against London United in 1879, and they were languishing in the early 1880s.

The original UNEE followed the pattern set by the older itinerant elevens, with a preponderance of matches against "odds", yet, considering their fairly short span of life, they played a remarkable number of first-class fixtures, thirteen in all. Four were got up in the first season (1870), three of them against the United South of England Eleven, and further eleven-a-side matches were arranged every year, except 1873. Contending against the

United South on no less than ten occasions, their other opponents were a team raised by Richard Daft (1870), the All England Eleven (1871), and Derbyshire (1875). Two of the three fixtures recorded for the UNEE in the closing season of 1876 were first-class. Played at Huddersfield and Hull, these were the final encounters with the USEE, and the personnel involved suggest that at least one of the games was merely a financial speculation with little regard for nomenclature. Only four of those appearing at Huddersfield also played at Hull, and none of the remaining seven had assisted the UNEE previously in 1876. Further, at least eight of the Hull side had also turned out for the All England Eleven the same season, and one of the contemporary annuals, calling the teams "North" and "South", describes the contest as "An illegitimate match, and one more properly to be designated as United South v. All England Eleven". The weight of evidence implies, on the whole, that the opponents were generally regarded as the United North and United South of England Elevens, but the divergence over nomenclature points to the difficulties of determining exactly which matches are to be included in the complete records of some of the itinerant elevens.

The usual reasons, such as a diminution of interest and a loss of support, accounted for the extinction of the original United North of England Eleven, plus another factor: they encountered some unusual opposition on their own doorstep. A new organization, entitled in full the Yorkshire United County Cricket Club—usually abridged to Yorkshire United—was founded at York, in January 1874. At the outset, there was evidently little desire to launch yet another itinerant eleven, since Yorkshire United had much more laudable aims, set forth in the following declaration:

> The above-named club has been formed for the purpose of generally advancing the interests of cricket in the county.
>
> It is not intended to have any ground, but to play county and first-class matches on any such grounds as may be deemed convenient and desirable.
>
> By this we hope to spread the interest taken in this noble game throughout the whole county, and to give to rising players opportunities for distinguishing themselves.

In their first season (1874), Yorkshire United played at least eleven matches—*at least*, since their activities were not over-publicized. Four were against "odds", two near Lyndhurst (Hampshire), under the auspices of Lord Londesborough, one at Harrogate, and one at Hull, but the other seven were eleven-a-side contests. None has so far been awarded first-class status, a somewhat harsh decision: the opponents included Derbyshire (twice) and Lancashire, both sides containing a good proportion of men to be found also in their teams contending against other leading counties.

In establishing the Yorkshire United programme, care was taken to avoid any conflict with official county fixtures, but nevertheless the new team found little favour in the land of broad acres. Notwithstanding the averred intention of serving as an agency dedicated to revealing the talents of possible recruits for the county side, and the respectability conferred by the presidency and patronage of Lord Londesborough—who had acted in the same capacity for the UNEE in 1870—Yorkshire United probably encountered some hostility from different quarters. The formation at, and connection with, York were grounds for jealousy in Sheffield and other towns, and Yorkshire United could easily have been regarded as a rival providing unwanted competition with Yorkshire CCC as well as the United North of England Eleven. Suspicions were also aroused by the election as paid secretary of Roger Iddison, then a resident of York. This appointment presented the intriguing spectacle of Roger wearing two hats. Founding secretary of the UNEE in 1870, he is still shown as occupying the post without a break in the editions of *Lillywhite's Cricketers' Annual* from 1872 to 1875. On the other hand, the same publication for 1876–78 names Joseph Rowbotham as the secretary of "Yorkshire County", the title by which Yorkshire United was subsequently known.

The praiseworthy intentions predicated in the document issued at the foundation of Yorkshire United seem to have gone by the board at an early date, coinciding, perhaps, with the replacement of Iddison by Rowbotham. A limited number of inter-county fixtures left gaps in the season, which the Yorkshire professionals were only too anxious to fill. Consequently, the original objective of encouraging promising young cricketers receded into the background, and Yorkshire United became an itinerant team, providing extra wages for regular members of the county side.

Yorkshire United expired around 1877, unable to compete with the still popular United South of England Eleven, and any further chance of survival was snuffed out in the following season by the numerous engagements fulfilled in the county by the Australian touring team. The formation of Yorkshire United in 1874 may well have exerted an adverse influence on the fortunes of the original United North of England Eleven, while, in all probability, Yorkshire United's final death blow—a nice touch of irony—was dealt by the foundation of the new, or second UNEE, under George Pinder's leadership.

Although the appeal of travelling elevens—the United South apart—had dwindled, there were still a few optimists continuing to manage organizations operating on a limited scale, such as the United Midland Counties Eleven and London United, which existed around 1880. London United played an eleven-a-side match against Pinder's (second) UNEE at Birmingham, in 1879, but otherwise little is known of the history of the two teams, and only one or two brief, casual references have survived.

Slightly more is known of another side, bearing the touching title of the Veterans of Yorkshire. Got up on an *ad hoc* basis in 1872 to contend against 11 Juniors of Yorkshire, at Sheffield, the Veterans were revived some years later, with two matches in 1876—under the patronage of the ever generous Lord Londesborough—two in 1877, and two in 1878 of which no details have been preserved. Loyal spectators would doubtless have overlooked the creaking joints and slowness in the field and indulged in waves of nostalgia at the pleasure of seeing some of their old favourites in action once more. The team for the 1872 match included several still to be found in the Yorkshire side, and there was one name from the dim and distant past—George Chatterton, who had played for 20 of Sheffield against the All England Eleven as far back as 1846, when William Clarke began his operations. Old John Thewlis and George Atkinson assisted the Veterans on several occasions, and William Slinn, the famous Given Man, appeared in the two fixtures of 1877. Exactly how many matches were played is uncertain, but it is unlikely that the team's existence was prolonged much after 1878. The Veterans were a completely harmless organization, posing no threat to the development of first-class cricket nor the activities of a well established itinerant eleven, such as the USEE. Their operations were largely confined within the boundaries of Yorkshire, and, while the standard of cricket was not of the best, some impecunious old professionals were given the occasional opportunity to earn a welcome supplement to their meagre resources.

CHAPTER FOURTEEN
The Healing of the Wounds

THE re-appearance of the rump of Parr's "clique" on southern grounds from 1870 onwards was a visible sign of the amelioration of hostile relations between North and South. More tangible evidence of a determined effort to repair the breach emerged from the arrangement of three first-class matches featuring teams representative of the two warring factions. The first encounter was witnessed by a boy, who would in later years achieve fame as a writer on sporting topics.

Short of stature and deficient of physique, James Alfred Henry Catton showed no signs of possessing the natural aptitude of a cricketer. Attempts at coaching by Tom Plumb, the United All England Eleven wicket-keeper, yielded but indifferent success in developing latent skills or even much enthusiasm for the game. Like many another boy, Catton's interest was kindled by overhearing a conversation between his elders. A leisurely breakfast at the family home, situated near Lord's, was interrupted by a sudden remark from Catton *père*. Tossing his newspaper down on the table, he addressed his spouse, expressing amazement that "old George Parr" was still playing cricket. Young Catton was confused. Did his father mean Old Parr, the famous centenarian, who lived to a great age? Laughter, followed by explanations, from which it transpired that the elder Catton was referring to a famous cricketer. As a reward for good behaviour, young James would be taken to see the famous George Parr, should he ever play in London again. But George had already made his final appearance at Lord's, so the youngster was taken to see another match.

Prolonged negotiations had evidently taken place between Roger Iddison and George Freeman on the one hand, and Edgar Willsher on the other. Attempts to put the clock back and revive a well established tradition were about to be realized. There would be, the promoters decided, a contest between two itinerant elevens at Lord's for the benefit of the Cricketers' Fund. Since the All England Eleven were not involved, and the United Eleven had been disbanded, their places would be taken by the United North and United South of England Elevens. The match could hardly be regarded as a genuine encounter of North *v* South at their full strength. Though some of their members were getting a little long in the tooth, the

USEE were able to field a fairly strong side, without, however, some of the amateurs, who would have been automatic choices for a team representing the South. Similarly, Richard Daft, Carpenter, Hayward, and J. C. Shaw—the "cracks" of the AEE—would have been assured of places in a real North side, but were necessarily absent. The UNEE were nevertheless strong enough: the team, including six Yorkshire professionals, consisted largely of former members of the old United All England Eleven.

The dates scheduled for the match were July 4, 5, and 6, 1870, and the attendance at Lord's on the first day was fairly large, but, said one reporter, "hardly so large as we should like to have seen on the occasion of a benefit set apart for so laudable a purpose". Iddison won the toss, elected to bat, and sent in two Toms, Bignall, a forcing bat from Nottinghamshire, and Plumb, the wicket-keeper. Opposing them was James Southerton of Surrey (also Hampshire and Sussex), a part-time barber residing at Mitcham. A slow, round-arm right-hander capable of bowling unchanged for lengthy spells, Southerton was renowned for his skill in pinning down his opponents. His partner at the Nursery end was Edgar Willsher, the captain. Though not so fast and deadly as of yore, Ned was still regarded as one of the leading left-handers in England, but on this occasion he posed few problems for the batsmen, and his second delivery, dispatched by Bignall to the wood-stacks with a mighty off drive, cost five runs. The first wicket fell at 14, when Plumb was stumped for 4 off one of Southerton's "slows", and Ephraim Lockwood joined Bignall. A dominating partnership burgeoned, the batsmen taking few liberties with Southerton, but treating Willsher with disdain, scoring 18 off him in two overs. Once, fortune favoured Bignall, who played an uppish shot into the hands of Tom Humphrey at deep point, "but that usually prehensile fieldsman failed to hold the ball". With 48 runs in the book, all but 10 conceded by Willsher, the captain took himself off. His replacement was Frank Silcock.

Fastish, round-armed, with a low delivery, bowling round the wicket and breaking from leg, Silcock soon found his length. A rare loose one from Southerton presented Bignall with five more runs—a lusty leg-hit to the bat stacks—but the batsman's generous portion of luck deserted him in Silcock's third over, when he was caught off his glove at point for 36. Two for 60. Joe Rowbotham came to the crease, scored a single and was then parted from Lockwood, who gave a steepling catch to "Ben" Griffith at mid-on. Three for 61. Enter Roger Iddison, who saw Rowbotham drive Southerton for four, only to succumb to a "bailer" from the same bowler. Four for 70. Luke Greenwood tried to live up to his reputation as a forcing batsman and failed. Badly missed at mid-on, he dashed out impetuously to one of Southerton's "slows" and was stumped by Ted Pooley for a single. Half the northern wickets gone for only 72.

The newcomer was Cornelius "Kerr" Coward, who had shared a

productive partnership with Iddison at Old Trafford, on the occasion of the last match played by the AEE and UAEE for the benefit of the Cricketers' Fund in 1867. They were confined to dogged defence by the tight bowling of Southerton and Silcock, who conceded only 28 runs in as many overs. Then Roger, who was beginning to emerge from his shell, had the misfortune to deflect a ball from Silcock into his stumps and departed for 18. Coward went on to reach 35 (21 singles), when Silcock tempted him into lofting a catch to Willsher at long-off. The innings closed at 4:10 p.m. for a total of 158, with Silcock and Southerton each claiming five wickets.

In after years, James Catton was able to recall the memory of three incidents from this match played in his boyhood. The first was his reintroduction to Tom Plumb, the United North stumper, who had once endeavoured to teach him the rudiments of batting. The second and third occurred at the start of the United South's first innings. Willsher had succeeded in engaging the services of W. G. Grace, who had played only a few times for the USEE in previous seasons. W. G.'s younger brother Fred was also in the side. Catton was impressed by the talk of the spectators around him, most of them southerners, who were gleefully anticipating the number of runs W. G. would score off his opponents' trundling. The thin sprinkling of northern supporters retaliated by boasting that their champion fast bowler, George Freeman, would soon be rattling W. G.'s stumps.

The USEE began their innings at 4:25, and Catton never forgot the thunderous acclamation that welcomed the appearance of W. G., striding to the wickets accompanied by Harry Jupp. Freeman (Pavilion end) and George Howitt opened the United North bowling. Somewhat surprisingly, the dour Jupp outpaced his illustrious partner, "who appeared to play with but little of his wonted fire". Seemingly ill at ease, W. G. scraped a couple of singles, while Jupp forged ahead to reach double figures. Shortly afterwards, abashed by a Howitt bumper, the Surrey batsman tipped a simple catch to Iddison at point. One for 16. His place was taken by Charlwood, an attacking batsman from Sussex, who was badly missed by Bignall at long-stop when marking a single off Freeman.

The next delivery produced the third incident that stuck in Catton's memory. A horrifying shooter from Freeman flattened the Champion's leg-stump, and the mighty roar greeting this feat far eclipsed the welcome given to W. G. when he emerged from the Pavilion. Two for 17.

Charlwood had another life, but the new batsman ("Ben" Griffith) soon surrendered to Howitt. Three for 19. Fred Grace now "joined issue", and the United North suffered a temporary set-back. Feeling the effects of a recurring strain in his bowling arm, Freeman was unable to continue, and Iddison was compelled to call upon Wootton to take over at the Pavilion end. Howitt, however, remained as the battering ram of the attack.

T. Humphrey and H. Jupp, Surrey and United South of England Eleven. Both toured North America, 1868. Jupp toured Australia, 1873–74 and 1876–77, playing in the first ever Test *v* Australia, 1877.

Admirably supported by his new partner, he pitilessly exposed the frailty of the United South Batting, and the southern supporters witnessed in shocked silence a sorry procession to and from the wickets. Six batsmen failed to score, and only Fred Grace (19) and Silcock (5 not out in dogged fashion) showed any resistance. The innings ended shortly before 6:00 p.m. for the miserable total of 52. Howitt, the fast left-hander, was largely responsible for this rout, capturing 6 wickets for 21 runs in 25 overs.

Having failed to save the follow-on, the United South began their second innings by sending the Grace brothers to the wickets. Since Freeman was still *hors de combat*, Iddison continued with the partnership of Howitt and Wootton. The roles of W. G. and G. F. were reversed in the second hands. With no threat from his bogeyman Freeman, the Champion fought successfully to keep his wicket intact. Not so Fred, who lost his off-stump to Howitt for a single. One for 3. Jupp, at first wicket down, showed signs of promise once more until he was deftly stumped by Plumb off Howitt for 8. Two for 13. A miniature partnership between W. G. and Charlwood ensued, taking the total to 30, when the latter was bowled off his pads by Howitt, a wicked delivery scattering the middle and off-stumps. "Ben" Griffith made two singles and was snapped up by Greenwood at short-leg off Wootton. Four for 35. Ted Pooley just managed to avoid a pair before losing his off-stump to Howitt. Five for 36. Much was expected of the next batsman, Frank Silcock, who had kept up his end throughout 25 overs in the first innings to carry out his bat for 5. W. G., now well set and "warming to his work", opened his shoulders to punish both bowlers with a cut and two off drives, but the hapless Silcock was clean bowled by Howitt for a cipher shortly before 7:00 p.m., when stumps were drawn to end an eventful day. With 6 wickets gone for only 43, the United South could only pin their hopes on the Champion (22 not out)—or pray for rain.

Their supplications did not go unanswered. Daybreak brought a steady downpour lasting several hours, but, with brighter weather supervening, the agonies of the USEE were resumed in mid-afternoon. Howitt completed an unfinished over by bowling two balls to the new batsman, James Lillywhite, junior. Wootton, at the Pavilion end, conceded 5 runs, then Howitt, in the next over, uprooted Lillywhite's middle stump. Seven for 49. His place was taken by Tom Humphrey, once the darling of the Oval and Harry Jupp's dashing partner, but now little more than a spent force, deserted by most of his erstwhile lustre. W. G. went onto the attack, scoring off both bowlers. Facing Wootton again, he placed the first ball of the over to the on for two, only to meet his downfall with the third, dismissed by a magnificent catch at the wicket by Tom Plumb. Eight for 57, to which W. G. had contributed 32, the only double figure on his side.

Ned Willsher joined Humphrey, and the latter, once famous for the brilliance of his cutting, revived memories of former glory by scoring four with his favourite stroke down towards the printing office. He added three singles for good measure, and Willsher succeeded in getting off the mark with a brace of ones. Now was the time for a captain's innings, but Ned was as impotent as his team-mates in the face of Howitt's onslaught and soon edged a catch to Freeman, standing rather deep at short-slip. Nine for 66. Southerton, last man in, survived the final ball of Howitt's over, the field changed, and Wootton resumed the attack against Humphrey. The first three deliveries passed by without incident, but the batsman misjudged the fourth and cocked up a return catch to the bowler. Little more than half-an-hour had sufficed to complete the final humiliation of the USEE, "the United North winning the match in a most hollow style by an innings and 40 runs". Iddison's men had proved themselves superior in all departments of the game, especially in fielding, but most of the credit for their victory attached to the magnificent bowling of George Howitt, whose fast, left-handed thunderbolts accounted for 13 wickets at a cost of only 39 runs.

The United South's collapse in both innings on the first day, the rain and the speedy termination of the contest on the second, all combined to make the match a failure as regards yielding any benefit to the Cricketers' Fund. With the result virtually a foregone conclusion, the paucity of spectators braving the inclement weather on the Tuesday was restricted to "a few enthusiastic supporters of the rival interests". James Catton was evidently not one of them, since his recollections contain no hint that he witnessed the final stages of the game.

In a limited sense, then, the match was abortive, with the promoters probably incurring some financial loss. Viewed in the wider spectrum of English cricket, however, it was an unqualified success. Breaking out of intangible barriers, a team of northern professionals had demonstrated their ability to set aside old animosities and their willingness to contend against a team from the South on a southern ground. And the South, to their credit, reciprocated their gesture and were prepared to meet them half-way in this attempt to repair the disastrous schism of 1864.

The score card for this match is as follows:

The United North of England Eleven

Ist Innings

T. Bignall, c W. G. Grace, b Silcock	36	C. Coward, c Willsher, b Silcock		35
†T. Plumb, st Pooley, b Southerton	4	G. Freeman, c Pooley, b Southerton		9
E. Lockwood, c Griffith, b Silcock	20	G. R. Atkinson, not out		14
Joseph Rowbotham, b Southerton	7	G. Wootton, st Pooley, b Southerton		6
*R. Iddison, b Silcock	18	G. Howitt, b Silcock		4
L. Greenwood, st Pooley, b Southerton		Lb 4		4
	1	Total		158

United South Bowling

	Runs	Wickets
Southerton	63	5
Willsher	38	0
Silcock	53	5

The United South of England Eleven

1st Innings		2nd Innings	
Mr W. G. Grace, b Freeman	2	c Plumb, b Wootton	32
H. Jupp, c Iddison, b Howitt	10	(3) st Plumb, b Howitt	8
H. R. J. Charlwood, c Howitt, b Wootton	9	(4) b Howitt	6
G. Griffith, b Howitt	0	(5) c Greenwood, b Wootton	2
Mr G. F. Grace, b Howitt	19	(2) b Howitt	1
†E. Pooley, b Wootton	0	b Howitt	1
Frank Silcock, not out	5	b Howitt	0
James Lillywhite, junior, b Howitt	0	b Howitt	3
T. Humphrey, c Greenwood, b Howitt	0	c & b Wootton	7
*E. Willsher, b Howitt	0	c Freeman, b Howitt	2
J. Southerton, run out	0	not out	0
B 4, lb 3	7	B 2, lb 2	4
Total	52	Total	66

United North Bowling

	Runs	Wickets		Runs	Wickets
Freeman	8	1			
Howitt	21	6	Howitt	18	7
Wootton	16	2	Wootton	44	3

Another account shows Howitt conceding 19 runs and Wootton 43 in the second innngs, but 18 and 44 are given in almost all the contemporary reports and *Scores and Biographies*.

Undeterred by the outcome of the encounter at Lord's, the promoters persisted with their desire to recapture the pattern of days gone by. The match in aid of the Cricketers' Fund was succeeded by two fixtures got up in August for the benefit of individuals, one from the North and one from the South. At Sheffield, the beneficiary was Edwin Stephenson, of Yorkshire, the All England, and United All England Elevens. The sum accruing to Ned can have been little more than modest, since the United South (without W. G.) were once more overwhelmed in two days, losing by an innings and 5 runs. Inevitably, George Howitt was principally responsible for the *débâcle*, taking 13 wickets again. In the third meeting, with W. G. back in the side, the United South could claim a moral victory in an unfinished match at the Oval, played for the benefit of William Mortlock, of Surrey, the UAEE, and the USEE. A minor curiosity—one of those fascinating items of trivia—occurred on the second day: Henry Charlwood, batting for the United South, hit one ball high and handsome into the deep and "was missed, made one run, ran a short run, and was run out all from one hit!!"

Shortly afterwards, yet another benefit match—this time a genuine North v South contest—was got up at Dewsbury in honour of George Anderson, the Yorkshire and All England veteran. The North triumphed once more, trouncing the South by an innings and 154 runs, and their opening pair, Roger Iddison (71) and John Smith of Cambridge (96), put on 161 for the first wicket, an aggregate exceeding the combined totals of the South (75 and 74).

Seven more contests took place between the UNEE and the USEE in the next few years, three in 1872, two in 1874, and two in 1876. In a final assessment, the former were slightly superior with four victories; the United South won three times, and three games were unfinished. The original scheme initiated by the promoters in 1870 to revive the old tradition of arranging benefit matches seems to have been tacitly abandoned. Six of the encounters played between 1872 and 1876 may have been purely financial speculations—there is at any rate no mention of any connection with individuals or the Cricketers' Fund—while the other was got up to provide relief for two Yorkshire professionals (A. Hill and G. Pinder), whose earning capacity had been curtailed by illness throughout part of the 1874 season. Mere mercenary considerations, however, should not obscure the contribution made by the UNEE and USEE is cementing harmonious relations between North and South.

CHAPTER FIFTEEN
The Twilight of the Gods

ALTHOUGH there were still not quite enough first-class matches in the 1870s to yield a completely adequate income for even the best professionals, the decade represented a period of degeneration for most of the itinerant elevens. After the collapse of the United All England Eleven in 1869, the first important casualty was the United North, followed by the Yorkshire United Eleven, while the second United North, founded by George Pinder, lasted but a few years and enjoyed only limited popularity. Others were to follow, as the time of their inevitable extinction approached.

Further evidence of the decline is manifested by the gradual loosening of the bonds between individuals and a particular team. Rigid distinctions were largely preserved in Old Clarke's time: a player was above all an All England man or a United man, with no opportunities for maintaining a footing in both camps. The lines became blurred after Clarke's death, and professionals, such as Bob Carpenter, accepted employment with the AEE as well as the UAEE. As far as the great series between the two teams was concerned, Carpenter kept faith with the United, but no less than eight players appeared for both sides. Gradually, especially in the late 1860s and the 1870s, the importance of team loyalties was diminishing, and in some instances even regional ties yielded before the overriding consideration of earning wages. Many individuals assisted two or three of the four principal itinerant elevens against "odds", and at least five professionals—G. Howitt, T. Plumb, E. Pooley, Joseph Rowbotham, and Alfred Shaw—played at one time or another for the All England, United All England, United South of England, and United North of England Elevens. Special circumstances account for the inclusion of Ted Pooley's name in the list. A brilliant wicket-keeper and a forcing batsman, he was nevertheless prone to personal lapses and had a chequered career. Banned from playing for Surrey and subsequently the USEE in 1873 for allegedly laying a bet against his own side in a county fixture, Ted sought desperately for other sources of income. The invitation to appear for the United North was possibly an act of sympathetic generosity by the team manager—perhaps even a gesture of professional solidarity.

Judging by the evidence available, the United South of England Eleven commanded the greatest measure of popularity in the 1870s, and the managers betrayed no scruples over periodically engaging the services of northerners, such as R. G. Barlow of Lancashire. Their programme was never so ambitious as All England's in the 1860s, but the number of fixtures ran into double figures each season. Most were "odds" matches, many of them played in the North and Midlands, and long journeys were never considered to be a problem. Their opponents were not, however, exclusively local sides, reinforced sometimes by Given Men. Between 1870 and 1880, more or less in alternating seasons, the USEE pitted their strength against first-class opposition on thirteen occasions. Their principal adversary in ten of these encounters was, as previously mentioned, the United North of England Eleven. The other three matches, against Yorkshire (1874), the All England Eleven (1876), and a team entitled the North (1880), all resulted in defeats. Since the dates of the final match, played at Rotherham, coincided with those of the Test between England and Australia at the Oval, the United South, deprived of their two leading "cracks", experienced difficulties over selection and were compelled to field a weak, makeshift side. More than half the North team were Derbyshire professionals, among them a certain A. Smith, possibly Alfort Smith. One of the most unsuccessful batsmen ever to appear in first-class cricket at one time, he supplied the inspiration for one of those excruciating Victorian puns, enshrined in *Lillywhite's Cricketers' Companion*, 1879 (italics in the original): "Probably no player has ever made more *noughts* in a season—not even J. C. Shaw in the zenith of his fame—than A. Smith, of Glossop, the wicket-keeper; it is a wonder that he is not *crossed* out of the eleven".

The administration of the USEE throughout most of the 1870s lay with James Lillywhite, junior, of Sussex, England's captain in the first ever Test with Australia in 1877 and a promoter of tours to the Antipodes. His name is published as the secretary of the United South from 1872 to 1879, a post usually combined with the captaincy, and Lillywhite certainly led the side several times in the first-class matches played between 1872 and 1876. It is not unlikely, however, that his influence may have declined to a certain extent not long after he assumed office. G. F. Grace was a permanent member of the team throughout the decade, while his brother W. G. and cousin W. R. Gilbert also played regularly from 1873 onwards. Thus, the United South became to all intents and purposes the property of the Grace family, with Gilbert becoming the secretary around 1879. Nominally amateurs, all three were without doubt paid match fees for their services. This anomaly caused a measure of heart burning among some of the professionals and eventually produced a ruling from MCC that anybody receiving more than his expenses would be disqualified from representing the Gentlemen against the Players at Lord's. Gilbert, perhaps on the grounds of ability, was never selected to appear in this fixture, G. F. was omitted from the team in 1879 and 1880, but W. G. assisted the Gentlemen in every match at headquarters in the 1870s—a case of customs curtseying to great kings.

While rival organizations fell by the wayside, the United South continued to flourish. One factor above all created a cast-iron guarantee of protracted existence—the presence of W. G. Matches against "odds" had lost much of their appeal for the general public, but anybody would eagerly pay the price of admission for the opportunity of seeing the Champion. Yet, though W.G. was the team's star performer, Fred Grace was just as instrumental, perhaps even more so than his elder brother, in maintaining the USEE as a going concern. He played a considerable part in the management of the team, hardly ever missed a match, and assumed the captaincy at times in the late 1870s. So closely was he identified with the side, that R. G. Barlow entitled it "G. F. Grace's United South of England XI". At the time of the United South's last first-class contest in 1880, Fred Grace, already suffering from the effects of a cold, was playing for England against Australia at the Oval. Immediately afterwards, he participated in an "odds" match at Stroud, where his illness was further aggravated by fielding in the rain. A few days later, he was attacked by severe congestion of the lungs and died on September 22, 1880, at the age of twenty-nine.

With the death of Fred Grace the United South of England Eleven expired also. For about two years, W. G. tried to maintain the status quo with a team usually known as W. G. Grace's United Eleven. The absence of any regional qualification in the title justified the occasional inclusion of northern players, such as R. G. Barlow and Arthur Shrewsbury. Most of the matches were played against "odds", but there were two eleven-a-side contests against the Australians in 1882, one at Chichester, the other at Tunbridge Wells. The first gave rise to proceedings in the Chichester County Court, where Charlie Howard, a Sussex professional, objected to a payment of £5 for assisting the United and entered a claim for £10. When it transpired that Howard had received a fee of £6 for representing his county against the Australians in 1880, the court ruled that he should be paid the same amount in 1882. The defendant in the case, responsible for the financial arrangements and getting up the team, was rather ominously W.G.'s cousin, W. R. Gilbert, destined in a few years to appear in less savoury circumstances in a trial culminating in a conviction for theft from his team-mates, followed by emigration to Canada.

Meanwhile, the All England Eleven continued to operate in the 1870s, but on a much reduced scale. Twelve matches were played in 1870 and sixteen the following year. Thereafter, apart from 1874, the number of fixtures recorded fell into single figures. There may, of course, have been more; if so, however, they attracted no attention. As might be expected, most were contests against "odds", but the AEE also undertook four first-class engagements. At Bolton, in 1871, they trounced the United North but were defeated by Yorkshire at Huddersfield, in 1874. Lord's, in 1876, was the scene of their solitary encounter with the United South, whom they overwhelmed, and two years later they achieved an easy victory over Derbyshire at Derby.

Like most of the travelling elevens, the AEE suffered from the seasonal increase of first-class matches, but the other cause of their decline was their inability to compete with their principal rival, the USEE. Apart from a few fixtures in Ireland, most of the All England matches were played against local teams in the North and Midlands. But so, also, were many undertaken by the United South, who shamelessly invaded the traditional All England territory, exploiting that infallible advantage denied to their competitors in the person of W. G.

George Parr continued to hold the office of secretary of the AEE in the first half of the 1870s, but from 1876 onwards the duties passed to another Nottinghamshire man, William Oscroft. His task cannot have been too onerous, judging by the number of fixtures fulfilled. Although he is still listed as the All England secretary in 1879, the last recorded match of the previous season—the only one—was the game against Derbyshire. To Oscroft, then, fell the melancholy assignment of winding up the affairs of the mighty All England Eleven. Once a dominant force in the world of cricket, it lapsed seemingly into oblivion. Oblivion? Not so, for there was a curious aftermath.

Richard Daft first played for the AEE as far back as 1857, and he assisted them also in their final first-class match against Derbyshire in 1878. Even longer was his association with Nottinghamshire, beginning in 1858 and lasting until 1891, though he ceased playing regularly after 1880. Occasionally during the 1860s, he led the county side in the absence of George Parr, and he was the official captain from 1870 to 1880. Nevertheless, Daft's membership of the AEE seems to have held pride of place in his eyes. Throughout much of the period of his tenure of the Nottinghamshire captaincy, he inserted advertisements in *Lillywhite's Cricketers' Companion*, soliciting custom for his business as a dealer in sporting goods, and his name is followed by the sole qualification, "Member of (the) All England Eleven". This, however, is replaced in the editions for 1882–84 with the rubric, "Late Captain of Notts County Eleven", which might imply that the AEE was ceasing to operate from around 1880–81. In his book, *Kings of Cricket*, published in 1893, Daft harks back to the popularity of the AEE in their days of glory, saying, "and now this great and powerful organization has passed entirely away".

This valediction may well have been true for the early 1890s, but in the years following Daft's virtual retirement from first-class cricket a brief, interim period was followed by a veritable renaissance. Like the United

North of England Eleven, the AEE experienced a revival under new management. Reconstituted probably around 1882–83, the All England Eleven Mark II lasted up to the end of the decade. Little remains of the team's history and the record of their doings, but evidently the traditional system of playing "odds" matches was adopted, since no trace survives of any first-class fixture involving a side entitled the All England Eleven in the 1880s. The very evidence of existence is extremely limited, comprising advertisements in such publications as *Wisden*, 'Red' and 'Green Lilly', and *Cricket Chat*, a photograph, and scattered references to matches. These, however, furnish several clues relating to the new enterprise sustained by two well known cricket entrepreneurs, James Lillywhite, junior, and Arthur Shrewsbury, partners with Alfred Shaw in the promotion of more than one tour to Australia.

Daft's successor as captain of the Nottinghamshire team was William Oscroft, who held that office in the seasons of 1881 and 1882. Though secretary of the AEE at the same time, so to speak, Oscroft was doubtless absorbed in his new duties with the county side and had little inclination to devote much energy to a moribund organization. Additionally, he may then have already been a sick man, since the onset of a crippling disease terminated his career at the end of the 1882 season.

Although Oscroft may have been content to let things slide, his sentiments were not shared by Arthur Shrewsbury. In 1880, the latter formed a partnership with Alfred Shaw, establishing a business for the sale of sporting goods at Nottingham. The firm of Shaw and Shrewsbury advertised their wares in *Wisden* and *Lillywhite's Annual* (1881–86), and *Lillywhite's Companion* (1883–85). Both partners append their credentials in brackets after their names, and in *Wisden* and 'Red Lilly' for 1881 and 1882 Shrewsbury designates his membership of the touring teams to North America (1879) and Australia (1881–82) as well as the Nottinghamshire County Eleven. The two advertisements also contain a sentence reading, "Secretaries of Clubs wishing to arrange Matches with All-England teams, including the leading professionals, may do so by applying to the above address". At this stage, then, Shrewsbury was prepared to raise sides on an ad hoc basis.

A subtle but significant change has crept into the wording of the advertisements in the volumes for 1883 and also *Lillywhite's Companion*, by which time Oscroft was out of the picture, and W.G.'s United Eleven (successor to the USEE) was apparently in limbo. Shrewsbury gives his credentials in all three publications as "Member of Anglo-Australian and *All England Elevens*", while the exhortation now reads, "Secretaries wishing to arrange Matches with *the All England Team* can do so by applying to Shaw and Shrewsbury" (italics supplied in both instances). The sentence has vanished from *Wisden* of 1884 and the two *Lillywhites* for 1885, but up to that final year Shrewsbury was still declaring his membership of the AEE. *Lillywhite's Annual* and *Wisden* for 1886—the *Companion* had by now been incorporated in the former—contain neither the sentence nor any mention of Shrewsbury's All England connection. The firm of Shaw and Shrewsbury seems thereafter to have cancelled its advertising contract with both publications.

Additional convincing proof of the revival of the AEE appears in an advertisement inserted in *Lillywhite's Companion* for 1884 (three entries) and 1885, reading as follows:

ALL ENGLAND ELEVEN. // For matches with the above Eleven, application // should be made to // JAMES LILLYWHITE, // WESTERTON, CHICHESTER, SUSSEX; // OR TO // A. SHREWS-BURY, // CARRINGTON STREET BRIDGE, // NOTTINGHAM.

Advertisements proclaiming the merits of Shaw and Shrewsbury's sporting gear were not confined to the pages of *Wisden* and 'Red' and 'Green Lilly'. The partners also bought space in *Cricket Chat*, a booklet containing a selection from the biographical sketches and portraits of cricketers previously printed in the journal *Cricket*. In the volumes issued in 1884 and 1885, Shrewsbury included membership of the All England Eleven among his credentials, but all team affiliations were excluded from the 1886 edition. Shaw and Shrewsbury, however, were not the only dealers to solicit custom in *Cricket Chat*. Another was the Lancashire and England all-rounder R. G. Barlow, whose notice in the 1886 and 1888 issues stated that he also was a member of the AEE. Yet another individual to claim this distinction in the volumes for 1888 and 1889 was Walter Wright, of Nottinghamshire (1879–86) and Kent (1888–99). The indications are, then, that the (second) AEE was still in being as the decade drew to its close.

One further item of documentary evidence remains. Arthur Shrewsbury's membership of the All England Eleven under the old organization was not very extensive. He first played for them apparently in 1873, but from then until 1878 his name appears in the team list in less than one-quarter of the recorded matches. With the revival in 1882–83, for which he was partly responsible, he was evidently proud of the connection and willing to publicize it. The journal *Cricket*, 1883, printed an appreciation of Shrewsbury, which was later reproduced in the appropriate volume of *Cricket Chat*. Accompanying the text is a portrait of the subject wearing a cap with a badge bearing the device 'AEE'.

As to the (second) All England Eleven's performances in the field, the number of fixtures, and the identity of their opponents, the annals are largely silent. Several matches had been played against university teams at Dublin in the 1870s, and this custom was maintained to a certain extent by the new organization, with games against Dublin University in 1887 and 1888, in the second of which William Gunn scored 191 not out. It is likely that the team's existence came to an end not long afterwards, unless it were continued on the same sort of ad hoc basis obtaining in the early 1880s, before Lillywhite and Shrewsbury "officially" revived a famous name and tried to recapture some of its traditional splendour. Throughout much of their life, particularly up to about 1870, the original AEE had provided wages during the weeks when there were few county or other important fixtures. The first-class programme became more extensive, as time passed, and it may be supposed that the Lillywhite–Shrewsbury venture was more limited in its scope, yielding the occasional match fees to individuals on rest days.

So the first became the last, and the last was the first. Of all the touring teams, William Clarke's original All England Eleven was unquestionably the greatest of its kind. Nothing could be more appropriate than the assumption of that same proud name by the last of the itinerant elevens.

An institution characteristic of the Victorian age, the first All England Eleven and its offshoots accelerated the development of cricket throughout England at a time when the game was in its infancy. Yet the enthusiasm they stimulated was merely a by-product of their activities, for nobody could claim that Clarke and his fellow organizers were disinterested in their motivation. Philanthropy and altruism were alien to their mental processes. Their energies were concentrated exclusively on the foundation and management of a successful venture, whose primary concern was the creation of wealth, and in the pursuit of this objective they provided the opportunity for individuals, originating usually on the lower rungs of the social ladder, to market their skills on a more extended basis, stretching far beyond the range of occasional match fees.

Cricket, beyond doubt, received an enormous fillip from the institution of the itinerant elevens. Without them, the progress towards the form assumed by the game would probably have been delayed for some considerable time. That evolution, nevertheless, spelt inevitable extinction to the All England Eleven and similar organizations, once they had far outlived their usefulness. For well over half a century and more, there was no place for the itinerant eleven in the ethos of cricket. In recent years, however, the state of the game and its financial rewards have not inspired untrammelled satisfaction in the hearts of all its adherents, and the spirit of Clarke's creation has surfaced once more. Prominent cricketers have elected to capitalize on their talents in operations divorced from the established order by taking part in Kerry Packer's World Series and the so-called 'rebel' tour to South Africa. Latterly, according to report, a wealthy enthusiast hatched plans for setting up a circus of star players, who were becoming

Arthur Shrewsbury, Nottinghamshire, England, second All England Eleven, wearing cap with AEE badge

disenchanted by the treadmill of the county championship and limited-overs contests. In return for generous wages, these twentieth-century "cracks" would band together to form a kind of road show, touring the country and playing matches got up at popular seaside resorts. The sympathetic shade of William Clarke, one imagines, would stir on some celestial cricket field. Another All England Eleven in the making?

APPENDIX I

Fashion, Costume, and Equipment

WHEN Leicester, assisted by Fuller Pilch, defeated Sheffield by 7 wickets in 1828, one member of the victorious home side incurred a crushing rebuke in the columns of the leading sporting journal. "It would be much better", said the report in *Bell's Life*, "if H. Davis would appear in a cricketing dress instead of that of a sailor". Bell-bottoms, blouse with spreading collar, knotted neckerchief, straw hat, luxuriant hair and whiskers, perhaps, and was the ostentatious H. Davis the only offender to affect this nautical garb? Possibly not, but some twenty years later William Clarke's All England Eleven presented a much more sober appearance, judging by the famous picture executed by Nicholas Felix. Hair and whiskers are not over-abundant, and the preferred head-dress is a top hat, though the artist himself and one other player are sporting baggy caps, while a youthful George Parr has also adopted a less austere covering. Shirts with a collar and bow or cravat, and trousers in most instances supported by wide braces, are white, and almost all the shoes are black. The bats appear to have no splice, and no protective gear is in evidence. This spruce, idealized turn-out, however, was not necessarily maintained in its entirety throughout the course of a match.

In his treatise, *Felix on the Bat* (1845), the author/artist discusses dress and equipment at length, including such details as the best type of socks to wear and the correct fitting of spikes to the shoes. He departs in two important instances from the habits of most of his contemporaries. For the head, he recommended not a topper but "a cap made of chequered woollen . . . light and cool to the head . . . and . . . not likely to blow off and hit the wicket". This precept was no doubt reinforced by his recollection of the occasions in Gentlemen *v* Players, at Lord's, when he witnessed the discomfiture of Fuller Pilch (1837) and Mr C. G. Taylor (1843), both ignominiously dismissed "hat knocked on wicket". Nor were his animadversions confined to the subject of headgear, for Felix also deplored the means favoured by many of his fellow players for supporting their flannel trousers. It was, he felt, infinitely preferable for them to be fitted

145

with "six loops round the waistband, through which an Indian-rubber belt may pass, and help to do the duty of braces, which must be exploded whilst in the active exercise of hitting". Advice of eminent good sense, but these loops were not the only adjustment he recommended for the trousers. The wide-spread use of the fast, round-arm delivery ("the present system of throwing bowling") could inflict crippling injuries to the legs, necessitating some protection for batsmen. Leg-guards, at that time crude and in their infancy, lacked the aesthetic appeal to an artist, and the best method, according to Felix, was to have sockets of linen sewn into the inside of the trouser-legs into which long strips of rubber could be inserted to safeguard the lower limbs from above the knee down to the ankle. And finally, Felix was also the inventor of a pattern of batting gloves. Much of his advice, in one form or another, gained acceptance in the years to come.

The period of the heyday of the itinerant elevens (c. 1855–1875) had its own distinctive characteristics, and its appearance, costume, and equipment have been well documented. John Corbet Anderson's famous lithographs constitute a mine of information for the 1850s, illustrating the evolution of fashion with the abandonment of those articles of dress that were anathema to Felix—compare, for instance, the Anderson print of the United All England Eleven (c. 1855) with the Felix picture of the All England Eleven (1847). Of equal importance are the wood engravings, based on early photographs, published in some of the illustrated journals. In addition, there are some of the old photographs themselves, either rare originals or reproductions in books. Like Felix's All England group, most of these are posed pictures, representing a certain standard of "Sunday best", and it is evident that some of the bandbox trappings were discarded when players went into action.

Hair was worn fairly short by most cricketers at this time, and at first beards and moustaches were not common. Many players affected side-whiskers, some of them slight, others of the mutton-chop variety. One popular style was the "Newgate fringe", in which the upper and lower lips and part of the face were shaved, but the whiskers were allowed to grow down the sides to meet eventually under the chin. There were exceptions: George Anderson, George Parr, and H. H. Stephenson all wore moustaches with their whiskers, and in the more hirsute 1860s R. C. Tinley, Edgar Willsher, and John Wisden cultivated beards of varying shape. Fashions changed with the years according to personal tastes, and different styles were adopted by individuals throughout the years. H. H. Stephenson is sometimes portrayed with a complete beard, sometimes with the lower lip shaved, and, after adding a moustache to his whiskers, William Caffyn later settled for a beard. Towards the end of the period, some of the younger cricketers were clean shaven or wore only moustaches, though Alfred Shaw, in his early thirties, still sported luxuriant Dundreary whiskers—to be grown out eventually into a full beard.

Top hats had practically vanished from first-class matches by about 1857. This, doubtless, gave intense satisfaction to George Parr, who abominated them so much that he was once moved to discard a portrait of himself crowned with a topper. Many players favoured caps similar to the type previously recommended by Felix. A little more capacious than those fashionable in later years and the twentieth century, they resembled the head-dress of the working man of the period. Some were of a vaguely military pattern, and occasionally individual tastes were indulged: John Lillywhite often tilted his cap (and hat) at a rakish angle, and James Grundy frequently wore a black velvet cap, which he tucked into his belt while bowling. Straw hats of various shapes sometimes made their appearance, but for several years the chief rival to the cap was the pot hat or billycock, a type of bowler hat. It was usually dark in colour and round in the crown, though now and then different styles were seen: at times, Roger Iddison wore a light-coloured, round-crowned hat, at others a dark-coloured one with a flat top, though often enough he exchanged these for a cap. Some players continued wearing billycocks after the majority of their colleagues had abandoned them, and George Parr, who played until 1870, remained attached to his for many years. In the well known photograph of the English Twelve who toured North America in 1859, eleven of the team are wearing an assortment of caps, but the twelfth (George Parr) is bareheaded and holds what looks like a billycock in his right hand. Some of these eleven, however, appeared in billycocks on other occasions.

Sweaters were not fashionable much before the 1870s, and when the weather was cold, it was not uncommon for white, flannel jackets to be worn. These could be quite short, like a waistcoat with sleeves, or the usual length. Both styles may be seen in some of the portraits of Tom Lockyer, the Surrey wicket-keeper, and Ted Pooley, his successor, also wore one at times. On occasions, even the ordinary jacket did duty out of sheer necessity, example impecunious John Thewlis batting in his first match for Lascelles Hall ("They shouted to me to doff me coat, but Ah warn't going to show 'em t'oles in me shirt"). As an alternative form of protection against the cold, players would don extra shirts or an everyday waistcoat. When not actively participating in the play, some professionals in the 1860s habitually wore their ordinary morning tailcoats, long, usually black, and buttoned high up to the neck.

Shirts, of cotton, linen, and flannel, came in a wide variety of tints and designs: plain white, grey, red, and darker hues, such as brown; white or some pale material with small spots or thin stripes of different shades; broader stripes of white and a contrasting colour, such as black; checks—all these were to be found. On his first appearance for Yorkshire against Surrey in 1868, Ephraim Lockwood dazzled the Oval crowd by featuring "a shirt with red, black, and green squares like a church window". There were some attempts at uniformity, though these were more common with some of the leading amateur clubs and teams touring abroad. Most shirts were the collarless, tunic style, to which stand-up, turn-down, and later butterfly collars were fastened and supplemented by ties or neck-cloths often knotted in a bow. But were collars and ties worn on the field of play? They would have been very restricting, especially for fast bowling and big hitting, and there are several pictures of both amateurs and professionals, in which the subjects have collarless shirts secured at the neck with buttons or studs. At least some cricketers evidently preferred to sacrifice elegance for the sake of comfort by discarding collars and ties while actually playing, though sometimes a neckerchief was worn around the throat. Eventually, plain white shirts with attached collars were generally adopted.

Flannel trousers, usually white, were universally worn. The wide braces, always associated with top hats, began to lose favour around the middle of the century, when both items were gradually being abandoned. Felix would have been gratified, but his recommendation that trousers should be provided with loops to retain a belt gained little ground at first. A photograph of Alfred Mynn and a print of William Clarke show they had followed their team-mate's advice, but they were exceptions, judging by many pictures of cricketers, whose belts encircle trousers not fitted with loops. Worn in this manner, belts would surely have been very precarious as the sole means of support. In moments of great exertion, whether batting, bowling, or fielding, a girdle lacking the vital security of retaining loops would be liable to slide up above the top of the trousers, giving rise to feelings of acute anxiety, if not actual embarrassment. Normally made of elastic or webbing, the belts had metal buckles often decorated with cricketing motifs—"a batsman or a bowler . . . usually represented in the most improbable attitude conceivable", according to one instructional manual of the mid-1860s, which states that belts were "fast going out", adding that a waistband at the back was the best method of keeping the trousers in their proper position. The author of another handbook declares categorically that "Belts are now out of fashion, the trousers being fastened by a waistband which may be drawn tight or loosened at the back at pleasure". This work was published in 1867, but pictures earlier than this date show players without belts, whose trousers, fitting snugly around the middle, were almost certainly maintained by a waistband of the type described. Some belts were probably more ornamental than functional and could be worn or discarded on the field without disturbing the peace of mind. Later, when belts were completely out of favour—the bat handle coming into contact with the buckle could make a sound like a snicked catch—many cricketers followed the new fashion of wearing sashes at the waist.

Spiked boots, occasionally white, usually black or brown, were the regular footwear of the period, though sometimes a more fancy pattern of "striped" appearance was to be seen. These boots had a brown or black toe-cap, then a strip of white, then another dark strip, followed by more white on the instep, slightly similar to the type of shoe popularly supposed to be affected by co-respondents in the 1920s. Around 1865, a boot was introduced with a "new-fashioned sole, barred diagonally with alternate strips of leather and India-rubber".

A photograph of the Yorkshire side for a county match in 1875 provides an excellent representation of the variety of costume to be found in one team and the changes dictated by current fashions. Most of the players are clean shaven or wearing a moustache of moderate proportions. Three kinds of head-dress are featured: two veterans from the previous decade cling to the sort of cap popular in the early 1860s (they are also the only ones with beards or "Newgate fringes"); younger players have opted for the more modern, closer fitting cap, but three others are sporting billycocks. Some of the shirts are white, others striped, and whereas several individuals are attired in sweaters, two men have donned ordinary waistcoats. At least two members of the group are wearing belts and all the boots visible are uniformly dark.

Umpires were dressed in their sombre, everyday garments, and though white coats were worn for the first time apparently in the early 1860s, this practice did not become general for quite a number of years afterwards.

The fiery nature of some pitches and the fast bowling of the period made some form of personal protection eminently desirable. A few amateurs often scorned the use of gloves and leg-guards when batting, but most of the leading professionals took the necessary precautions to avoid injuries and a temporary loss of livelihood. Batting gloves had the palms cut away and fitted closely at the wrist or were secured there by a wrap-around strap. For a right-handed batsman, the right glove had strips of rubber running along the fingers and most of the thumb. There was no rubber on the thumb of the left-hand glove, but the strips on the fingers were longer, with one continuous U-shaped band to protect the first and fourth fingers. For a left-hander, the position of the strips was reversed, with rubber on the left thumb, and so on. Wicket-keepers wore gauntlets covering the wrists. They were gradually improved with the addition of extra padding and ventilation, but they gave less protection than the gloves in use to-day.

Felix's suggestion that a batsman's legs should be protected with thin strips of rubber inside the trousers does not seem to have caught on, though occasionally a type of shin-guard was worn under the trouser-legs. The vast majority of first-class cricketers donned leg-guards, which were not quite so bulky as those worn a hundred years later and did not come so far above the knee. The best ones were made of buckskin, and those sold by John Lillywhite, one of the leading outfitters as well as a professional cricketer, were "stuffed with the finest Virginia cotton, not hay and other rubbish". At least three forms of fastening existed at one time. The first consisted of separate sets of tape or twine, one round the ankle, two round the knee, and sometimes another round the shin. This clumsy method of securing the guards—shown in the Anderson print of George Chatterton and W. Bromley's portrait of George Parr in the Long Room at Lord's—soon fell out of favour because of the time required to attach them to the legs, and because a pad was rendered useless whenever one of the ties frayed or broke. The second form consisted of three elastic straps fitted with catches for instantaneous fastening. This pattern was perfectly satisfactory at the outset, but after a time the straps lost their elasticity and stretched, leaving the pads dangling loosely on the legs. The third type—straps pierced with holes and secured by a buckle—proved the best and has survived to the present day.

An obvious and understandable desire, as much at this period as any other, impelled cricketers to prevent themselves "from being cut over in that part which takes all the batting out of you". Some form of abdominal protector or box was certainly in use at this time, though Victorian modesty naturally militated against much mention of such an article. A discreet allusion appeared as early as 1855 in Fred Lillywhite's *Guide to Cricketers*, and the same publication for 1863 contained an announcement, "ALL KINDS OF GUARDS made to order on the shortest notice". An instructional manual issued in 1867 refers to "protectors for the abdomen", and another of approximately the same date ends a description of pads by noting the existence of several other guards, "such as elbow and private-guards, but they are scarcely ever used". One cannot help wondering if the leading batsmen of the day agreed with the last statement. With a means of self-preservation available, were they prepared to risk the danger of "being badly cut over", when facing the expresses of Jackson, Tarrant, Freeman, and J. C. Shaw? One has only to recall that occasion (previously mentioned), when George Freeman inflicted so much damage on "the inside of 'W. G.'s' thigh, above the pad". Advertisements extolling the efficacy of improved patterns of abdominal protectors became more common from the 1880s onwards, by which time the travelling elevens had virtually passed away.

Caps were of little use against bumping deliveries. As a kind of rudimentary helmet, the billycock provided a measure of protection—probably one of the reasons why it retained its popularity until more attention was given to the preparation of pitches. Some improvisation was called for in a dire emergency: at Lord's, in 1870, when a kicking ball struck a batsman on the temple—fatally, as it turned out—Richard Daft came to the crease with towels swathed around his head and secured by a scarf under his chin. The first delivery he received was a hair-raising bouncer, and Daft addressed the offending bowler with a few choice observations expressed in the Anglo-Saxon vernacular.

The ball was slightly larger than the twentieth-century pattern, but the seam was less pronounced. The spliced bats used in first-class matches had cane handles bound in twine—the rubber sheath had not been invented—and the handles were sometimes fitted with strips of whalebone to make them more springy. Viewed in profile, the bats of the 1860s and 1870s were much flatter than those of to-day. As regards the wicket, Law III stated that: "The STUMPS must be three in number; twenty-seven inches out of the ground; the Bails eight inches in length; the Stumps of equal and sufficient thickness to prevent the ball from passing through".

APPENDIX II

Statistics

Contents

The statistics for this Appendix have been compiled from the following sources:

Matches before 1860:- *Scores and Biographies*, IV, V, and VI.

Matches from 1860 onwards:- *Cricket Matches 1860–1863*, and for the period 1864–1880 the volumes of scores printed in *First Class Cricket Matches* (Association of Cricket Statisticians).

The classification of matches is based on the principles defined in *A Guide to Important Cricket Matches Played in the British Isles 1709–1863* and, beginning in 1864, *A Guide to First Class Cricket Matches Played in the British Isles* (Association of Cricket Statisticians).

Information on the identification of some of the early fixtures has been obtained from details in the notices appended by Haygarth to the scores of matches in *Scores and Biographies*, e.g. "This match was one of those 'got up' by W. Clarke among his All England Players . . ." Contests such as

North v South got up by the All England or United All England Eleven have been excluded.

A complete and uninterrupted summary of the series All England Eleven v United All England Eleven appears in section B. From the first match of the series played in 1857, the United All England Eleven's only opponents in first-class contests were the All England Eleven. The averages for this series are given in section G.

The enumeration of first-class matches played by the All England Eleven from 1864 onwards appears in *A Guide to First Class Cricket Matches Played in the British Isles*. Among this list are three fixtures with Cambridge University, one in 1872 and two in 1873. In *First Class Cricket Matches* and *Scores and Biographies*, the sides opposing the University are called "An Eleven of All England", "An All England Eleven", and "An Eleven of All England", but the titles vary considerably in the press and elsewhere. Moreover, these teams seem to have been got up on an ad hoc basis, consisting as they do of several amateurs and various professionals, the latter temporarily engaged at Cambridge to provide coaching and practice for the undergraduates. It is far from certain, therefore, that these three fixtures are genuine All England Eleven matches, and consequently they have not been included in sections A and E of this appendix.

On the other hand, the Association's *Guide* omits from the list of the United South of England Eleven's fixtures the match between the USEE and the North in September 1880, the score of which is, however, printed in *First Class Cricket Matches 1879–1880*. This match has been included in sections C and H.

The statistics for the United North of England Eleven (sections D and I) relate entirely to the first organization bearing that name, founded by Roger Iddison and George Freeman, and the figures for the solitary first-class match played by the (second) UNEE, founded by George Pinder, have not been included.

The bowling analyses for some matches have not so far been discovered, and a bowler's figures on these occasions are recorded as, for example, 8–?

The number of wickets taken by a bowler appears at times in the averages with two totals, e.g., 92 (+ 32), signifying that the analyses are available for the 92 wickets but not for the 32. The number of wickets given in brackets is not used in assessing the bowling average.

A THE ALL ENGLAND ELEVEN SUMMARY OF RESULTS IN IMPORTANT AND FIRST-CLASS MATCHES

Played 47—won, 20; lost, 14; drawn, 12; tied, 1 (all matches)
    19—won, 8; lost, 8; drawn, 3 (v UAEE)

August 7, 8, and 9, 1848, at The Oval, v 14 of Surrey
    AEE 129 (G. Parr 39, F. Pilch 29) and 77 (G. Parr 41)
    14 of Surrey 131 (Mr N. Felix 40, Mr W. J. Hammersley 27) and 76–5
    (J. Chester 42*)
    14 of Surrey won by 8 wickets
September 28, 29, and 30, 1848, at Itchen, near Southampton, v 14 of
    Hampshire (D. Day's Benefit)
    AEE 93 (G. Parr 30) and 22 (Sir F. H. H. Bathurst 6–13)
    14 of Hampshire 53 (W. R. Hillyer 8–26, F. W. Lillywhite 5–27) and
    44–12 (W. R. Hillyer 6–22, J. Wisden 5–17)
    Match drawn
May 21, 22, and 23, 1849, at Cambridge, v Cambridge Undergraduates and
    Cambridge Town Club
    AEE 198 (G. Parr 86*, Rev J. Bradshaw 30; F. P. Fenner 6–?)
    Cambridge 73 (W. R. Hillyer 5–?, W. Martingell 5–?) and 30–3
    Match drawn
June 21 and 22, 1849, at Gravesend, v Kent
    AEE 112 (J. Dean 25; W. R. Hillyer 6–?) and 116 (J. Hodson 30,
    T. Box 25; W. Martingell 5–?)
    Kent 57 (J. Wisden 5–?) and 128 (W. Martingell 32*; J. Wisden 5–?)
    AEE won by 43 runs
June 28, 29, and 30, 1849, at Itchen, near Southampton, v 14 of Hampshire
    14 of Hampshire 74 (W. Clarke 7–29, W. R. Hillyer 6–45) and 83
    (W. Clarke 7–46)
    AEE 83 (G. Parr 32*) and 75–8 (D. Day 5–32)
    AEE won by 2 wickets
September 13, 14, and 15, 1849, at Brighton, v Sussex
    Sussex 101 (J. Dean 33; W. Clarke 6–40) and 131 (Mr W. J. Humphry
    30; W. Clarke 6–80)
    AEE 277 (G. Parr 85, Mr N. Felix 67, G. Chatterton 25; T. Box 5–45)
    AEE won by an innings and 45 runs
June 10 and 11, 1850, at Sheffield, v 14 of Yorkshire
    AEE 107 (G. Armitage 5–28) and 38
    14 of Yorkshire 118 (W. Clarke 9–34) and 28–2
    14 of Yorkshire won by 11 wickets

July 18, 19, and 20, 1850, at Cranbrook, *v* Kent
AEE 137 (T. Box 37; F. Hollands 5–?) and 92 (W. Clarke 28; T. M. Adams 5–?)
Kent 99 (W. Clarke 6–?) and 44–5
Match drawn

July 25, 26, and 27, 1850, at The Oval, *v* 14 of Surrey
AEE 119 (D. Day 8–?) and 84 (D. Day 5–?, T. Sherman 5–?)
14 of Surrey 115 (Mr C. H. Hoare 27, Mr E. Reeves 25; W. Clarke 5–?, J. Wisden 5–?)
Match drawn

August 22 and 23, 1850, at Itchen, near Southampton, *v* 14 of Hampshire
14 of Hampshire 74 (W. Clarke 5–?) and 57 (W. R. Hillyer 8–?, J. Wisden 5–?)
AEE 131 (J. Guy 46, Mr H. Vernon 33; Sir F. H. H. Bathurst 6–?) and 1–1
AEE won by 9 wickets

May 5 and 6, 1851, at Lord's, *v* 15 of MCC and the Metropolitan Clubs
AEE 30 and 47 (J. Dean 7–19)
15 of MCC 95 (G. Chatterton 35; W. Clarke 8–35)
15 of MCC won by an innings and 18 runs

May 12, 13, and 14, 1851, at Sheffield, *v* 14 of Yorkshire
14 of Yorkshire 183 (John Berry 51, H. Sampson 48; J. Wisden 10–58)
AEE 47 (Mr R. F. Skelton 8–29) and 83
14 of Yorkshire won by an innings and 53 runs

June 9, 10, and 11, 1851, at Lord's, *v* 14 of MCC
14 of MCC 169 (Mr A. Haygarth 40, T. Nixon 34, J. Dean 30; W. R. Hillyer 7–?, W. Clarke 5–?) and 98 (G. Chatterton 29; W. Clarke 7–?, W. R. Hillyer 6–?)
AEE 153 (G. Parr 41, J. Guy 32*, Mr A. Mynn 31) and 114–5 (F. Pilch 50, T. Box 38*)
Match tied

June 12, 13, and 14, 1851, at The Oval, *v* 14 of Surrey
AEE 94 (J. Guy 37; T. Sherman 5–38) and 183–9 (R. C. Tinley 35, H. Sampson 32, J. Guy 26; T. Sherman 7–72)
14 of Surrey 142 (Julius Caesar 38, W. Martingell 30; W. R. Hillyer 6–48)
Match drawn

July 25 and 26, 1851, at Cranbrook, *v* Kent
AEE 122 (W. Caffyn 35, H. Sampson 35, G. Parr 28) and 84–9
Kent 107 (F. Pilch 37, E. G. Wenman 30)
Match drawn

May 17, 18, and 19, 1852, at Sheffield, *v* 14 of Yorkshire
14 of Yorkshire 162 (G. Berry 40, G. Anderson 30, A. Crossland 28;

W. Clarke 8–80) and 150 (H. Sampson 40*, G. Berry 40; W. Clarke 9–80)

AEE 78 (Mr N. Felix 30) and 58–4 (Julius Caesar 25)

Match drawn

June 3, 4, and 5, 1852, at The Oval, *v* Surrey, with J. Bickley, W. Clarke, and G. Parr

    AEE 86 (J. Bickley 5–33) and 77 (T. Sherman 7–32)

    Surrey 106 (T. Lockyer 42; Mr A. Mynn 6–16) and 58–3 (Mr N. Felix 29)

    Surrey won by 7 wickets

June 8, 1852, at Priory Park, Chichester, *v* 16 of Sussex (For the Benefit of G. Brown, sen)

    16 of Sussex 89 (J. Dean 44; W. Martingell 5–14, W. Clarke 5–42)

    AEE 37–2

    Match drawn

July 21 and 23, 1853, at Tunbridge Wells, *v* Kent and Sussex

    Kent and Sussex 124 (E. Bushby 41; C. Arnold 6–43) and 89

    AEE 138 (S. Parr 53) and 29–2

    Match drawn

June 1 and 2, 1855, at The Oval, *v* Surrey

    Surrey 68 (J. Bickley 5–24) and 166 (W. Caffyn 52, Mr F. P. Miller 31; W. Clarke 5–61, J. Bickley 5–73)

    AEE 148 (G. Parr 50; W. Martingell 6–43) and 87–9

    AEE won by 1 wicket

August 16, 17, and 18, 1855, at Nottingham, *v* Nottinghamshire

    Nottinghamshire 138 (J. Grundy 60) and 162 (R. C. Tinley 45, S. Parr 39, G. Parr 29; F. Hollands 6–?)

    AEE 190 (T. M. Adams 43, G. Anderson 36, H. H. Stephenson 36; W. Clarke 6–?) and 111–3

    AEE won by 7 wickets

August 21, 22, and 23, 1856, at Newark, *v* Nottinghamshire

    AEE 84 and 84 (Julius Caesar 25; J. Grundy 7–?)

    Nottinghamshire 82 (E. Hinkly 7–?) and 79 (James Chatterton 26; E. Hinkly 6–?)

    AEE won by 7 runs

June 1, 2, and 3, 1857, at Lord's, *v* UAEE (Cricketers' Fund)

    UAEE 143 (W. Caffyn 38, J. Dean 36; J. Jackson 6–31) and 140 (F. W. Bell 33, J. Grundy 27; E. Willsher 5–45)

    AEE 206 (G. Parr 56*, H. H. Stephenson 51; W. Caffyn 7–69) and 78–5

    AEE won by 5 wickets

July 27, 28, and 29, 1857, at Lord's, *v* UAEE (J. Dean's Benefit)

    AEE 99 (G. Parr 48; J. Wisden 8–49) and 214 (A. J. D. Diver 46, R. C. Tinley 46, G. Parr 36)

UAEE 126 and 54 (E. Willsher 5–16)

AEE won by 133 runs

June 7 and 8, 1858, at Lord's, *v* UAEE (Cricketers' Fund)

AEE 111 (A. J. D. Diver 41; W. Caffyn 7–39) and 143 (G. Parr 52;
W. Caffyn 5–64)

UAEE 155 (R. P. Carpenter 45, W. Caffyn 26; J. Jackson 5–50) and
100–6 (T. Hearne 54*)

UAEE won by 4 wickets

July 26 and 27, 1858, at Lord's, *v* UAEE (G. Parr's Benefit)

AEE 254 (J. Jackson 45, E. Stephenson 33, E. Willsher 33, G. Parr 28)

UAEE 87 (W. Caffyn 29; J. Jackson 6–40) and 70 (J. Jackson 6–28)

AEE won by an innings and 97 runs

June 6 and 7, 1859, at Lord's, *v* UAEE (Cricketers' Fund)

UAEE 82 (J. Wisden 26; J. Jackson 8–32) and 70 (J. Jackson 6–29)

AEE 63 (E. Stephenson 25; W. Caffyn 6–31) and 52 (G. R. Atkinson
5–17, W. Caffyn 5–32)

UAEE won by 37 runs

July 4, 5, and 6, 1859, at Lord's, *v* UAEE (Mr Dark's Benefit)

AEE 165 (T. Hayward 46, A. J. D. Diver 41) and 130 (A. Clarke 37*,
R. C. Tinley 32; W. Caffyn 6–58)

UAEE 262 (R. P. Carpenter 97, T. Hearne 62, W. Mortlock 25*) and
34–1

UAEE won by 9 wickets

May 28, 29, and 30, 1860, at Lord's, *v* UAEE (Cricketers' Fund)

AEE 71 (W. Caffyn 7–44) and 131 (G. Parr 55, J. Jackson 29)

UAEE 89 (T. Hearne 31; G. F. Tarrant 6–28) and 92 (J. Grundy 27,
G. Griffith 26)

AEE won by 21 runs

July 19, 20, and 21, 1860, at The Oval, *v* UAEE (W. Martingell's Benefit)

AEE 156 (E. Willsher 55, T. Hayward 28, G. Parr 26; J. Grundy 8–42)
and 221 (T. Hayward 67, G. Parr 44, R. C. Tinley 26)

UAEE 123 (John Lillywhite 32) and 102–8 (R. P. Carpenter 39;
J. Jackson 7–40)

Match drawn

June 3, 4, and 5, 1861, at Lord's, *v* UAEE (Cricketers' Fund)

AEE 74 (W. Caffyn 5–41) and 152 (R. Daft 48, J. Jackson 41;
W. Buttress 5–66)

UAEE 61 (J. Jackson 7–31) and 160 (G. Griffith 45, R. P. Carpenter 29)

AEE won by 5 runs

July 11, 12, and 13, 1861, at Old Trafford, *v* UAEE (For the Benefit of the
Two Teams)

AEE 131 (G. Parr 37, T. Hayward 29; J. Grundy 7–38) and 190–7
(R. Daft 66, G. Anderson 54*, G. Parr 36)

UAEE 101 (G. Griffith 30, R. P. Carpenter 27; J. Jackson 5–64)
Match drawn

August 5, 6, and 7, 1861, at The Oval, v UAEE (T. Barker's Benefit)
UAEE 171 (J. Grundy 72, W. Mortlock 32*, G. Griffith 31;
T. Hayward 5–90) and 260 (W. Caffyn 63, R. P. Carpenter 44,
F.W. Bell 28*, T. Lockyer 26; G. F. Tarrant 5–45)
AEE 106 (T. Hayward 36; G. Griffith 6–27) and 210 (Julius Caesar 72,
H. H. Stephenson 40, R. Daft 25)
UAEE won by 115 runs

June 9, 10, and 11, 1862, at Lord's, v UAEE (Cricketers' Fund)
UAEE 126 (R. P. Carpenter 63*; E. Willsher 5–46) and 129
(R. P. Carpenter 39, G. Griffith 25)
AEE 203 (H. H. Stephenson 70*, R. Daft 36) and 53–6 (G. Anderson
25*)
AEE won by 4 wickets

August 25, 26, and 27, 1862, at Barnsley, v 14 of Yorkshire
AEE 47 (I. Hodgson 7–23) and 205 (G. Parr 60, G. F. Tarrant 60,
Joseph Rowbotham 29)
14 of Yorkshire 136 (E. Dawson 30, John Berry 28; R. C. Tinley 6–45)
and 86 (G. F. Tarrant 7–26)
AEE won by 30 runs

May 25 and 26, 1863, at Lord's, v UAEE (Cricketers' Fund)
UAEE 109 (R. P. Carpenter 26; J. Jackson 7–48) and 150 (T. Hearne
44; G. Wootton 5–46)
AEE 92 (T. Hayward 30; G. Griffith 6–44) and 97 (H. H. Stephenson
26)
UAEE won by 70 runs

May 16, 17, and 18, 1864, at Lord's, v UAEE (Cricketers' Fund)
AEE 218 (C. Brampton 45, R. Daft 44, G. Bennett 39, H. H. Stephen-
son 34) and 166 (G. Wootton 60)
UAEE 181 (T. Sewell, jun 55, G. R. Atkinson 32*, C. H. Ellis 31;
E. Willsher 5–55) and 206–8 (W. Mortlock 65, R. Iddison 44)
UAEE won by 2 wickets

June 5, 6, and 7, 1865, at Lord's, v UAEE (Cricketers' Fund)
AEE 207 (E. Stephenson 59, G. F. Tarrant 40, R. Daft 25) and 186
(G. Parr 48, G. F. Tarrant 26)
UAEE 176 (J. Grundy 57*, G. R. Atkinson 43, R. Iddison 30) and 151
(C. Brampton 36, J. Thewlis 34; R. C. Tinley 6–58)
AEE won by 66 runs

July 17, 18, and 19, 1865, at Sheffield, v Yorkshire
AEE 524 (R. P. Carpenter 134, T. Hayward 112, G. Parr 78,
W. Oscroft 54, J. Smith (Cambs) 32, T. Bignall 27; I. Hodgson 5–127)
Yorkshire 125 (J. Thewlis 34, W. Cuttell 25) and 144 (T. Darnton 81*;

G. Wootton 10–54)
AEE won by an innings and 255 runs

May 21, 22, and 23, 1866, at Lord's, *v* UAEE (Cricketers' Fund)
UAEE 186 (J. Smith (*Cambs*) 62, R. P. Carpenter 38★, S. Biddulph 30)
and 148 (R. Iddison 40)
AEE 112 (G. Howitt 7–63) and 153 (W. Oscroft 86; G. Howitt 6–66)
UAEE won by 69 runs

May 23, 24, and 25, 1867, at Old Trafford, *v* UAEE (Cricketers' Fund)
UAEE 208 (R. Iddison 63, R. P. Carpenter 28, C. Coward 25;
J. C. Shaw 7–82) and 81 (C. Coward 34, R. Iddison 26; J. Jackson 6–50)
AEE 232 (R. Daft 111★, J. Smith (*Cambs*) 34) and 58–6
AEE won by 4 wickets

June 1 and 2, 1868, at Dewsbury, *v* UAEE (For the Benefit of
R. P. Carpenter and T. Hayward)
AEE 95 (R. Daft 36; G. Freeman 6–44) and 106
UAEE 159 (T. Plumb 40★, T. Darnton 29, R. P. Carpenter 27;
G. F. Tarrant 6–76) and 43–2
UAEE won by 8 wickets

May 17 and 18, 1869, at Dewsbury, *v* UAEE (G. Anderson's Benefit)
AEE 131 (T. Hayward 43; G. Freeman 5–53)
UAEE 24–2
Match drawn

July 20 and 22, 1871, at Bolton, *v* UNEE
UNEE 108 (E. B. Rawlinson 26; J. C. Shaw 5–44) and 27 (T. Emmett
6–14)
AEE 156 (R. P. Carpenter 39, John Selby 35, T. Hayward 33)
AEE won by an innings and 21 runs

July 23, 24, and 25, 1874, at Huddersfield, *v* Yorkshire
Yorkshire 236 (Joseph Rowbotham 70, Mr G. Savile 38, Joseph Berry
30, G. Ulyett 30)
AEE 131 (T. Plumb 53★, Martin McIntyre 38) and 94
Yorkshire won by an innings and 11 runs

May 22 and 23, 1876, at Lord's, *v* USEE
AEE 287 (Mr R. P. Smith 87, Alfred Shaw 41, Mr A. N. Hornby 39,
E. Lockwood 32)
USEE 86 (W. Mycroft 5–31) and 117 (G. F. Elliott 27★)
AEE won by an innings and 84 runs

July 1 and 2, 1878, at Derby, *v* Derbyshire
AEE 190 (R. G. Barlow 63, A. Shrewsbury 44) and 35–3
Derbyshire 110 (T. Foster 30, Mr R. P. Smith 25; Alfred Shaw 5–41)
and 113 (Mr R. P. Smith 40)
AEE won by 7 wickets

B THE UNITED ALL ENGLAND ELEVEN SUMMARY OF RESULTS IN IMPORTANT AND FIRST-CLASS MATCHES

Played 23—won, 12; lost, 8; drawn, 3 (all matches)
     19—won, 8; lost, 8; drawn, 3 (v AEE)

June 6 and 7, 1853, at Sheffield, v 14 of Yorkshire
    14 of Yorkshire 53 (J. Wisden 9–27) and 41 (J. Wisden 8–19)
    UAEE 130 (J. Dean 62)
    UAEE won by an innings and 36 runs

September 12, 13, and 14, 1853, at Brighton, v 14 Gentlemen of England,
    with 3 Players
    14 Gentlemen 110 (Mr H. L. Nicholson 41, Mr F. P. Miller 31) and 89
    (Mr F. P. Miller 26; J. Wisden 5–38)
    UAEE 85 (E. Willsher 6–47) and 115–3 (T. Lockyer 60*, G. H. Wright
    27)
    UAEE won by 7 wickets

August 24, 25, and 26, 1854, at Gravesend, v 15 Young Players of Kent
    15 Young Players of Kent 121 (G. Chatterton 7–21) and 226 (G. Bennett
    58, Mr H. W. Andrews 32)
    UAEE 70 (E. Willsher 7–28) and 279–8 (J. Dean 99, G. H. Wright 68)
    UAEE won by 2 wickets

September 4, 5, and 6, 1854, at Lewes, v 16 of Sussex
    16 of Sussex 78 (J. Wisden 6–33) and 108 (Mr H. L. Nicholson 34;
    J. Dean 6–41)
    UAEE 132 (T. Lockyer 38, W. Mortlock 27) and 55–2 (T. M. Adams 30)
    UAEE won by 8 wickets

June 1, 2, and 3, 1857, at Lord's, v AEE (Cricketers' Fund)
    UAEE 143 (W. Caffyn 38, J. Dean 36; J. Jackson 6–31) and 140
    (F. W. Bell 33, J. Grundy 27; E. Willsher 5–45)
    AEE 206 (G. Parr 56*, H. H. Stephenson 51; W. Caffyn 7–69) and 78–5
    AEE won by 5 wickets

July 27, 28, and 29, 1857, at Lord's, v AEE (J. Dean's Benefit)
    AEE 99 (G. Parr 48; J. Wisden 8–49) and 214 (A. J. D. Diver 46,
    R. C. Tinley 46, G. Parr 36)
    UAEE 126 and 54 (E. Willsher 5–16)
    AEE won by 133 runs

June 7 and 8, 1858, at Lord's, v AEE (Cricketers' Fund)
    AEE 111 (A. J. D. Diver 41; W. Caffyn 7–39) and 143 (G. Parr 52;
    W. Caffyn 5–64)

UAEE 155 (R. P. Carpenter 45, W. Caffyn 26; J. Jackson 5–50) and
100–6 (T. Hearne 54*)
UAEE won by 4 wickets

July 26 and 27, 1858, at Lord's, *v* AEE (G. Parr's Benefit)
AEE 254 (J. Jackson 45, E. Stephenson 33, E. Willsher 33, G. Parr 28)
UAEE 87 (W. Caffyn 29; J. Jackson 6–40) and 70 (J. Jackson 6–28)
AEE won by an innings and 97 runs

June 6 and 7, 1859, at Lord's, *v* AEE (Cricketers' Fund)
UAEE 82 (J. Wisden 26; J. Jackson 8–32) and 70 (J. Jackson 6–29)
AEE 63 (E. Stephenson 25; W. Caffyn 6–31) and 52 (G. R. Atkinson
5–17, W. Caffyn 5–32)
UAEE won by 37 runs

July 4, 5, and 6, 1859, at Lord's, *v* AEE (Mr Dark's Benefit)
AEE 165 (T. Hayward 46, A. J. D. Diver 41) and 130 (A. Clarke 37*,
R. C. Tinley 32; W. Caffyn 6–58)
UAEE 262 (R. P. Carpenter 97, T. Hearne 62, W. Mortlock 25) and
34–1
UAEE won by 9 wickets

May 28, 29, and 30, 1860, at Lord's, *v* AEE (Cricketers' Fund)
AEE 71 (W. Caffyn 7–44) and 131 (G. Parr 55, J. Jackson 29)
UAEE 89 (T. Hearne 31; G. F. Tarrant 6–28) and 92 (J. Grundy 27,
G. Griffith 26)
AEE won by 21 runs

July 19, 20, and 21, 1860, at The Oval, *v* AEE (W. Martingell's Benefit)
AEE 156 (E. Willsher 55, T. Hayward 28, G. Parr 26; J. Grundy 8–42)
and 221 (T. Hayward 67, G. Parr 44, R. C. Tinley 26)
UAEE 123 (John Lillywhite 32) and 102–8 (R. P. Carpenter 39;
J. Jackson 7–40)
Match drawn

June 3, 4, and 5, 1861, at Lord's, *v* AEE (Cricketers' Fund)
AEE 74 (W. Caffyn 5–41) and 152 (R. Daft 48, J. Jackson 41;
W. Buttress 5–66)
UAEE 61 (J. Jackson 7–31) and 160 (G. Griffith 45, R. P. Carpenter 29)
AEE won by 5 runs

July 11, 12, and 13, 1861, at Old Trafford, *v* AEE (For the Benefit of the
Two Teams)
AEE 131 (G. Parr 37, T. Hayward 29; J. Grundy 7–38) and 190–7
(R. Daft 66, G. Anderson 54*, G. Parr 36)
UAEE 101 (G. Griffith 30, R. P. Carpenter 27; J. Jackson 5–64)
Match drawn

August 5, 6, and 7, 1861, at The Oval, *v* AEE (T. Barker's Benefit)
UAEE 171 (J. Grundy 72, W. Mortlock 32*, G. Griffith 31;
T. Hayward 5–90) and 260; (W. Caffyn 63, R. P. Carpenter 44,

F. W. Bell 28*, T. Lockyer 26; G. F. Tarrant 5–45)

AEE 106 (T. Hayward 36; G. Griffith 6–27) and 210 (Julius Caesar 72, H. H. Stephenson 40, R. Daft 25)

UAEE won by 115 runs

June 9, 10, and 11, 1862, at Lord's, v AEE (Cricketers' Fund)

UAEE 126 (R. P. Carpenter 63*; E. Willsher 5–46) and 129 (R. P. Carpenter 39, G. Griffith 25)

AEE 203 (H. H. Stephenson 70*, R. Daft 36) and 53–6 (G. Anderson 25*)

AEE won by 4 wickets

May 25 and 26, 1863, at Lord's, v AEE (Cricketers' Fund)

UAEE 109 (R. P. Carpenter 26; J. Jackson 7–48) and 150 (T. Hearne 44; G. Wootton 5–46)

AEE 92 (T. Hayward 30; G. Griffith 6–44) and 97 (H. H. Stephenson 26)

UAEE won by 70 runs

May 16, 17, and 18, 1864, at Lord's, v AEE (Cricketers' Fund)

AEE 218 (C. Brampton 45, R. Daft 44, G. Bennett 39, H. H. Stephenson 34) and 166 (G. Wootton 60)

UAEE 181 (T. Sewell, jun 55, G. R. Atkinson 32*, C. H. Ellis 31; E. Willsher 5–55) and 206–8 (W. Mortlock 65, R. Iddison 44)

UAEE won by 2 wickets

June 5, 6, and 7, 1865, at Lord's, v AEE (Cricketers' Fund)

AEE 207 (E. Stephenson 59, G. F. Tarrant 40, R. Daft 25) and 186 (G. Parr 48, G. F. Tarrant 26)

UAEE 176 (J. Grundy 57*, G. R. Atkinson 43, R. Iddison 30) and 151 (C. Brampton 36, J. Thewlis 34; R. C. Tinley 6–58)

AEE won by 66 runs

May 21, 22, and 23, 1866, at Lord's, v AEE (Cricketers' Fund)

UAEE 186 (J. Smith (*Cambs*) 62, R. P. Carpenter 38*, S. Biddulph 30) and 148 (R. Iddison 40)

AEE 112 (G. Howitt 7–63) and 153 (W. Oscroft 86; G. Howitt 6–66)

UAEE won by 69 runs

May 23, 24, and 25, 1867, at Old Trafford, v AEE (Cricketers' Fund)

UAEE 208 (R. Iddison 63, R. P. Carpenter 28, C. Coward 26; J. C. Shaw 7–82) and 81 (C. Coward 34, R. Iddison 26; J. Jackson 6–50)

AEE 232 (R. Daft 111*, J. Smith (*Cambs*) 34) and 58–6

AEE won by 4 wickets

June 1 and 2, 1868, at Dewsbury, v AEE (For the Benefit of R. P. Carpenter and T. Hayward)

AEE 95 (R. Daft 36; G. Freeman 6–44) and 106

UAEE 159 (T. Plumb 40*, T. Darnton 29, R. P. Carpenter 27; G. F. Tarrant 6–76) and 43–2

UAEE won by 8 wickets

May 17 and 18, 1869, at Dewsbury, *v* AEE (G. Anderson's Benefit)
    AEE 131 (T. Hayward 43; G. Freeman 5–53)
    UAEE 24–2
    Match drawn

C THE UNITED SOUTH OF ENGLAND ELEVEN SUMMARY OF RESULTS IN FIRST-CLASS MATCHES

Played 13—won, 3; lost, 7; drawn, 3

July 4 and 5, 1870, at Lord's, *v* UNEE (Cricketers' Fund)
    UNEE 158 (T. Bignall 36, C. Coward 35; Frank Silcock 5–53,
    J. Southerton 5–63)
    USEE 52 (G. Howitt 6–21) and 66 (Mr W. G. Grace 32; G. Howitt 7–18)
    UNEE won by an innings and 40 runs
August 1 and 2, 1870, at Sheffield, *v* UNEE (E. Stephenson's Benefit)
    UNEE 173 (G. Freeman 50, Joseph Rowbotham 30; J. Southerton
    7–105)
    USEE 75 (G. Howitt 7–36) and 93 (G. Howitt 6–50)
    UNEE won by an innings and 5 runs
August 22, 23, and 24, 1870, at The Oval, *v* UNEE (W. Mortlock's Benefit)
    UNEE 185 (G. Freeman 35, Joseph Rowbotham 34; E. Willsher 6–63)
    and 122 (E. Lockwood 38, Joseph Rowbotham 29, G. Wootton 28★;
    J. Southerton 6–77)
    USEE 177 (H. Jupp 54, Mr W. G. Grace 42; Alfred Shaw 5–55) and
    98–2 (Mr W. G. Grace 51★, E. Pooley 34★)
    Match drawn
June 10 and 12, 1872, at Bishop's Stortford, *v* UNEE
    USEE 81 (H. Jupp 36; E. Lockwood 6–47) and 51 (E. Lockwood 7–35)
    UNEE 74 (J. Southerton 5–34)
    Match drawn
August 8, 9, and 10, 1872, at Hunslet, *v* UNEE
    USEE 119 (James Lillywhite, jun 35; A. Hill 5–41) and 123 (H. Jupp 37,
    R. Humphrey 35)
    UNEE 203 (A. Greenwood 69, Joseph Rowbotham 61; Mr G. F. Grace
    5–45) and 40–2
    UNEE won by 8 wickets
September 2, 3, and 4, 1872, at Northampton, *v* UNEE
    UNEE 142 (A. Hill 35, R. P. Carpenter 31) and 30 (Mr G. F. Grace
    6–13)

USEE 97 (H. R. J. Charlwood 28; A. Hill 5–41, J. C. Shaw 5–53) and
76–2 (Frank Silcock 36*)
USEE won by 8 wickets
June 22, 23, and 24, 1874, at Bradford, *v* Yorkshire
Yorkshire 64 (E. Willsher 5–26, James Lillywhite, jun 5–30) and 148
(E. Lockwood 38, T. Armitage 25; James Lillywhite, jun 6–58)
USEE 147 (E. Willsher 34, H. Killick 28; G. Ulyett 7–82) and 39
(A. Hill 6–9)
Yorkshire won by 26 runs
July 30, 31, and August 1, 1874, at Todmorden, *v* UNEE
UNEE 201 (Joseph Rowbotham 56, E. B. Rawlinson 44*, J. Hicks 28)
and 46 (Mr W. G. Grace 7–28)
USEE 277 (H. R. J. Charlwood 100, Mr W. R. Gilbert 57, R. Hum-
phrey 42, J. Phillips 29)
USEE won by an innings and 30 runs
September 10, 11, and 12, 1874, at Wellingborough, *v* UNEE (For the
Benefit of A. Hill and G. Pinder)
USEE 208 (H. Jupp 72, Mr W. G. Grace 27) and 36–1
UNEE 120 (E. Lockwood 33, A. Greenwood 31) and 122 (J. Hicks 26;
Mr W. G. Grace 6–57)
USEE won by 9 wickets
May 22 and 23, 1876, at Lord's, *v* AEE
AEE 287 (Mr R. P. Smith 87, Alfred Shaw 41, Mr A. N. Hornby 39,
E. Lockwood 32)
USEE 86 (W. Mycroft 5–31) and 117 (G. F. Elliott 27*)
AEE won by an innings and 84 runs
July 13, 14, and 15, 1876, at Huddersfield, *v* UNEE
USEE 102 (H. R. J. Charlwood 29; A. Hill 5–25) and 211 (Mr
G. F. Grace 95, James Lillywhite, jun 25; W. Mycroft 5–78)
UNEE 240 (A. Greenwood 111, D. Eastwood 35, E. Lockwood 29) and
74–3 (G. Ulyett 26*)
UNEE won by 7 wickets
August 3, 4, and 5, 1876, at Hull, *v* UNEE
USEE 159 (Mr W. G. Grace 126) and 207 (Mr W. G. Grace 82, Mr
W. R. Gilbert 37)
UNEE 242 (E. Lockwood 108*, W. Oscroft 51, A. Greenwood 37; Mr
W. R. Gilbert 7–65) and 31–1
Match drawn
September 6 and 7, 1880, at Masbrough, Rotherham, *v* The North
The North 102 (A. Shrewsbury 38; Mr W. R. Gilbert 7–28) and 100
(W. Clarke (Old Basford) 5–42)
USEE 37 (A. Watson 5–8) and 112 (W. E. Midwinter 35; G. Nash 8–31)
The North won by 53 runs

D THE UNITED NORTH OF ENGLAND ELEVEN SUMMARY OF RESULTS IN FIRST-CLASS MATCHES

Played 13—won, 6; lost, 4; drawn, 3

July 4 and 5, 1870, at Lord's, *v* USEE (Cricketers' Fund)
UNEE 158 (T. Bignall 36, C. Coward 35; Frank Silcock 5–53, J. Southerton 5–63)
USEE 52 (G. Howitt 6–21) and 66 (Mr W. G. Grace 32; G. Howitt 7–18)
UNEE won by an innings and 40 runs

August 1 and 2, 1870, at Sheffield, *v* USEE (E. Stephenson's Benefit)
UNEE 173 (G. Freeman 50, Joseph Rowbotham 30; J. Southerton 7–105)
USEE 75 (G. Howitt 7–36) and 93 (G. Howitt 6–50)
UNEE won by an innings and 5 runs

August 22, 23, and 24, 1870, at The Oval, *v* USEE (W. Mortlock's Benefit)
UNEE 185 (G. Freeman 35, Joseph Rowbotham 34; E. Willsher 6–63) and 122 (E. Lockwood 38, Joseph Rowbotham 29, G. Wootton 28★; J. Southerton 6–77)
USEE 177 (H. Jupp 54, Mr W. G. Grace 42; Alfred Shaw 5–55) and 98–2 (Mr W. G. Grace 51★, E. Pooley 34★)
Match drawn

September 12, 13, and 14, 1870, at Holbeck, Leeds, *v* R. Daft's Eleven
R. Daft's Eleven 71 (W. McIntyre 28; G. Freeman 5–25, R. Iddison 5–42) and 115 (F. Wild 40; G. Freeman 8–43)
UNEE 166 (G. R. Atkinson 66, Joseph Rowbotham 34) and 21–1
UNEE won by 9 wickets

July 20 and 22, 1871, at Bolton, *v* AEE
UNEE 108 (E. B. Rawlinson 26; J. C. Shaw 5–44) and 27 (T. Emmett 6–14)
AEE 156 (R. P. Carpenter 39, John Selby 35, T. Hayward 33)
AEE won by an innings and 21 runs

June 10 and 12, 1872, at Bishop's Stortford, *v* USEE
USEE 81 (H. Jupp 36; E. Lockwood 6–47) and 51 (E. Lockwood 7–35)
UNEE 74 (J. Southerton 5–34)
Match drawn

August 8, 9, and 10, 1872, at Hunslet, *v* USEE
USEE 119 (James Lillywhite, jun 35; A. Hill 5–41) and 123 (H. Jupp 37, R. Humphrey 35)

UNEE 203 (A. Greenwood 69, Joseph Rowbotham 61; Mr G. F. Grace 5–45) and 40–2

UNEE won by 8 wickets

September 2, 3, and 4, 1872, at Northampton, *v* USEE

UNEE 142 (A. Hill 35, R. P. Carpenter 31) and 30 (Mr G. F. Grace 6–13)

USEE 97 (H. R. J. Charlwood 28; A. Hill 5–41, J. C. Shaw 5–53) and 76–2 (Frank Silcock 36*)

USEE won by 8 wickets

July 30, 31, and August 1, 1874, at Todmorden, *v* USEE

UNEE 201 (Joseph Rowbotham 56, E. B. Rawlinson 44*, J. Hicks 28) and 46 (Mr W. G. Grace 7–28)

USEE 277 (H. R. J. Charlwood 100, Mr W. R. Gilbert 57, R. Humphrey 42, J. Phillips 29)

USEE won by an innings and 30 runs

September 10, 11, and 12, 1874, at Wellingborough, *v* USEE (For the Benefit of A. Hill and G. Pinder)

USEE 208 (H. Jupp 72, Mr W. G. Grace 27) and 36–1

UNEE 120 (E. Lockwood 33, A. Greenwood 31) and 122 (J. Hicks 26; Mr W. G. Grace 6–57)

USEE won by 9 wickets

August 30 and 31, 1875, at Chesterfield, *v* Derbyshire, with R. G. Barlow

UNEE 83 (W. Hickton 5–42) and 130 (E. Lockwood 47; W. Mycroft 6–44)

Derbyshire 56 (T. Armitage 7–27) and 67 (T. Foster 32; A. Hill 5–24, T. Armitage 5–34)

UNEE won by 90 runs

July 13, 14, and 15, 1876, at Huddersfield, *v* USEE

USEE 102 (H. R. J. Charlwood 29; A. Hill 5–25) and 211 (Mr G. F. Grace 95, James Lillywhite, jun 25; W. Mycroft 5–78)

UNEE 240 (A. Greenwood 111, D. Eastwood 35, E. Lockwood 29) and 74–3 (G. Ulyett 26*)

UNEE won by 7 wickets

August 3, 4, and 5, 1876, at Hull, *v* USEE

USEE 159 (Mr W. G. Grace 126) and 207 (Mr W. G. Grace 82, Mr W. R. Gilbert 37)

UNEE 242 (E. Lockwood 108*, W. Oscroft, 51, A. Greenwood 37; Mr W. R. Gilbert 7–65) and 31–1

Match drawn

E THE ALL ENGLAND ELEVEN
AVERAGES IN IMPORTANT AND FIRST-CLASS MATCHES

	BATTING									BOWLING AND FIELDING									
	M	I	TNO	Runs	HS	Average	25s	50s	100s	IBI	Runs	Wkts	Average	BBi	BBm	5wi	10wm	C	St
Adams, T. M.	6	11	1	87	43	8.70	1	—	—	Did not bowl								6	—
Anderson, G.	17	32	3	379	54*	13.06	2	1	—	Did not bowl								9	—
Arnold, C.	1	1	0	5	5	5.00	—	—	—	2	53	9	5.88	6-43	9-53	1	—	—	—
Barlow, R. G.	1	2	1	67	63	67.00	—	1	—	1	19	3	6.33	3-19	3-19	—	—	—	—
Barnes, W.	1	2	2	25	15*		—	—	—	2	47	3	15.66	2-39	3-47	—	—	1	—
Bartholomew, A.	1	1	0	2	2	2.00	—	—	—	Did not bowl								1	—
Bell, F. W.	1	2	0	10	10	5.00	—	—	—	Did not bowl								1	—
Bennett, G.	6	8	2	40	39	20.00	1	—	—	1	34	2	17.00	2-34	2-34	—	—	1	—
Bickley, J.	5	6	0	50	16	8.33	—	—	—	8	271	20	13.55	5-24	10-97	2	1	7	—
Biddulph, S.	1	1	1	16	16*	—	—	—	—	Did not bowl								1	1
Bignall, T.	2	3	0	46	27	15.33	1	—	—	Did not bowl								1	—
Box, T.	17	32	2	328	38*	10.93	3	—	—	Did not bowl								18	22
Bradshaw, Rev J.	1	1	0	30	30	30.00	1	—	—	Did not bowl								1	—
Brampton, C.	3	6	0	70	45	11.66	1	—	—	3	22	1	22.00	1-8	1-8	—	—	2	—
Brown, G.	1	2	1	12	8*	12.00	—	—	—	Did not bowl								—	—
Butler, G.	2	4	1	33	12*	11.00	—	—	—	Did not bowl								1	—
Buttress, W.	1	1	0	5	5	5.00	—	—	—	1	—	—(+3)	—	3-?	3-?	—	—	1	—
Caesar, Julius	17	31	3	369	72	13.17	2	1	—	2	—	—(+5)	—	3-?	5-?	—	—	9	—
Caffyn, W.	8	14	2	174	35	14.50	1	—	—	1	22	2	11.00	2-22	2-22	—	—	5	—
Carpenter, R. P.	3	4	0	195	134	48.75	1	—	1	Did not bowl								3	—
Chatterton, George	8	14	3	131	25	11.90	1	—	—	Did not bowl								6	8
Chester, J.	1	2	0	5	5	2.50	—	—	—	Did not bowl								2	—
Clarke, A.	14	26	4	215	37*	9.77	1	—	—	Did not bowl								6	—
Clarke, W.	18	29	6	197	28	8.56	1	—	—	27	895	92 (+32)	9.72	9-34	17-160	15	5	3	—
Clifford, F.	1	1	0	17	17	17.00	—	—	—	Did not bowl								—	—
Crossland, A.	2	4	0	40	24	10.00	—	—	—	Did not bowl								1	—
Curteis, Mr H. M.	1	2	0	2	2	1.00	—	—	—	Did not bowl								—	—

	BATTING											BOWLING AND FIELDING							
	M	I	TNO	Runs	HS	Average	25s	50s	100s	IBI	Runs	Wkts	Average	BBi	BBm	5wi	10wm	C	St
Daft, C. F.	2	4	0	35	13	8.75	–	–	–	Did not bowl								1	–
Daft, Richard	17	30	1	551	111*	19.00	6	1	1	Did not bowl								10	–
Day, D.	3	5	0	9	5	1.80	–	–	–	3	47	2	23.50	2–20	2–20	–	–	–	–
Dean, J.	3	6	0	49	25	8.16	1	–	–	3	69	6 (+2)	11.50	2–9	3–28	–	–	–	–
Diver, A. J. D.	14	26	2	285	46	11.87	3	–	–	2	–	– (+6)	–	3–?	6–?	1	–	11	–
Emmett, T.	1	1	0	1	1	1.00	–	–	–	2	70	10	7.00	6–14	10–70	1	1	1	–
Felix, Mr N.	9	14	1	160	67	12.30	1	1	–	Did not bowl								13	–
Flowers, W.	1	1	0	19	19	19.00	–	–	–	Did not bowl								1	–
Fryer, W. H.	1	1	0	0	0	0.00	–	–	–	Did not bowl								1	–
Gibson, R.	1	1	1	5	5*	–	–	–	–	Did not bowl								–	–
Guy, J.	17	31	2	296	46	10.20	4	–	–	Did not bowl								5	–
Hammersley, Mr W. J.	2	3	0	13	11	4.33	–	–	–	Did not bowl								3	–
Hayward, D., jun	1	2	0	22	22	11.00	–	–	–	Did not bowl								–	–
Hayward, Thomas	16	29	0	614	112	21.17	7	1	1	11	305	21	14.52	5–90	7–138	1	–	9	–
Hill, A.	1	1	0	4	4	4.00	–	–	–	2	41	3	13.66	2–19	3–41	–	–	2	–
Hillyer, W. R.	13	22	4	95	14	5.27	–	–	–	20	384	41 (+30)	9.36	8–26	14–48	8	3	11	–
Hinkly, E.	2	3	1	18	18	9.00	–	–	–	3	35	3 (+13)	11.66	7–?	13–?	2	1	–	–
Hodson, J.	1	2	0	31	30	15.50	1	–	–	Did not bowl								2	–
Hollands, F.	1	1	0	12	12	12.00	–	–	–	2	–	– (+8)	–	6–?	8–?	–	–	–	–
Hornby, Mr A. N.	1	1	0	39	39	39.00	1	–	–	Did not bowl								2	–
Howitt, G.	1	2	0	9	6	4.50	–	–	–	1	24	1	24.00	1–24	1–24	–	–	–	–
Humphrey, T.	2	2	0	11	6	5.50	–	–	–	Did not bowl								2	–
Hunt, T.	2	4	0	17	9	4.25	–	–	–	1	–	– (+1)	–	1–?	1–?	–	–	1	–
Iddison, R.	2	2	0	6	6	3.00	–	–	–	1	–	– (+1)	–	1–?	1–?	–	–	6	–
Jackson, J.	17	28	6	307	45	13.95	3	–	–	31	1215	110	11.04	8–32	14–61	11	3	16	–
King, Mr R. T.	2	4	0	2	1	0.50	–	–	–	Did not bowl								1	–
Layton, Mr R.	1	1	0	15	15	15.00	–	–	–	Did not bowl								–	–
Lillywhite, F. W.	3	6	5	4	2	4.00	–	–	–	5	55	9 (+5)	6.11	5–27	5–27	1	–	–	–
Lillywhite, John	2	4	0	46	16	11.50	–	–	–	Did not bowl								2	–
Lindow, Mr H. W.	2	4	0	7	5	1.75	–	–	–	Did not bowl								1	–
Lockwood, E.	1	1	0	32	32	32.00	1	–	–	Did not bowl								2	–
Martin, G. N.	1	2	0	0	0	0.00	–	–	–	Did not bowl								–	–
Martingell, W.	9	12	1	61	14	5.54	–	–	–	6	66	7 (+6)	9.42	5–14	6–?	2	–	9	–

McIntyre, Martin	2	3	0	70	38	23.33	1	–	–	1	34	3	11.33	3–34	3–34	–	–	1	–
McIntyre, W.	4	5	0	25	7	5.00	–	–	–	3	171	8	21.37	4–59	5–79	–	–	1	–
Morley, F.	1	1	0	4	4	4.00	–	–	–	Did not bowl								1	–
Morton, G.	1	1	0	2	2	2.00	–	–	–	Did not bowl								2	2
Mycroft, W.	1	1	1	18	18*	–	–	–	–	2	83	9	9.22	5–31	9–83	1	–	1	–
Mynn, Mr A.	13	23	3	175	31	8.75	1	–	–	4	61	8 (+0)	7.62	6–16	6–38	1	–	4	–
Napper, Mr E.	1	2	0	21	15	10.50	–	–	–	Did not bowl								1	–
Nixon, T.	1	2	1	3	3	3.00	–	–	–	2	40	1	40.00	1–15	1–40	–	–	1	–
Oscroft, J. T.	1	2	0	6	6	3.00	–	–	–	Did not bowl								–	–
Oscroft, W.	9	14	2	232	86	19.33	–	2	–	Did not bowl								3	–
Parr, G.	38	68	7	1416	86*	23.21	14	8	–	3	51	2	25.50	1–6	1–20	–	–	19	–
Parr, S.	2	3	0	58	53	19.33	–	1	–	Did not bowl								2	–
Pell, Mr O. C.	1	2	0	9	6	4.50	–	–	–	Did not bowl								–	–
Pilch, F.	7	13	0	110	50	8.46	1	1	–	Did not bowl								5	–
Pilch, W.	3	6	0	38	18	6.33	–	–	–	Did not bowl								3	–
Pinder, G.	4	6	1	34	11	6.80	–	–	–	Did not bowl								4	2
Plumb, T.	1	2	1	67	53*	67.00	–	1	–	Did not bowl								–	–
Reynolds, F. R.	1	1	0	1	1	1.00	–	–	–	1	53	1	53.00	1–53	1–53	–	–	1	–
Rowbotham, Joseph	7	14	0	141	29	10.07	1	–	–	Did not bowl								6	3
Sampson, H.	3	6	0	71	35	11.83	2	–	–	Did not bowl								–	–
Scotton, W. H.	1	2	0	0	0	0.00	–	–	–	Did not bowl								1	–
Selby, John	2	2	0	44	35	22.00	1	–	–	Did not bowl								–	–
Shaw, Alfred	4	5	0	88	41	17.60	1	–	–	5	157	17	9.23	5–41	9–75	1	–	5	–
Shaw, J. C.	6	9	6	11	8	3.66	–	–	–	10	390	31	12.58	7–82	11–113	2	1	1	–
Sherman, T.	1	2	1	27	18*	27.00	–	–	–	1	–	– (+2)	–	2–?	2–?	–	–	1	–
Shrewsbury, A.	1	2	0	48	44	24.00	1	–	–	Did not bowl								–	–
Slinn, W.	1	2	0	1	1	0.50	–	–	–	2	127	2	63.50	1–53	2–127	–	–	–	–
Smith, J. (of ?)	1	2	1	2	2*	2.00	–	–	–	Did not bowl								–	–
Smith, J. (*Cambs*)	4	6	0	103	34	17.16	2	–	–	Did not bowl								2	–
Smith, Mr R. P.	1	1	0	87	87	87.00	–	1	–	Did not bowl								–	–
Stephenson, E.	6	11	1	181	59	18.10	2	1	–	Did not bowl								3	2
Stephenson, H. H.	16	30	3	433	70*	16.03	4	2	–	10	217	13	16.69	3–40	4–54	–	–	12	4
Story, Mr W. F.	1	2	0	5	3	2.50	–	–	–	Did not bowl								2	3
Summers, G.	1	1	0	9	9	9.00	–	–	–	Did not bowl								–	–
Tarrant, G. F.	11	19	1	229	60	12.72	2	1	–	14	449	41	10.95	7–26	10–67	4	1	9	–

	BATTING									BOWLING AND FIELDING									
	M	I	TNO	Runs	HS	Average	25s	50s	100s	IBI	Runs	Wkts	Average	BBi	BBm	5wi	10wm	C	St
Thewlis, J.	1	2	0	9	5	4.50	–	–	–	Did not bowl								–	–
Thoms, R.	1	2	1	0	0*	0.00	–	–	–	Did not bowl								1	–
Tinley, F.	1	1	1	23	23*	–	–	–	–	2	36	3	12.00	3–21	3–36	–	–	–	–
Tinley, R. C.	21	39	3	343	46	9.52	4	–	–	23	610	42	14.52	6–45	7–65	2	–	14	1
Vernon, Mr H.	1	1	0	33	33	33.00	1	–	–	Did not bowl								1	–
Wadsworth, W.	1	1	0	7	7	7.00	–	–	–	Did not bowl								–	–
Walker, Mr John	1	2	1	0	0*	0.00	–	–	–	Did not bowl								–	–
Walton, Mr E.	1	1	0	1	1	1.00	–	–	–	Did not bowl								–	–
Whittaker, Mr E.	1	1	0	13	13	13.00	–	–	–	Did not bowl								1	–
Whymper, Mr F. H.	1	1	0	0	0	0.00	–	–	–	Did not bowl								–	–
Wild, F.	4	4	0	43	22	10.75	–	–	–	Did not bowl								4	–
Willsher, E.	16	30	3	288	55	10.66	1	1	–	29	892	59 (+1)	15.11	5–16	9–62	4	–	14	–
Wisden, J.	11	22	3	143	23	7.52	–	–	–	15	256	27 (+28)	9.48	10–58	10–58	6	2	9	–
Wootton, G.	6	11	2	141	60	15.66	–	1	–	11	467	34	13.73	10–54	11–78	2	1	7	–
Wright, G. H.	2	4	0	33	22	8.25	–	–	–	3	33	5	6.60	3–12	3–12	–	–	–	–

Errors in bowling analysis (7 innings):

5 runs too many conceded by bowlers (W. Clarke, Hillyer, F. W. Lillywhite, Dean)
2 runs too many conceded by bowlers (Wisden, Hillyer, W. Clarke)
1 run too many conceded by bowlers (Hillyer, W. Clarke)
2 runs too many conceded by bowlers (Wisden, W. Clarke, Day, Hillyer, Martingell)
1 run too few conceded by bowlers (W. Clarke, R. C. Tinley, Hillyer, Wisden)
2 runs too many conceded by bowlers (W. Clarke, Arnold, F. Tinley)
2 runs too many conceded by bowlers (Jackson, R. C. Tinley, Willsher)

Appearances:
In 1 match the names of 4 of the players are not known

F THE UNITED ALL ENGLAND ELEVEN AVERAGES IN IMPORTANT AND FIRST-CLASS MATCHES

	BATTING									BOWLING AND FIELDING									
	M	I	TNO	Runs	HS	Average	25s	50s	100s	IBI	Runs	Wkts	Average	BBi	BBm	5wi	10wm	C	St
Adams, T. M.	4	7	0	90	30	12.85	1	—	—	3	24	4	6.00	3-8	4-18	—	—	4	—
Atkinson, G. R.	12	20	4	182	43	11.37	2	—	—	18	674	39	17.28	5-17	8-46	1	—	3	—
Bell, F. W.	10	17	2	137	33	9.13	2	—	—	8	164	9	18.22	4-40	4-40	—	—	5	—
Bennett, G.	2	4	0	26	11	6.50	—	—	—	3	143	5	28.60	3-49	3-49	—	—	3	—
Biddulph, S.	1	1	0	61	30	20.33	1	—	—	Did not bowl								2	—
Bignall, T.	1	1	0	8	8	8.00	—	—	—	Did not bowl								—	—
Brampton, C.	3	6	0	70	36	11.66	1	—	—	Did not bowl								2	—
Brown, G.	2	2	0	11	11	5.50	—	—	—	Did not bowl								1	—
Buttress, W.	1	2	0	1	1	0.50	—	—	—	2	95	9	10.55	5-66	9-95	1	—	—	—
Caffyn, W.	13	24	0	293	63	12.20	3	1	—	23	1059	73	14.50	7-39	12-103	8	3	8	—
Carpenter, R. P.	16	27	2	611	97	24.44	10	2	—	1	6	0	—	0-6	0-6	—	—	25	—
Chatterton, George	2	3	0	35	16	11.66	—	—	—	2	74	9	8.22	7-21	9-74	1	—	3	—
Chatterton, James	1	2	0	14	7	7.00	—	—	—	Did not bowl								—	—
Cheesman, Mr R.	1	1	0	0	0	0.00	—	—	—	Did not bowl								—	—
Coates, G.	1	1	0	2	2	2.00	—	—	—	Did not bowl								1	—
Coward, C.	3	4	1	81	34	27.00	2	—	—	Did not bowl								—	—
Coward, F.	1	1	0	3	3	3.00	—	—	—	Did not bowl								1	—
Dakin, S.	2	3	0	6	4	2.00	—	—	—	Did not bowl								—	—
Darnton, T.	2	4	1	56	29	18.66	1	—	—	6	117	12	9.75	6-41	11-53	2	1	1	—
Dean, J.	7	12	1	272	99	24.72	1	2	—	Did not bowl								8	—
Ellis, C. H.	3	6	1	76	31	15.20	1	—	—	3	130	7	18.57	4-46	4-73	—	—	3	—
Emmett, T.	2	1	0	5	5	5.00	—	—	—	6	244	20	12.20	6-44	9-94	2	—	1	—
Freeman, G.	4	5	0	23	12	4.60	—	—	—	2	50	5	10.00	3-32	5-50	—	—	2	—
Greenwood, L.	1	2	0	11	8	5.50	—	—	—	11	256	25	10.24	6-27	10-73	2	2	—	—
Griffith, G.	12	20	1	285	45	15.00	5	—	—	25	668	56	11.92	8-42	10-89	2	1	9	—
Grundy, J.	20	36	4	429	72	13.40	2	2	—	Did not bowl								13	—
Halton, W.	2	3	1	29	14*	14.50	—	—	—	1	3	1	3.00	1-3	1-3	—	—	—	—
Hearne, T.	10	19	2	285	62	16.76	2	2	—	Did not bowl								9	—

	BATTING									BOWLING AND FIELDING									
	M	I	TNO	Runs	HS	Average	25s	50s	100s	IBI	Runs	Wkts	Average	BBi	BBm	5wi	10wm	C	St
Hodgson, I.	1	2	0	0	0	0.00	–	–	–	1	15	3	5.00	3-15	3-15	–	–	–	–
Holmes, H.	1	2	0	5	3	2.50	–	–	–	Did not bowl								1	–
Howitt, G.	4	5	0	10	7	2.00	–	–	–	6	300	26	11.53	7-63	13-129	2	1	3	–
Hunt, T.	3	5	0	21	13	4.20	–	–	–	1	9	0	–	0-9	0-9	–	–	1	–
Hyde, J.	1	1	0	0	0	0.00	–	–	–	2	16	5	3.20	4-8	5-16	–	–	–	–
Iddison, R.	8	14	1	299	63	23.00	4	1	–	6	121	12	10.08	3-9	5-65	–	–	6	1
Jupp, H.	1	2	0	6	6	3.00	–	–	–	Did not bowl								2	–
Lillywhite, John	10	19	1	140	32	7.77	1	–	–	3	80	6	13.33	4-27	4-27	–	–	4	–
Lockyer, T.	16	27	5	367	60*	16.68	2	1	–	1	4	0	–	0-4	0-4	–	–	23	6
Martingell, W.	3	6	3	27	11*	9.00	–	–	–	4	102	4	25.50	2-47	2-47	–	–	1	–
Miller, Mr. F. P.	1	1	0	0	0	0.00	–	–	–	Did not bowl								–	–
Mortlock, W.	12	22	4	235	65	13.05	3	1	–	1	4	0	–	0-4	0-4	–	–	5	–
Newman, C	1	2	0	1	1	0.50	–	–	–	Did not bowl								1	–
Nicholson, Mr H. L.	1	2	1	19	19	9.50	–	–	–	1	2	0	–	0-2	0-2	–	–	1	–
Nixon, T.	2	2	0	0	0*	0.00	–	–	–	2	72	6	12.00	4-40	6-72	–	–	–	–
Oscroft, J. T.	2	2	0	16	9	8.00	–	–	–	Did not bowl								–	–
Paling, G.	2	2	0	25	15	12.50	–	–	–	Did not bowl								–	–
Picknell, G.	3	4	0	23	10	5.75	–	–	–	2	9	0	–	0-3	0-9	–	–	3	–
Plumb, T.	3	5	3	59	40*	29.50	1	–	–	Did not bowl								5	2
Reynolds, F. R.	1	2	0	19	11	9.50	–	–	–	2	121	5	24.20	3-66	5-121	–	–	–	–
Ricketts, J.	1	1	0	2	2	2.00	–	–	–	Did not bowl								–	–
Royston, H.	1	2	1	4	4*	4.00	–	–	–	Did not bowl								1	–
Sewell, T., jun	4	7	2	114	55	22.80	–	1	–	5	26	1	26.00	1-26	1-26	–	–	–	–
Shaw, Alfred	2	4	2	34	21	11.33	–	–	–	5	155	7	22.14	4-44	5-67	–	–	1	–
Sherman, T.	2	2	2	8	6*	–	–	–	–	Did not bowl								–	–
Silcock, Frank	1	2	1	18	10*	18.00	–	–	–	1	19	3	6.33	3-19	3-19	–	–	1	–
Slinn, W.	1	2	1	0	0*	0.00	–	–	–	1	41	1	41.00	1-41	1-41	–	–	1	–
Smith, John (*Cambs*)	2	2	0	72	62	18.00	–	1	–	2	56	4	14.00	3-24	4-56	–	–	1	–
Stephenson, E.	3	6	0	55	19	9.16	–	–	–	Did not bowl								2	–
Thewlis, J.	1	2	0	34	34	17.00	1	–	–	Did not bowl								3	–
Wells, G.	1	2	0	1	1	0.50	1	1	–	Did not bowl								–	–
Wisden, J.	14	23	3	181	26	9.05	1	–	–	21	691	64	10.79	9-27	17-46	5	2	12	1
Wright, G. H.	5	10	1	160	68	17.77	1	1	–	1	20	2	10.00	2-20	2-20	–	–	9	–

THE ALL ENGLAND ELEVEN

	BATTING									BOWLING AND FIELDING								
	M	I	TNO	Runs	HS	Average	25s	50s	100s	IBI Runs	Wkts	Average	BBi	BBm	5wi	10wm	C	St
Adams, T. M.	1	2	1	0	0*	0.00	1	1	–	Did not bowl							3	–
Anderson, G.	9	18	2	218	54*	13.62	1	1	–	Did not bowl							4	–
†Bennett, G.	1	2	0	40	39	20.00	1	–	–	1 34	2	17.00	2-34	2-34	–	–	1	–
Bickley, J.	3	5	1	37	16	9.25	–	–	–	1 58	2	29.00	1-11	2-41	–	–	1	–
†Brampton, C.	3	6	0	70	45	11.66	1	–	–	3 22	1	22.00	1-8	1-8	–	–	2	–
Caesar, Julius	12	22	1	256	72	12.19	–	1	–	Did not bowl							6	–
Clarke, A.	10	19	4	152	37*	10.13	1	–	–	Did not bowl							2	–
Crossland, A.	2	4	0	40	24	10.00	–	–	–	Did not bowl							1	–
Daft, C. F.	1	2	0	26	13	13.00	–	–	–	Did not bowl							–	–
Daft, Richard	14	27	1	529	111*	20.34	6	1	1	Did not bowl							9	–
Diver, A. J. D.	11	20	1	226	46	11.89	3	–	–	Did not bowl							5	–
Gibson, R.	1	1	1	5	5*	–	–	–	–	Did not bowl							–	–
Hayward, Thomas	14	27	0	469	67	17.37	6	1	–	11 305	21	14.52	5-90	7-138	1	–	6	–
Humphrey, T.	1	2	0	11	6	5.50	–	–	–	Did not bowl							2	–
Jackson, J.	16	27	6	292	45	13.90	3	–	–	29 1174	107	10.97	8-32	14-61	11	3	16	–
McIntyre, W.	1	1	0	0	0	0.00	–	–	–	Did not bowl							–	–
Oscroft, W.	5	9	1	134	86	16.75	–	1	–	Did not bowl							–	–
Parr, G.	17	32	3	622	56*	21.44	8	3	–	3 51	2	25.50	1-6	1-6	–	–	7	–
Pinder, G.	3	5	1	24	11	6.00	–	–	–	Did not bowl							3	2
†Reynolds, F. R.	1	1	0	1	1	1.00	–	–	–	1 53	1	53.00	1-53	1-53	–	–	1	–
Rowbotham, Joseph	6	12	0	111	17	9.25	–	–	–	Did not bowl							4	–
†Shaw, Alfred	2	3	0	37	18	12.33	2	–	–	1 7	0	–	0-7	0-7	–	–	–	–
Shaw, J. C.	4	6	4	10	8	5.00	–	–	–	7 257	22	11.68	7-82	11-113	1	1	1	–
†Slinn, W.	1	2	0	1	1	0.50	–	–	–	2 127	2	63.50	1-53	2-127	–	–	–	–
†Smith, John (*Cambs*)	3	5	0	71	34	14.20	1	–	–	Did not bowl							2	–
†Stephenson, E.	6	11	1	181	59	18.10	2	1	–	Did not bowl							3	2
Stephenson, H. H.	14	27	3	386	70*	16.08	3	2	–	10 217	13	16.69	3-40	4-54	–	–	8	4
Summers, G.	1	1	0	9	9	9.00	–	–	–	Did not bowl							–	–
Tarrant, G. F.	10	17	1	163	40	10.18	2	–	–	12 382	31	12.32	6-28	7-102	3	–	9	–
†Thewlis, J.	1	2	0	9	5	4.50	–	–	–	Did not bowl							–	–
Tinley, R. C.	16	30	3	277	46	10.25	3	–	–	18 387	31	12.48	6-58	7-100	1	–	11	1
Wadsworth, W.	1	1	0	7	7	7.00	–	–	–	Did not bowl							–	–
Willsher, E.	14	26	3	243	55	10.56	1	1	–	27 868	59	14.71	5-16	9-62	4	–	13	–
Wootton, G.	4	8	1	124	60	17.71	–	1	–	7 311	16	19.43	5-46	5-46	1	–	4	–

† a player who appeared for both Elevens in this series
In the analysis of one innings, the total of the runs conceded by three bowlers (Jackson, Tinley, and Willsher) is 2 runs too many.

THE ALL ENGLAND ELEVEN v THE UNITED ALL ENGLAND ELEVEN
THE UNITED ALL ENGLAND ELEVEN

	BATTING									BOWLING AND FIELDING									
	M	I	NO	Runs	HS	Average	25s	50s	100s	I	Runs	Wkts	Average	BBi	BBm	5wi	10wm	C	St
Atkinson, G. R.	12	20	4	182	43	11.37	2	—	—	18	674	39	17.28	5–17	8–46	1	—	3	—
Bell, F. W.	9	15	2	114	33	8.76	2	—	—	7	154	9	17.11	4–40	4–40	—	—	4	—
†Bennett, G.	2	4	0	26	11	6.50	—	—	—	3	143	5	28.60	3–49	3–49	—	—	3	—
Biddulph, S.	2	4	1	61	30	20.33	1	—	—	Did not bowl								2	—
Bignall, T.	1	1	0	8	8	8.00	—	—	—	Did not bowl								—	—
†Brampton, C.	3	6	0	70	36	11.66	1	—	—	Did not bowl								2	—
Buttress, W.	1	2	0	1	1	0.50	—	—	—	2	95	9	10.55	5–66	9–95	1	—	—	—
Caffyn, W.	13	24	0	293	63	12.20	3	1	—	23	1059	73	14.50	7–39	12–103	8	3	—	—
Carpenter, R. P.	16	27	2	611	97	24.44	10	2	—	1	6	0	—	0–6	0–6	—	—	25	—
Chatterton, James	1	2	0	14	7	7.00	—	—	—	Did not bowl								—	—
Coward, C.	3	4	1	81	34	27.00	2	—	—	Did not bowl								1	—
Coward, F.	1	1	0	3	3	3.00	—	—	—	Did not bowl								1	—
Darnton, T.	2	4	0	56	29	18.66	1	—	—	Did not bowl								1	—
Dean, J.	3	5	1	50	36	12.50	1	—	—	2	47	0	—	0–14	0–14	—	—	3	—
Ellis, C. H.	3	6	1	76	31	15.20	1	—	—	Did not bowl								1	—
Emmett, T.	2	1	0	5	5	5.00	—	—	—	3	130	7	18.57	4–46	4–73	—	—	1	—
Freeman, G.	4	5	0	23	12	4.60	—	—	—	6	244	20	12.20	6–44	9–94	2	—	2	—
Greenwood, L.	1	2	0	11	8	5.50	—	—	—	2	50	5	10.00	3–32	5–50	—	—	—	—
Griffith, G.	12	20	1	285	45	15.00	5	—	—	11	256	25	10.24	6–27	10–73	2	2	9	—
Grundy, J.	17	31	2	375	72	12.93	2	2	—	19	501	37	13.54	8–42	10–89	2	2	11	—
Halton, W.	2	3	1	29	14*	14.50	2	—	—	Did not bowl								—	—
Hearne, T.	10	19	2	285	62	16.76	2	2	—	1	3	1	3.00	1–3	1–3	—	—	9	—
Hodgson, I.	1	2	0	0	0	0.00	—	—	—	1	15	3	5.00	3–15	3–15	—	—	—	—
Holmes, H.	1	2	0	5	3	2.50	—	—	—	Did not bowl								—	—
Howitt, G.	4	5	0	10	7	2.00	—	—	—	6	300	26	11.53	7–63	13–129	2	2	3	—
Hunt, T.	2	4	0	19	13	4.75	—	—	—	Did not bowl								1	—
Iddison, R.	8	14	1	299	63	23.00	4	1	—	6	121	12	10.08	3–9	5–65	—	—	6	—

Player	Matches	Innings	Not Outs	Runs	Highest	Average	Mdns	Runs	Wkts	Average	Best (inns)	Best (match)	5wi	Ct	St
Jupp, H.	1	2	0	6	6	3.00	Did not bowl							2	1
Lillywhite, John	9	18	1	129	32	7.58	3	80	6	13.33	4–27	4–27	—	4	—
Lockyer, T.	13	23	4	255	26	13.42	1	4	0	-	0–4	0–4	—	21	4
Martingell, W.	3	6	3	27	11*	9.00	4	102	4	25.50	2–47	2–47	—	1	—
Mortlock, W.	11	21	4	208	65	12.23	1	4	0	-	0–4	0–4	—	5	—
Newman, C.	2	2	0	1	1	0.50	Did not bowl							1	—
Oscroft, J. T.	1	2	0	16	9	8.00	Did not bowl							—	—
Paling, G.	2	2	0	25	15	12.50	Did not bowl							5	—
Plumb, T.	3	5	3	59	40*	29.50	2	121	5	24.20	3–66	5–121	—	—	—
†Reynolds, F. R.	1	2	0	19	11	9.50	Did not bowl							—	—
Ricketts, J.	1	1	0	2	2	2.00	5	155	7	22.14	4–44	5–67	—	1	—
Sewell, T., jun	4	7	2	114	55	22.80	Did not bowl							—	—
†Shaw, Alfred	2	4	1	34	21	11.33	1	41	1	41.00	1–41	1–41	—	1	—
Silcock, Frank	1	2	1	18	10*	18.00	2	56	4	14.00	3–24	4–56	—	1	—
†Slinn, W.	1	2	1	0	0*	0.00	Did not bowl							—	—
†Smith, John (*Cambs*)	2	4	0	72	62	18.00	Did not bowl							2	—
†Stephenson, E.	3	6	0	55	19	9.16	Did not bowl							3	—
†Thewlis, J.	1	2	0	34	34	17.00	Did not bowl							—	—
Wells, G.	1	2	0	1	1	0.50	Did not bowl							1	—
Wisden, J.	10	18	1	142	26	8.35	13	411	29	14.17	8–49	12–96	1	8	4
Wright, G. H.	2	4	0	42	21	10.50	Did not bowl							4	—

† a player who appeared for both Elevens in this series

H THE UNITED SOUTH OF ENGLAND ELEVEN AVERAGES IN FIRST-CLASS MATCHES

	BATTING									BOWLING AND FIELDING									
	M	I	TNO	Runs	HS	Average	25s	50s	100s	IBI	Runs	Wkts	Average	BBi	BBm	5wi	10wm	C	St
Bennett, G.	1	1	0	1	1	1.00	—	—	—	Did not bowl								1	—
Carter, W. J.	1	2	0	14	9	7.00	—	—	—	Did not bowl								5	—
Charlwood, H. R. J.	11	20	1	318	100	16.73	2	—	1	Did not bowl								1	—
Clarke, W. (Old Basford)	1	2	1	24	18	24.00	—	—	—	2	67	7	9.57	5–42	7–67	1	—	1	—
Day, Mr L. M.	1	2	0	5	3	2.50	—	—	—	Did not bowl								—	—
Elliott, G. F.	3	6	1	55	27*	11.00	1	—	—	Did not bowl								1	—
Fillery, R.	4	7	1	20	11*	3.33	—	—	—	Did not bowl								1	—
Gilbert, Mr W. R.	6	11	1	182	57	18.20	1	1	—	2	92	4	23.00	4–78	4–78	—	—	7	—
Grace, Mr G. F.	10	17	0	176	95	10.35	1	1	—	5	191	21	9.09	7–28	11–81	2	1	9	—
Grace, Mr W. G.	8	14	1	427	126	32.84	3	2	1	7	206	19	10.84	6–13	10–24	2	1	9	—
Griffith, G.	4	6	0	9	4	1.50	—	—	—	9	439	28	15.67	7–28	10–80	2	2	2	—
Hearne, T.	1	1	1	20	20*	—	—	—	—	Did not bowl								—	—
Henty, E.	1	2	2	1	1*	—	—	—	—	Did not bowl								—	—
Holmes, H.	1	2	0	17	17	8.50	—	—	—	Did not bowl								1	—
Humphrey, R.	8	14	0	154	42	11.00	2	—	—	Did not bowl								—	—
Humphrey, T.	7	12	2	84	17	8.40	—	—	—	Did not bowl								5	—
Humphreys, W. A.	2	4	0	29	20	7.25	—	—	—	Did not bowl								1	—
Hunter, J.	1	2	1	3	3	3.00	—	—	—	Did not bowl								2	1
Jupp, H.	11	19	0	362	72	19.05	2	2	—	Did not bowl								2	—
Jupp, W. T.	1	2	0	2	2	1.00	—	—	—	Did not bowl								2	—
Killick, H.	2	4	0	37	28	9.25	1	—	—	Did not bowl								6	—
Lillywhite, James, jun	10	17	1	162	35	10.12	2	—	—	12	500	37	13.51	6–58	11–88	2	1	6	—
Marten, W. G.	1	2	1	7	7	7.00	—	—	—	—	13	0	—	0–13	0–13	—	—	1	—
Midwinter, W. E.	1	2	0	44	35	22.00	1	—	—	1	33	1	33.00	1–33	1–33	—	—	1	—
Palmer, W. T.	1	2	0	25	13	12.50	—	—	—	Did not bowl								—	—
Phillips, H.	2	4	1	14	9*	4.66	—	—	—	Did not bowl								6	5
Phillips, J.	4	7	1	91	29	15.16	1	—	—	Did not bowl								7	—

								Bowling									
Pooley, E.	11	19	2	157	34*	9.23	1	Did not bowl								8	6
Pooley, F. W.	1	2	0	3	3	1.50	—	Did not bowl								1	—
Reed, A. A.	1	2	0	3	2	1.50	—	Did not bowl								—	—
Silcock, Frank	10	18	4	133	36*	9.50	1	11	297	18	16.50	5-53	5-53	1		—	8
Southerton, J.	9	14	4	75	24	7.50	—	13	746	40	18.65	7-105	10-194	4		1	7
Stephenson, H. H.	1	2	0	9	9	4.50	—	Did not bowl								—	2
Titchmarsh, V. A.	1	2	0	8	5	4.00	—	Did not bowl								—	4
Willsher, E.	4	7	2	43	34	8.60	1	6	209	15	13.93	6-63	8-71	2		—	2
Woof, W. A.	1	2	0	3	2	1.50	—	1	15	0	—	0-15	0-15	—		—	—

Errors in bowling analysis (3 innings):

Runs conceded by bowlers (Willsher, Lillywhite, Messrs W. G. and G. F. Grace) are 2 too many

Runs conceded by bowlers (Midwinter, Woof, Clarke, Mr W. R. Gilbert) are 3 too many

Runs conceded by bowlers (Clarke, Mr W. R. Gilbert) are 3 too few

I THE UNITED NORTH OF ENGLAND ELEVEN AVERAGES IN FIRST-CLASS MATCHES

	BATTING									BOWLING AND FIELDING									
	M	I	TNO	Runs	HS	Average	25s	50s	100s	IBI	Runs	Wkts	Average	BBi	BBm	5wi	10wm	C	St
Armitage, T.	1	2	0	21	18	10.50	—	—	—	2	61	12	5.08	7-27	12-61	2	2	2	—
Atkinson, G. R.	4	5	2	88	66	29.33	—	1	—	3	56	5	11.20	2-16	2-16	—	—	3	—
Bignall, T.	5	8	0	94	36	11.75	1	—	—	Did not bowl								1	—
Blackburn, J. S.	1	2	0	20	20	10.00	—	—	—	2	45	1	45.00	1-28	1-45	—	—	—	—
Butler, R.	1	2	0	22	19	11.00	—	—	—	Did not bowl								2	—
Carpenter, R. P.	2	3	0	40	31	13.33	—	—	—	Did not bowl								2	—
Clayton, R. O.	1	2	0	21	21	10.50	1	—	—	1	14	3	4.66	3-14	3-14	—	—	1	—
Coward, C.	1	1	0	35	35	35.00	1	—	—	Did not bowl								—	—
Daft, Richard	2	3	0	28	24	9.33	—	—	—	Did not bowl								1	—
Eastwood, D.	1	1	0	35	35	35.00	1	—	—	Did not bowl								1	—
Emmett, T.	3	5	0	66	24	13.20	1	—	—	3	63	2	31.50	2-36	2-45	—	—	2	—
Freeman, G.	4	5	0	97	50	19.40	1	1	—	6	157	18	8.72	8-43	13-68	2	1	1	—
Greenwood, A.	8	14	1	306	111	23.53	2	1	1	Did not bowl								5	—
Greenwood, L.	9	15	2	102	24	7.84	—	—	—	5	134	9	14.88	3-25	4-33	—	—	3	—
Hayward, Thomas	3	2	0	0	0	0.00	—	—	—	Did not bowl								—	—
Hicks, J.	3	5	0	61	28	12.20	1	—	—	2	53	3	17.66	2-53	2-53	—	—	1	—
Hill, A.	7	10	0	88	35	8.80	1	—	—	10	360	28	12.85	5-25	7-46	4	—	8	—
Hornby, Mr A. N.	1	2	0	7	5	3.50	—	—	—	Did not bowl								—	—
Howitt, G.	7	11	3	51	13*	6.37	—	—	—	10	405	37	10.94	7-18	13-39	4	2	4	—
Iddison, R.	10	15	2	117	23	9.00	4	—	—	5	157	7	22.42	5-42	6-108	1	—	12	—
Lockwood, E.	13	21	3	413	108*	22.94	—	—	1	9	249	18	13.83	7-35	13-82	2	1	7	—
Morley, F.	2	3	1	19	14*	9.50	—	—	—	3	118	6	19.66	4-58	4-58	—	—	2	—
Mycroft, W.	2	3	0	18	11	6.00	—	—	—	3	179	9	19.88	5-78	8-120	1	—	2	—
Oscroft, W.	2	2	0	62	51	31.00	—	1	—	2	34	6	5.66	3-10	6-34	—	—	1	—
Pinder, G.	3	4	3	19	13	19.00	—	—	—	Did not bowl								3	2
Plumb, T.	9	15	4	156	23*	14.18	2	—	—	Did not bowl								11	3
Rawlinson, E. B.	6	8	1	111	44*	15.85	2	—	—	1	17	3	5.66	3-17	3-17	—	—	5	—
Rowbotham, Joseph	11	18	1	321	61	18.88	4	2	—	Did not bowl								2	—

Batting and Fielding

Player	M	I	NO	Runs	HS	Avge	Ct
Rylott, A.	1	1	0	10	10	10.00	—
Shaw, Alfred	2	3	0	4	3	1.33	2
Shaw, J. C.	2	3	1	2	2*	1.00	1
Shrewsbury, A.	1	2	1	16	8*	16.00	—
Smith, John (*Cambs*)	5	8	1	21	7*	3.00	4
Smith, Mr R. P.	3	5	0	26	14	5.20	—
Thewlis, J.	1	2	0	0	0	0.00	—
Tye, J.	1	1	0	14	14	14.00	1
Ullathorne, C. E.	3	5	0	12	4	2.40	3
Ulyett, G.	2	4	1	45	26*	15.00	—
Wootton, G.	2	3	1	58	28*	29.00	1

Bowling

Player	Maidens	Runs	Wkts	Avge	Best (innings)	Best (match)	5wi
Rylott, A.	2	41	2	20.50	1-16	2-41	—
Shaw, Alfred	4	192	13	14.76	5-55	7-102	1
Shaw, J. C.	4	140	9	15.55	5-53	5-91	1
Shrewsbury, A.	Did not bowl						
Smith, John (*Cambs*)	Did not bowl						
Smith, Mr R. P.	Did not bowl						
Thewlis, J.	Did not bowl						
Tye, J.	2	59	1	59.00	1-45	1-59	—
Ullathorne, C. E.	Did not bowl						
Ulyett, G.	Did not bowl						
Wootton, G.	4	117	8	14.62	3-44	5-60	—

SELECT BIBLIOGRAPHY

The principal publications consulted are the following:

1. Collections of Scores, Annuals, and Reference Works

Cricket Scores and Biographies, 15 vols.
Cricket Matches 1860–1863, First Class Cricket Matches 1864–1866, and succeeding volumes covering the period 1867–1880, comp. and pub. by the Association of Cricket Statisticians.
A Guide to Important Cricket Matches Played in the British Isles 1709–1863, and *A Guide to First Class Cricket Matches Played in the British Isles*, comp. and pub. by the Association of Cricket Statisticians.
The Guide to Cricketers, ed. Frederick Lillywhite.
James Lillywhite's Cricketers' Annual
John Lillywhite's Cricketers' Companion (later *John & James* . . . , and finally *James Lillywhite's Cricketers' Companion*)
John Wisden's Cricketers' Almanack

2. Newspapers

Bell's Life in London
The Berkshire Chronicle
The Cambridge Chronicle and University Journal, Isle of Ely Herald, and Huntingdonshire Gazette
The Cambridge Independent Press
The Daily Telegraph
The Field, the Country Gentleman's Newspaper
The Illustrated London News
The Illustrated Sporting News
The Illustrated Times
The Leeds Mercury
The Manchester Guardian
The Reading Mercury
The Sporting Life
The Sportsman
The Times

3. Journals and Periodicals containing articles and miscellaneous material

Baily's Magazine of Sports and Pastimes
Cricket: A Weekly Record of the Game

Cricket Chat
The Cricket Quarterly
The Cricket Statistician
The Cricketer
The Journal of the Cricket Society
The Playfair Cricket Monthly
Wisden Cricket Monthly

4. Books

Altham, H. S., and E. W. Swanton, *A History of Cricket* (2 vols., London: George Allen & Unwin Ltd, 1962).

Alverstone, The Rt. Hon. Lord, and C. W. Alcock, eds., *Surrey Cricket: Its History and Associations* (London: Longmans, Green, and Co., 1904).

Arlott, John, comp., *From Hambledon to Lord's: The Classics of Cricket* (London: Christopher Johnson, Publishers, Ltd., 1948. Contains John Nyren and Charles Cowden Clarke, *The Cricketers of My Time*; The Rev. James Pycroft, *The Cricket Field* (1851 ed.); The Rev. John Mitford, Review of Nyren's *The Young Cricketers' Tutor*).

—— comp., *The Middle Ages of Cricket* (London: Christopher Johnson, n.d. [1949]. Contains William Denison, *Sketches of the Players*; The Rev. James Pycroft, "Cricket Recollections", in *Oxford Memories*).

Arrowsmith, R. L., *A History of County Cricket: Kent* (London: Arthur Barker Limited, 1971)

Ashley-Cooper, F. S., *Edward Mills Grace Cricketer* (London: Chatto & Windus, 1916).

—— *Nottinghamshire Cricket and Cricketers* (Nottingham: Henry B. Saxton, n.d. [1923]).

—— *Cricket Highways and Byways* (London: George Allen & Unwin Ltd., 1927).

Barlow, Richard Gorton, *Forty Seasons of First-class Cricket . . .* (Manchester: John Heywood Ltd., n.d. [1908]).

Barty-King, Hugh, *Quilt Winders and Pod Shavers: The History of Cricket Bat and Ball Manufacture* (London: Macdonald & Jane's, 1979)

Bettesworth, W. A., *The Walkers of Southgate: A Famous Brotherhood of Cricketers*, ed. by E. T. Sachs (London: Methuen & Co., 1900).

—— *Chats on the Cricket Field*, with Explanatory Notes by F. S. Ashley-Cooper (London: Merritt & Hatcher, Limited, n.d. [1910]).

Birley, Derek, *The Willow Wand: Some Cricket Myths Explored* (London: Queen Anne Press, Macdonald and Jane's, 1979).

Blyth, Henry, *The Pocket Venus: A Victorian Scandal* (London: Sphere Books Limited, 1968).

Bowen, Rowland, *Cricket: A History of Its Growth and Development throughout the World* (London: Eyre & Spottiswoode, 1970).

Brodribb, Gerald, *Felix on the Bat: Being a Memoir of Nicholas Felix, together with the Full Text of the Second Edition of 'Felix on the Bat'*. (London: Eyre & Spottiswoode, 1962).

Brookes, Christopher, *English Cricket: The Game and Its Players through the Ages* (London: Weidenfeld and Nicolson, 1978).

Caffyn, William, *see* "Mid-on".

Catton, J. A. H. ("Tityrus"), *Wickets and Goals: Stories of Play* (London: Chapman and Hall Ltd., 1926).

Coldham, James D., *Lord Harris* (London: George Allen & Unwin, 1983).

Collins, W. E. W., *Leaves from . . . An Old Country Cricketers' Diary* (Edinburgh and London: William Blackwood & Sons, 1908).

Daft, Richard, *Kings of Cricket: Reminiscences and Anecdotes with Hints on the Game* (Bristol: J. W. Arrowsmith; London: Simpkin, Marshall, Hamilton, Kent & Company, Limited, n.d. [1893]).

—— *A Cricketer's Yarns, to Which Have Been Added a Few Genealogical Tables of Nottinghamshire Cricketing Families*, ed., with an Introduction, by F. S. Ashley-Cooper (London: Chapman and Hall Ltd., 1926).

Felix, Nicholas, *see* Brodribb, Gerald.

FitzGerald, R. A., *see* "Quid".

Gale, Frederick, *Echoes from Old Cricket Fields, or, Sketches of Cricket and Cricketers from the Earliest History of the Game to the Present Time* (London: Simpkin, Marshall, and Co., 1871; rpt. Wakefield: S. R. Publishers Ltd., 1972).

Grace, W. G., *Cricket* (Bristol: J. W. Arrowsmith; London: Simpkin, Marshall, Hamilton, Kent & Co. Limited, 1891).

—— *The History of a Hundred Centuries*, ed. by W. Yardley (London: L. Upcott Gill, 1895).

—— *"W. G.": Cricketing Reminiscences and Personal Recollections* (London: James Bowden, 1899).

Green, Stephen, ed., *Backward Glances: An Album of 60 Early Cricket Photographs 1857–1917* (Newport, I. W.: M. G. Richards, n.d. [1976]).

—— *Cricketing Bygones* (Princes Risborough: Shire Publications 90, 1982).

Hadfield, John, *A Wisden Century 1850–1950* (London: Sporting Handbooks Ltd., 1950).

Harris, The Right Hon. Lord, *The History of Kent County Cricket, Containing Contributions by the Several Captains of the Kent Team* (London: Eyre & Spottiswoode, 1907).

—— *A Few Short Runs* (London: John Murray, 1921).

Harris, Lord, and F. S. Ashley-Cooper, *Lord's and the M.C.C.: A Cricket Chronicle of 137 Years, Based on Official Documents, and Published with the Knowledge and Sanction of the Marylebone Cricket Club to Commemorate the Centenary of Their Present Ground* (London: London & Counties Press Association, 1914; rpt. London: Herbert Jenkins Limited, 1920).

—— eds., *Kent Cricket Matches 1719–1880* (Canterbury: Gibbs & Sons, 1929).

Hawke, Lord, *Recollections & Reminiscences* (London: Williams & Norgate, Ltd., 1924).

Hawke, Lord, Lord Harris, and Sir Home Gordon, Bart., eds., *The Memorial Biography of Dr. W. G. Grace* (London: Constable & Company, Ltd., 1919).

Holmes, The Rev. R. S., *Surrey Cricket and Cricketers 1773 to 1895* (London: "Cricket" Offices, 1896).

—— *The History of Yorkshire County Cricket 1833–1903* (London: Archibald Constable and Co. Ltd., 1904).

Hyndman, Henry Mayers, *The Record of an Adventurous Life* (London: MacMillan and Co., Limited, 1911).

Ledbrooke, A. W., *Lancashire County Cricket: The Official History of the Lancashire County & Manchester Cricket Club 1864–1953* (London: Phoenix House, 1954).

Lewis, W. J., *The Language of Cricket, with Illustrative Extracts from the Literature of the Game* (London: Oxford University Press, 1934).

Lillywhite, Fred., *The English Cricketers' Trip to Canada and the United States* (London: F. Lillywhite; Kent & Co., 1860; rpt., Introduction by Robin Marlar, Tadworth, Surrey: World's Work Ltd., 1980).

Lubbock, Alfred, *Memories of Eton and Etonians, Including My Life at Eton, 1854–1863, and Some Reminiscences of Subsequent Cricket, 1864–1874* (London: John Murray, 1899).

Lucas, E. V., ed., *A Hundred Years of Trent Bridge* (Privately Printed for Sir Julien Cahn, 1938).

Lyttelton, The Hon. R. H., *Cricket* (London: Duckworth & Co., 1898).

Lyttelton, The Hon. R. H .and others, *Giants of the Game: Being Reminiscences of the Stars of Cricket from Daft down to the Present Day* (London: Ward, Lock & Co., Limited, n.d. [1899]).

Martineau, G. D., *Bat, Ball, Wicket and All: An Account of the Origin and Development of the Implements, Dress and Appurtenances of the National Game* (London: Sporting Handbooks Ltd., 1950).

—— *The Valiant Stumper: A History of Wicket-keeping* (London: Stanley Paul, 1957).

"Mid-on" [R. P. Daft], ed., *Seventy-one Not Out: The Reminiscences of William Caffyn* (Edinburgh and London: William Blackwood and Sons, 1899).

Midwinter, Eric, *W. G. Grace: His Life and Times* (London: George Allen & Unwin, 1981).

Montgomery, H. H., *Old Cricket and Cricketers* (London: H. Stacey Gold; Wright & Co., n.d. [1890]).

Morrah, Patrick, *Alfred Mynn and the Cricketers of His Time* (London: Eyre & Spottiswoode, 1963).

"Old Ebor", *see* Pullin, A. W.

Pullin, A. W. ("Old Ebor"), *Talks with Old Yorkshire Cricketers*, 2nd ed. (Leeds: "The Yorkshire Post", 1898).

—— *Talks with Old English Cricketers* (Edinburgh and London: William Blackwood and Sons, 1900).

—— *Alfred Shaw Cricketer: His Career and Reminiscences* (London: Cassell and Company, 1902).

Pycroft, The Rev. James, *The Cricket-field, with Some Notes by H. H. Stephenson*, ed., with an Introduction, by F. S. Ashley-Cooper (London: St. James's Press Co., Ltd., 1922).

—— *Cricketana* (London: Longman, Green, Longman, Roberts, & Green, 1865).

"Quid" [R. A. FitzGerald], *Jerks in from Short-leg* (London: Harrison, 1866).

Rait Kerr, R. S., *The Laws of Cricket: Their History and Growth* (London: Longmans, Green and Co, 1950).

Read, W. W., *Annals of Cricket: A Record of the Game Compiled from Authentic Sources, and My Own Experiences during the Last Twenty-five Years* (London: Sampson Low, Marston & Company Limited, 1896).

Routledge, Edmund, *Handbook of Cricket* (London: George Routledge and Sons, n.d. [1866?]).

Rutter, Edward, *Cricket Memories: Rugby—Middlesex—Free Foresters* (London: Williams and Norgate, Ltd., 1925).

Selkirk, George H., *Guide to the Cricket Ground* (London and Cambridge: MacMillan and Co., 1867).

Shaw, Alfred, *see* Pullin, A. W. ("Old Ebor").

Spratt, A. W., *A Short Account of the Career of the Eminent Cricketer Robert Carpenter* (Cambridge: Cambridge University Press, 1897).

Steel, A. G., and the Hon. R. H. Lyttelton, and others, *Cricket*, 2nd ed., The Badminton Library of Sports and Pastimes (London: Longmans, Green, and Co., 1888).

Taylor, Alfred D., *Sussex Cricket in the Olden Time, with Glances at the Present* (Hove: Hove Printing and Publishing Company Ltd., n.d. [1900]).

—— *Annals of Lord's and History of the M.C.C.: A Concise Record of the Club's Progress Gleaned from Authentic Sources from the Date of Its Formation to the Present Time* (Bristol: J. W. Arrowsmith; London: Simpkin, Marshall, Hamilton, Kent & Company Limited, n.d. [1903]).

—— *The Story of a Cricket Picture (Sussex and Kent)* (Hove: Emery & Son, Ltd., 1923).

Thomas, Peter, *Yorkshire Cricketers 1839–1939* (Manchester: Derek Hodgson Publisher, 1973).

Warner, Sir Pelham, *Lord's 1787–1945* (London: George G. Harrap & Co. Ltd., 1946).

—— *Gentlemen v. Players 1806–1949* (London: George G. Harrap & Co. Ltd., 1950).

Washer, George, comp., *A Complete Record of Sussex County Cricket 1728 to 1957* (Hove: Sussex County Cricket Club, n.d. [1958]).

Wood, Frederick, *Beeton's Cricket Book* (London: Frederick Warne and Co., n.d. [1866]).

Wynne-Thomas, Peter, *Nottinghamshire Cricketers 1821–1914* (Haughton, Retford, Notts: The Author, 1971).

Index

(Text and Appendix I)
★=an Itinerant Eleven